MRE
Than
Forgiveness

STEVE DeNeff

M⊕RE
Than
Forgiveness

A Contemporary Call to Holiness
Based on the Life of Jesus Christ

WESLEYAN
PUBLISHING HOUSE

Indianapolis, Indiana

Copyright © 2002 by The Wesleyan Church
Published by Wesleyan Publishing House
Indianapolis, Indiana 46250
Printed in the United States of America
ISBN 0-89827-244-0

To My Mother

Contents

Preface

According to the newspaper, Professor Michael Christian of Boston College has gotten himself into quite a bind. He has finished his second book on the subject of kissing, covering twenty-five different kinds of kissing, from the lip-o-suction kiss to the upside down kiss. He is busy now designing the perfect smooch. And what is his problem?

"Women's expectations are too high," he says. Every time he kisses them, "they always say things like, 'You've got to be kidding. You wrote a book on the art of kissing and this is the best you can do?'"

Professor Christian is not the first to fall into this trap. For centuries, people have written about things they were not themselves able to do. When C. S. Lewis penned the preface to his book *The Problem of Pain,* he admitted that statements in the book "would become ridiculous if anyone knew who made them."[1] Even before that, the Anglican preacher John Wesley conceded that he himself had not reached the level of perfection he believed in and preached. And before him, the good Apostle Paul admitted that he had not "already been made perfect," and so he pressed on.

This is my albatross.

Since writing on the subject of holiness, I have met some of my readers who are, I imagine, a little disappointed that I am not as holy in reality as I seem to be in print. So let me begin by putting it bluntly. This is a book about holiness in the life of Christ. It is not about holiness in the life of this author, though I hope the gap between the two is narrowing.

For the past four years, I have studied the Gospels during Epiphany and it has transformed my life. I have watched the life of Jesus like a movie. It portrays the message of holiness more powerfully and more energetically than anything else I have seen. Jesus is no longer the poster child for my preconceived notions about faith and holiness. He is not a Baptist or a Lutheran or a Pentecostal or a Catholic or a Wesleyan. No, all of these wonderful traditions flow from Jesus; he does not flow from them. He is bigger and stronger than any of them. So while I have a deep appreciation for my own tradition (I am Wesleyan), I am moving toward the center, where all Christian traditions meet. This is not the same as being ecumenical, at least in the modern sense. Rather, I have one foot firmly grounded in my own biases—which will become evident throughout the book—and the other foot stepping toward my friends from the Roman Catholic, Lutheran, Reformed, and other traditions. I am not writing a defense of my own doctrine. I am describing a life that every disciple should recognize and, I pray, every convert will desire.

Nevertheless, I am biased. I come to the table with certain assumptions. The first is that Christian holiness does not and should not get more complicated than Jesus. In holiness, we call the believer to reproduce the life of Christ in his or her own life.

My second assumption is that this can happen, and it must. The word *holy* (*hagios*) means *set apart.* So I believe the holy life is one that is set apart from sin, self, and mediocrity. In the Bible, a person or item or piece of land was holy if it was set apart for God. It meant that God inhabited or used that person or thing as he did not use others. The opposite of holiness, then, was not merely sin but commonness. In the Fall, Adam not only sinned but also fell short of the glory of God. And to be holy, or *sanctified,* as it is properly called, is to be original and unique. It is to have God's glory returned to us. It is to return to a state of innocence similar to that from which we fell. It is the undoing of whatever evil sin has done. It is perfect love. In this sense, to be saved is more than to be forgiven. It is to be made extraordinary.

My third assumption is that Christian holiness should not be sectioned off from the rest of faith or theology. Nor should it be of interest only to the converted. I believe that sinners desire holiness, too—perhaps more so than saints—only they do not know what to call it. So while holiness may be attained in episodes of increasing measure, I do not argue for a "second work of grace."

Like Wesley, I believe that nothing impure can enter the kingdom of heaven and that neither death nor purgatory remove sin from the human soul. I believe we can actually be rid of sin in this lifetime, so that heaven is less moving up than moving over. I believe all people desire this cleansing from sin, even those who do not believe it possible. We did not create this desire in ourselves. It was given to us by God, who wants children after his own burning heart. And I believe that God did not give us the desire to be holy in order to mock us. It is not in his character to do so. So if I am asked to choose sides (as theologians are fond of asking us to do), I will choose the side of Wesley, believing that it really *is* possible to love the Lord our God with *all* of our heart, soul, mind, and strength, and to love our neighbor as authentically as we love ourselves. When one has reached this state of grace, he is properly called *entirely sanctified.*

Nevertheless, *perfect love* is a slippery term. If we speak of this as a "second work of grace," it seems too final, as if nothing should follow.

Those who profess sanctification will then believe their love needs no improvement, and those who believe their love is less than perfect will fear that they can never be sanctified. I write to challenge the one and encourage the other. Therefore, although I believe in a subsequent work of grace, I have avoided terminology that would cause any believer to think that his progress in grace is complete, or that real progress is not possible.

This is my fourth assumption: I do not believe that holiness can be achieved through a simple formula or prescribed prayer. The path toward holiness has defining moments, but it does not come in a moment's time. While I attempt to provide understanding and counsel, I stop short of offering multi-step plans for initiating this blessing. From my perspective, that is not the way Christians are made holy. Virtue is realized only through struggle. Like most gems, it is created by pressure, over time. That is, there is more to thirsting for holiness than saying the right words. These can come later, and they surely must (Matt. 7:7–8), but I have chosen to focus on the spirit of the seeker rather than the method for seeking. I suppose that when the seeker is finally ready, the methods will appear on their own.

So while I offer a biblical and sensible understanding of holiness, I do not intend to neatly answer every question I raise, because I do not intend for the reader to be done with this book, even after he has finished it. It is my hope that the reader will mature in his understanding of holiness, without feeling that he has mastered it. Like the woman at the well, many Christians desire God's filling so they won't get thirsty and have to keep coming back for more (see John 4:15). That was never Jesus' intention. He fully intends for us to continually thirst for holiness. As A. W. Tozer put it, "to have found God and still to pursue him is the soul's paradox of love."[2]

Yet I do hope these chapters will inspire us to action. I do not, like the good professor of kissing, want to create a symposium in which cerebral Christians discuss the theory of holiness but neglect its practice. It is fine to speak of holiness, but it is far better to experience it.

To be sure, these are not final answers. There is much more to holiness than what I know. There is much more to be said than what I could ever write. And what I have written may seem wrong. But where I am wrong, I hope to be wrong in ways that will help others get it right. While teaching, I want to remain teachable. So I submit these thoughts for the benefit of practicing Christians everywhere. May God use them to inspire those who seek to change the world through the love of Christ.

Acknowledgments

G.K. Chesterton once dedicated a book to his secretary, "without whose help this work would have been published upside down." He could have been speaking for me.

I, too, have people in my life who keep me right side up. And most are as subtle as a secretary.

I am thus indebted to those members of my church who have allowed me to share their lives. You would not recognize their names (and I would not give them), but their stories and struggles and candid confessions are very familiar to you. Most of this book was written while I pastored the North Lakeport Wesleyan Church. It was there, in front of a very patient audience, that I began to think seriously about holiness, attempting to blend Scripture and experience into a relevant message. My new family at College Wesleyan Church has been equally affirming. They have opened their hearts to me, have graciously allowed me the time to write, and have helped me to sharpen my thoughts before making them public. Private conversations have helped me immensely. Bret McAtee is a Reformed friend who plays Edwards to my Wesley. Stella Knak is a devoted parishioner with the mind of a student and the heart of God. Jackie White is a sister with an honest set of eyes who has critiqued this book and believed in it more than anyone, even me.

My friends at Wesleyan Publishing House have taken these thoughts and made them better. My editor, Larry Wilson, has poured unseen hours into this manuscript to make it read smarter and more poignantly than it would have.

I am also grateful to my family, my parents and siblings, whose lives are real, whose encouragement is refreshing, and whose love is reflected each time we speak. Their prayers have been the seedbed of this book.

My wife and children have patiently listened to most of the arguments contained herein and have helped hold them to the practical fires of reality. They have volunteered illustrations, cross-examined my logic, prayed in private, and often had supper without me. More than anyone, they are glad to see this project finished. *Honey, I'm home!*

And finally, to God: I am convinced that God has favorites, and I am just as sure that, for a little while, I have been one of them. I am not sure why, but God has given me more than I have desired, told me things I could not have conjured on my own, and shown me kindness I could not resist.

To Him, who makes all things possible.

PART I
THE END FROM THE BEGINNING
The Origin of Holiness

The "hour I first believed" is a critical time in the life of any disciple. These first few weeks in the believer's new life will likely determine the trajectory of his or her faith for a lifetime.

The three chapters that follow show that the quest for holiness begins even before the moment of faith, is present at the hour of conversion, and defines the subsequent life of the Christian.

Every genuine conversion begins with holiness in view. It is the goal toward which faith must inevitably lead. So those who do not think much of holiness make even their salvation suspect. For those who truly possess Christ at the beginning will be possessed by him in the end.

Chapter 1

FINDING THE HEART'S TRUE HOME
Our Instinctive Thirst for Holiness

They stood in line for twelve hours, nearly twenty thousand of them, to view the body of their friend and lover. He was Eugene "Big Daddy" Lipscomb, defensive lineman for the Baltimore Colts during the 1970s.

Dead at thirty-one, the Big Daddy had been known for his power. He was a six-foot-six-inch, three-hundred-plus-pound Bunyan with a seven-foot wingspan who moved forty-pound weights with his fingertips and tackled strong men with one arm.

"When Big Daddy wrapped a guy with those long arms, he stayed wrapped," said his coach, along with half of the league. "The best man I ever saw at knocking people over," said another.[1]

And there was more. One player remembered his "heart of gold," and another his "gentle spirit." He was the Babe Ruth of football, a man with big talent and a heart to match. More than once Big Daddy carried children on his shoulders or escorted whole families through the clothing store, buying them shoes, pants, and winter jackets. Unlike many of today's gladiators, Lipscomb helped his victims back to their feet after driving them into the turf, and often gave up his bed to derelicts caught in the cold Baltimore snow. But Big Daddy was a complex man with more than one side. This was his Dr. Jekyl.

His Mr. Hyde was evil and afraid. At night, when the demons came out, Lipscomb would slide his bed against the door so no one could get in. He kept a loaded gun under his pillow, and chained a friend's giant dog to the foot of his bed.

"I've been scared most of my life," he explained to confused roommates. "You wouldn't think so to look at me, [but] it gets so bad I cry myself to sleep."

One night while carousing through Baltimore with a friend, the big man suddenly broke down and started crying. "Ah, the Daddy ain't right," he mumbled over and again, "the Daddy ain't right."

"You'd walk up, and his mind would be somewhere else," remembered one teammate, "[then] you'd look and he was crying." His coaches reckoned that "the haunts of his childhood pursued him to the end of his life." Perhaps, but by the time he died, most of the Daddy's problems were of his own making.

In his worst moments, and there were lots of them, the Daddy drank to excess, trashed hotel rooms, gambled away his salary, and slept with prostitutes, girlfriends, ex-wives, and even hotel maids.

We have brawny reputations— but we are running scared.

"Willing women were all around and he was indiscriminate," a friend recalled. On the night of his death, he'd been in the company of two prostitutes before stopping at a friend's house to shoot up (twice) with what would become his final dose of heroine. According to the coroner's report, he died with enough smack in him to kill five people.

He was survived by a fiancée and three ex-wives, the second of whom he married while still wed to the first, whom he'd impregnated while dating the second. The second marriage ended in annulment after eight months of abuse. Like the good coach said, he was "the best man I ever saw at knocking people over."

The reason I bother to tell you about Big Daddy Lipscomb is that he is a *type* of modern man. We are big, powerful, fast, rich . . . hollow, afraid, haunted, angry, and dead.

We live fast and die faster. We have brawny reputations and lots of acquaintances we call "friends." But we are running scared, pursued by the haunts of a childhood that was lost in the Garden. We suffer deep problems with even deeper causes. Like a diabetic who drinks Kool-Aid thinking it will quench his thirst, modern people do not see the root of the problems that drive them. They do what they think they must to find relief, not fearing the consequences of tomorrow. They only know it feels better today.

"And where will you be in five years?" I asked a middle-aged woman contemplating divorce.

"I don't know," she said, "I never thought about that."

She is not alone. Many drift backwards into the fire only because they are tired of the frying pan. They try to solve deep and fundamental problems with fast and foolish answers. They act upon their instincts. They put off the pain. They bide their time. But very soon—ready or not—the rent will come due, because it must.

You see, human souls are working even when their minds are turned off. They are always keeping score, always measuring their chances of making it in the next world. As the holiness writer Daniel Steele put it, their consciences may be seared or even put to sleep, but they can never be changed.[2] That is, we may say that evil is good, but we will never get our souls to believe it. That is the gift of conscience. So even when we say "it doesn't matter," it does. Though we are never alone, we're still lonely. While we whistle in the dark, we tremble. Even as we terrify the league, we sleep with our bed against the door. We can have sex, but we can't make love. We are rich, yet always hungry; spiritual but not religious. We have sterling reputations, but inside we are insecure. And all we know is that "the Daddy ain't right."

Even in the Church we are committed, yet unfulfilled. Our lives are clean, but our thoughts are dirty. We sit together at worship, but seldom speak at home. We are all driven by the very desires, fears, and wounds of the Big Daddy, but some of us have hidden these under the rituals of our faith. Is this why one skeptic called modern conversions "a baptism of neurosis"?

But every now and then the soul of the modern person peeks out from under mounds of activity and whispers, "What about me?" And if we will put everything down and listen, we will find that Christ (and not religion), that holiness (and not good, clean living), that repentance (and not serial apologies) constitute the life we miss but cannot describe.

Like the Big Daddy, we have problems only holiness can fix. This is why our faith must be cloaked in terms of a "relationship." If it is not, it will have the same appeal as a Betty Ford clinic. It will be something to help us dry out, shape up, get back in line. Our lives will seem like a monastery, only with less fun and more furniture.

So what are the problems that modern people face? How are these deep needs met in those who lose themselves in Christ?

THE PERVERSION OF THE ORDINARY

To answer this, we must return to the Garden (Eden) from which we came. There is a reason for this. In Christian theology, we are always trying to balance two poles: sin and salvation; depravity and perfection. Like any good story, the Bible must unravel in the end whatever predicament it describes in the beginning. Whatever was ruined by the Fall must eventually be restored by conversion; for ultimately, that is the purpose of conversion, and *that* is the story of the Bible. If we do not balance these two opposites—that is, if we minimize sin in order to emphasize holiness (as the holiness movement has done), or if we minimize holiness in order to emphasize the depth and deceit of sin (as the Reformed tradition has done)—we skew the meaning and miracle of grace. We must always hold these two in balance. One is an action, the other an equal and opposite *re*action. Sin is the question. Holiness is the final answer. Sin is our journey away from God, and holiness is the homecoming in which we are granted all of our former privileges—and more (see Luke 15:21–24).

So what happened to "Big Daddy" in the Fall? How did he get this way? What does he need in life, and where can he get it?

The Effects of the Fall

Like Adam before the Fall, the Big Daddy was once not merely sinless, but innocent, transparent, and unselfish. Yet even before he'd finished eating the fruit from the forbidden tree, Adam was hiding from others ("they made coverings for themselves," Gen. 3:7) and running from God ("they hid from the LORD God among the trees," Gen. 3:8). Man's rebellion ("you will be like God," Gen. 3:5) had crystallized into fear ("I was afraid . . . so I hid," Gen. 3:10). Thus, the Big Daddy's problem is that he is smitten by sin in two ways. First, he is alienated from God, which, among other things, means that he is nearsighted (his "mind is on earthly things," thus he "cannot see the light of the gospel" Phil. 3:19, 2 Cor. 4:4), and he is dumb (that is, "darkened in [his] understanding," Eph. 4:18).

Second, and as a result of this, he is dreadfully selfish. To borrow Luther's poignant phrase, he is "curved inward upon himself." From the beginning, he has sewn fig leaves *for himself,* and he will likely continue with this fetish until the day he dies.[3]

But all is not lost. Solomon observed that God "has also set eternity in the hearts of men" (Eccl. 3:11), which means that we still carry the peculiar image of God. While human beings share many things with other creatures, there are distinctive needs that only we possess and that only God can fill. In other words, the problem with the Big Daddy is not that he has evil desires. His desires are the same as anyone else's. The problem with the Big Daddy (and every person) is that he is seeking to fulfill these normal desires in foolish and perverted ways. If and when the Daddy is converted, we must not expect him to have a new set of needs, but rather to meet the old, familiar needs in new and more satisfying ways. For if a person truly enjoys sinning, it is rarely the sin itself he enjoys. More likely, he enjoys the relief that he believes sin will bring to the deeper, more basic, human needs we call the image of God. These needs are the human being's trademark. They give him meaning and purpose. They make him human. They also make him vulnerable. And what does he need? I believe he is looking for significance, security, innocence, intimacy, and hope. And because he is nearsighted and dumb—that is, because he is affected by the Fall—he will always seek to meet these needs in selfish and perverted ways.

In order to find *significance* he will resort to power or pride, because both will make a person feel good about himself. When he feels the need for *security* he will hoard things (greed) or he will seek guarantees since both of these provide a sort of refuge. To recover *innocence* he will employ confession or therapy. To find *intimacy*, he will engage in sex. To feel *hope* he will seek pleasure.

BASIC HUMAN NEEDS	THROUGH THE FALL
Significance	Power/Pride
Security	Greed/Guarantees
Innocence	Confession
Intimacy	Sex
Hope	Pleasure

The Corruption of Desire

But just as there are perverted ways of gratifying natural desires, there are pure and more satisfying ways as well. In fact, "the reason the Son of God appeared was to destroy the devil's work" (1 John 3:8). In other words, anything sin can do, holiness can do better. For in true holiness, we are not only separated from sin, we are made fully human again. We are free to gratify our needs, this time through the cross. We are liberated from the bondage to our appetites. The hiding is over. We can search ourselves without being afraid of what we might find, for "whenever our hearts condemn us . . . God is greater than our hearts and he knows everything" (1 John 3:20). We are subject to genuine sorrow and thus to genuine joy (Luke 6:21).

In holiness, we find our *significance* not in power, but in service; not in pride, but in humility. We find our *security* neither in greed nor in

21

guarantees, but in simple trust. To recover our *innocence,* we have our sins forgiven and our sinful natures cleansed. We find *intimacy* as much in worship as in sex. To feel *hope,* we turn to suffering rather than to pleasure alone. We have the same basic needs, now redeemed through the Cross.

BASIC HUMAN NEEDS	THROUGH THE FALL	THROUGH HOLINESS
Significance	Power/Pride	Service/Humility
Security	Greed/Guarantees	Trust
Innocence	Confession	Cleansing
Intimacy	Sex	Worship
Hope	Pleasure	Suffering

This explains how Christ could be tempted without having evil desires, for temptation is merely the urge to fulfill an otherwise innocent need by perverted means. The temptation itself is not evil, nor is the need upon which the temptation preys. No, the evil occurs when a basic human need and the opportunity to fulfill it in unordained ways conceive an act or thought contrary to the will of God. As a human being, Christ carried within him every basic human need. And he was given ample opportunities to fulfill these needs in selfish, unordained ways. But as God, he resisted each opportunity and found his joy in holiness.

The Homecoming of Holiness

Each of us faces the same dilemma. By nature, we need what is ordinary and innocent. Through our sinful nature we have strong inclinations to fulfill these needs in perverted ways. To have our natures cleansed, that is, to be *sanctified*, is to have our inclinations miraculously changed, our minds reprogrammed, our appetites brought under control (now taking orders rather than giving them) so that even though we have the same basic needs, we see them for what they are and gratify them in the ways God originally intended. In this way, holiness restores us to a new yet familiar condition. The holy person, therefore, is not really different from the rest of us, neither is he faking his righteousness. He has the same needs as the rest of us, only he gratifies them through the Cross, the ultimate satisfier. Thus, the curse of the Garden is undone.

Once we view salvation and holiness in this way, it becomes clear that the search for the fulfillment of these needs does not belong exclusively to the Christian. Indeed, *everyone* is looking for the same things. The secular person does not need to become spiritual in order to try to meet these needs. He is already spiritual. He is incurably religious. Thus he will try to fill the void in his life, bouncing from one idea to the next, until he finds ultimate satisfaction in Christ. For one cannot know the whole content of any need until it is finally satisfied. One cannot fully describe thirst until he has discovered water. Until then, he will only know that sand cannot meet the need. In just this way, no one can fully understand his need for significance or intimacy until he has discovered service and worship. Until then, he can only know that power and sex do not quench these raging thirsts. Holiness then, is a homecoming. The restless heart finds its rest in Christ.

RESTORATION THROUGH HOLINESS

Let's look more closely at each of these five needs. In what ways do they make us vulnerable? And how are they satisfied by holiness?

Wholly Significant

To the Western person, the greatest insult is to tell him that he does not matter. You may call him names that disparage his ancestry. You may say he is stupid or uncivilized. But you must never ignore him. He is too much for that. He is *more* than an animal, so even the evolutionist will claim that while monkeys may evolve upward into people, people will never evolve downward into monkeys. The two species may have many things in common, but one of them is better than the other. Human beings do not belong to their world in the way that monkeys do. No, humans subdue the earth and rule over it. That is, people build zoos for monkey, monkeys do not build zoos for people. The instinctive belief that we were born just "a little lower than the angels" and higher than the animals was born in us at the beginning. So in the hell of an Auschwitz prison camp, the Swiss therapist Viktor Frankl noted that it was more humiliating to be ignored by the prison guards than to have them beat you half to death. One, he said, was the sting of hatred, but the other was the curse of an animal, a "nonhuman."[4]

When we try to gratify this need for dignity through our fallen nature, we resort to pecking orders and politics. We brag about ourselves and put others down. We take classes on improving our self-esteem. Our relationships are competitive. Our hearts are suspicious. Our spirits are critical. Our calendars are crammed. Our motives are misguided. All this has to do with power and pride. We want to impress others (power) and we want to be impressed with ourselves (pride).

But in holiness, our thirst for dignity is satisfied, oddly enough, through service. Our dignity is in our humility. We still want to matter. But to whom we matter is less important. We will find as much meaning in small things as in great things. Our significance is not found in making ourselves too busy for menial tasks. Rather it is grounded in the truth that we are loved by God, that he has taken up residence in us, that we are fulfilling our place in his plan. We want what we have and accept what we're given—with grace. We have realized that we cannot become more than we were destined to be. Thus, we take our place under his blue sky and seek only to accomplish what we were destined to accomplish, for as many years as we have.

The best leader reigns with a towel, not a scepter.

This humility is not founded in feeling rotten about ourselves, but in acting "in accordance with the measure of faith God has given" us (see Rom. 12:3). We still want to matter, to be important, only now have no need to be popular or famous. Our dignity comes from within. Anyone who has seen the well-ordered life of a true saint knows the dignity and the power such people possess.

"Why you?" asked the incredulous disciple of Saint Francis, "Why is the whole world running after you?"

The good saint replied that it was only because God could not find anyone more ordinary to bless. The world, then, does not always look for clever, intelligent people; neither is the best leader the one who is most prepared. Instead, it is the one whom God has exalted, who uses a towel rather than a scepter to reign.

Wholly Secure

In America, fear is big business. It sells insurance (what if something happens?), security alarms (who's watching your things when you aren't?), political campaigns (he's tough on crime!), and guns (never mind the dog, beware the owner!). Hollywood betrays our obsession with fear when it produces well-attended movies about twisters, earthquakes, meteorites, volcanoes, or killer epidemics.

But there is one deep and abiding fear that underlies them all, and one must turn to the philosophers in order to find it. The French existentialist Jean Paul Sartre describes a man who is caught from behind as he peeks through a keyhole in an act of voyeurism.

"All of a sudden I hear footsteps in the hall," writes Sartre. "Someone is looking at me!"

The result, said Sartre, is a feeling of shame, not for having spied upon another, but for having been spied upon. Sartre referred to this as being "naked before the Other." It strikes paranoia, fear, self-consciousness in the one being watched.[5]

Right here is the fear that modern people face. The unsettling question to them is not what to think about God, but what God must be thinking about them as he watches in silence. The answer that one gives himself at that moment will determine the whole course of his life. If he is at peace with this question, nothing can bother him for long. If he is not, if he is made to feel like an object—naked, observed, dispensable—he will become restless, even as he is entertained.

In my opinion, modern people still fear God. Only they have learned to deal with their fear in one of two futile ways: *fight* or *flight*. That is, they will argue with him (fight) or try to ignore him (flight). They will redefine him (fight) or avoid him (flight).

Whenever a culture avoids God it will talk about him less and its citizens will plan their lives without factoring him into the equation. As science has come of age, it has required more space in our lives and has tended to push God to the fringe or, as one writer put it, into the "gaps," where he is allowed to answer only those questions science cannot. After publishing a cover article on modern faith, the editors of one news magazine received an angry response from one reader who insisted that "religion should penetrate the cosmology of the day. To evoke awe and mystery, I turn to the great physicists. . . . They are the mystics of the 21st century."[6]

Most of those who avoid God do so by hiding behind shallow arguments about the need to see what they believe or the desire to avoid the confusion of the many religious arguments of the day. They profess to lead very simple lives when, in fact, their lives are complex and contradictory, since they have no governing principle. When they do concede the existence of God, they will spend little time figuring him out. They will have ideas about God, but very few convictions because, of course, mere ideas cannot frighten anyone. Legion are the ways in which modern man has fashioned God after his own image.

A fourteen-year-old Hindu boy from Chicago says he has pictures of all twenty-five gods tacked to the wall in his closet.

"Each one has a different purpose," he explains. "I have like a pitching rotation . . . but I left two of them out because I didn't think they were doing their job."[7] Come, let us make God in our image.

Of course, to have a God who fits into your pitching rotation or one who becomes whatever you need him to be at the moment is to have a four-sided triangle. It is a stark contradiction in terms. You may have one of these if you like, only you are not free to label it *God*. For part of what it means to be God is to remain holy, transcendent, and unchangeable.

There are others who venture to define God, but seldom in orthodox terms. According to one survey, 40 percent of Americans believe that "Jesus sinned while he was on earth."[8] Related to this is the new "open" view of God that insists he cannot know the future because he hasn't been there yet. The eminent philosopher Charles Hartshorne has said that God is always changing to become more of what he already is. He is incomplete. He is, if you will, "growing up." According to Hartshorne, "to memorize and honor everything that has ever happened is God's ultimate role."[9]

While that view may have advantages, it would be tough to get to know him or become like him since the target is always moving. And what if we get there first?

According to another writer, we have. "God isn't dead," he writes. "He just hasn't been born yet."

How did he come to that conclusion?

"In the future, life will include . . . computers powerful enough to achieve a state of consciousness," which will then blend itself "with other life forms until it envelops the universe."[10] Stranger things have happened, I guess.

It could be that one of the most dreadful symptoms of our fear of God is a "spiritual neuropathy" in which our souls are numb to his existence. We have talked ourselves out of fear, like children singing "who's afraid of the big bad wolf" while we wander wide-eyed into the black and eerie forest.

Christ's maxim about fearing not "those who kill the body" but "the one who can destroy both body and soul in hell" may come to us in the form of an either/or proposition. Either we will fear those who destroy the body, or we will fear God, who destroys the body and the soul. But we will never fear them both. To fear one is to virtually ignore the other.

Put another way, it is possible that we, who have failed to fear the one thing we should, have come to fear the many things we should not. We are waiting for the giant meteor to hit us. We are wondering when the terrorists will strike again. We are protecting ourselves from our enemies lest they drop "the big one." And we have compounded the problem by appealing to science as the answer for most of the things that frighten us. Kryonics will save us from the grave. Star Wars will save us from each other. A pill should save us from disease. Lawsuits will save us from the negligence of anyone who ruins our only chance at happiness. Satellites will save us from the meteor. The newsmagazine on my desk informs me that America has just landed a spacecraft on the asteroid Eros in order to see what it's made of. According to the "experts," this is a major achievement. For the paltry sum of $223 million, we will soon discover how dense is the rock about to destroy us.

But there is another way. The God who terrifies us also welcomes us onto his lap, where we are invited to blend our fear ("hallowed be thy name") with familiarity ("our father in heaven") and to make our wishes known. But it must come in this order: first fear, then familiarity. More than thirty times in the Bible when people conquered fear, they did so at the order (or permission) of God, who said, "Do not be afraid," and then promised them something in exchange for fear.

> The God who terrifies us also welcomes us onto his lap.

"Do not be afraid . . . I am your shield" (Gen. 15:1).

"Do not be afraid . . . for the battle is not yours, but God's" (2 Chron. 20:15).

"Do not be afraid . . . your prayer has been heard" (Luke 1:13)

"Do not be afraid . . . he has risen, just as he said" (Matt. 28:5–6). And so forth.

In every instance, the fear is not expelled. It is replaced by another, more powerful belief. Since fear is the result of believing that we are in danger, we can conquer our fear in one of only two ways. Either we must discover that our previous conclusions are wrong, or we must believe in something else, something *more*.

When my daughter was very young and still fearing the bogeyman, I tried both solutions and soon learned the power of the latter. I would tell her there was no bogeyman under her bed, and even pull up the covers so she could see for herself. But she was not consoled. For bogeymen only came out when everyone else was gone, she said. The last recourse then, was to sit myself at the foot of her bed and promise that I would stand guard while she slept.

"If the bogeyman comes out," I told her, "he'll have to get through me, and I am tougher than the bogeyman."

It worked like magic. There was no sense in denying her fear; it had to be replaced with trust in her father.

Now holiness is intimate trust in the One who sits at the foot of our bed and promises to protect us while we live in this world. God does not speak our fears out of existence. He does not lie about terrorists or diseases or the meteors that hide in the dark corners of our world. He promises simply that all of these will have to get past him if they are to get to us. And he tells us to close our eyes for the night and rest, not because there is no danger, but because we can trust the Father.

Wholly Innocent

By the grace of God, the human soul is always working. Because it is, a person will spend his life searching for a fresh start—a clean slate. It does not matter when or where he is born. Sociologists have long noted that every society constructs an ideal and then tries to live up to it. When it cannot, it will develop a system of atoning for sin and finding peace in spite of failure to a achieve the ideal.

In his drama *Traveler Without Luggage*, the existentialist playwright Annouilh tells the story of a young soldier who is wounded in battle and, as a result, loses his memory. He does not know who he is or where he came from. The case is publicized by the radio and newspaper and several people respond. The young man meets the respondents one by one to see whether he recognizes them. At first, there is nothing. Then suddenly, one family begins crying out, "That's him, that's our son, that's our brother." They recognize him. But there is no response from the wounded soldier.

Finally, they take him to visit the places of his childhood in order to jog his memory. They lead him to a stairway and explain how, years before, he had thrown a playmate down the steps in a fit of rage. The soldier is unmoved. A young woman from the neighborhood approaches and asks if he remembers anything he did to her when she was still a virgin. The soldier denies it. But the woman describes a birthmark he bears on his backside, and, after looking in the mirror, he discovers it is true. Now there is no more denying. He weeps. But he waits.

As he is about to resign himself to going home with his family, another couple approaches him. They are childless. In their desire to create a male heir for their family, they conspire with the young soldier to play the part of their son in exchange for a new start with no past.

Now the soldier must decide between the two families. With very little effort, he opts for the second and knowingly bids farewell to his real family. Why? Because he wants to live only for the moment. He does not want a past. He wants only a future. He desires to be what Anouilh calls "a traveler without luggage."

The modern person erases the past through confession. He will apologize to his neighbor or seek to repay him. He will promise to do better, as though his sinful actions were at variance with an otherwise perfect nature. Popular writers today encourage sinners to admit guilt but to quickly move past it by promising to improve. One such writer has just concluded that religion makes people feel bad about themselves when, in fact, they should not. He argues that the Christian doctrine of sin (i.e., that even angry and lustful *thoughts* are sinful) will ruin us because it will cause our lives to be dominated by guilt and fear—and guilt and fear don't bring out the best in anyone. Such feelings only drain the joy out of life and make us unpleasant companions. The writer does not, therefore, endorse repentance because repentance only makes one feel guilty.

> When we sin, there are two options— punishment and forgiveness.

While it is easier to confess our sins than to repent of our nature, only repentance will bring change. For the worst sinner of all, wrote Josh Billings, is the "one who spends half of his time sinning and the other half confessing."[11] Confession does not lessen the impulse to sin unless we are honest about the corruption of our nature that made sin possible in the first place.

It has been said that whenever people sin, there are two options. They must be either punished or forgiven. It is for want of forgiveness that many people punish themselves by sabotaging their careers, their marriages, or, as in the case of the Big Daddy, their very lives. Like children who push the limits until their father puts down the newspaper and paddles them, these people commit one sin after another until life finally spanks them. Others attempt to "confess our mistakes and move on." But as the writer above has suggested, this is futile since it does not appeal for forgiveness to anyone but ourselves. It is as though there is no standard but ours; as though ours is the only opinion that matters; as though we live only to ourselves.

But what if that's wrong? What if there is a God who is harder on sin than we imagine, and what if sin's most perverse quality is its ability to masquerade as self-righteousness? What then? How can we restore our innocence?

The gospel of the Cross is that we can be forgiven and cleansed from *all* our unrighteousness. To modern people, who are always seeking improvement, holiness is the standard by which they measure themselves and they are either moving toward it (which they call "getting better") or away from it (which they call "getting worse").

Sanctification—the cleansing of our sinful nature and the changing of our inclinations—is the confidence that the disease is cured, not merely under control. For where sin abounded, grace abounded more. For the one who seeks cleansing, holiness is the evidence that the Cross is as powerful as sin itself, that his Fall in the Garden has done nothing that his Savior on the Cross cannot undo.

Wholly Intimate

An anthropologist once asked a Hopi (member of a Native American tribe) why so many of their songs are about rain. The Hopi replied that it is because water is so scarce where they live, then added, "Is that why so many of your songs are about love?"

Well, something like that.

Actually, the modern person craves intimacy more than love. He wants to come out from hiding and to show himself to another trusted individual. He wants to be accepted. He wants to give himself away. He wants to matter to someone, to become one with another. He desires a religion of intimacy for which sex is only a sacrament. But too often he gives up the search for this true religion, deciding to settle for the sacrament.

The popular writer Max Lucado tells the story of Judy Bucknell, who was strangled and stabbed seven times in her Miami apartment in 1980. According to those who knew her, she had lived a quiet but fast life with several lovers and a hankering for real love. Among her scant belongings was a diary recording her final thoughts:

> Where are the men with flowers and champagne and music? Where are the men who call and ask for a date? Where are the men who would like to share more than my bed, my booze, my food. . . . I would like to have in my life, once before I pass through my life, the kind of relationship that is part of a loving relationship. . . . I see people together and I'm so jealous I want to throw up. What about me? Who is going to love Judy

Bucknell? I feel so old. Unloved. Unwanted. Abandoned. Used up. I want to cry and sleep forever.[12]

What do you say to Judy Bucknell? What do you have to offer that she has not already tried? How do you cure her deep, throbbing cry for acceptance?

The gospel for Judy Bucknell is that God loves her as she is, but he will not leave her in her mess. In Christian holiness, she will find the courage to confess her sins and the power to be free from them. In holiness, she can trust herself completely to God and know that he has accepted her. She can convert the rest of her life into a sacrament which she offers as a reasonable service to God.

Wholly Hopeful

It was Paul who said that lost people were "without hope and without God in the world" (Eph. 2:12), and as evidence of this, the Big Daddy—and all modern people with him—is exhibit A. Hope is the inner conviction that there is still a chance, a future, a purpose, a justice to life. It is more than optimism. It is the bedrock belief that our story has a plot, that all of the pain and nonsense in this life will one day converge at the feet of One who can make sense of it all. For want of this, people are not depressed: they are despairing.

A few years ago, two thirteen-year-old kids in Florida, a boy and his girlfriend, held hands as they waded into the murky waters near their home. Without looking back, they walked into water over their heads and inhaled it, drowning themselves because one of their parents insisted they break up. If they could not be together in this life, they wrote in a note, there was no hope.

Not far away, in another southern town, a young man attached himself to the end of a rope and hung himself from an old oak tree outside his rural community. Next to his body was a note that read: "this tree is about the only stable thing left in the world."

D. Martyn Lloyd-Jones observed that the singers and poets of any generation provided the truest idea of its ethos. Then he concluded that the lyrics of his day (the 1970s) were all about death, disaster, and lostness in this world.

Folk writer Garrison Keillor said the same thing after being asked to judge the poetry for a contest sponsored by *Atlantic Monthly*. Halfway through the pile of entries he observed, "hardly any poems were written for amusement, for the pleasure of language. Almost all were compelled, driven, winging up out of the poet's maimed past."[13]

If this is the ethos of our generation, we are in a world of hurt. Of course, a hopeless generation is never a dull one. More likely, it will be quite the opposite. While waiting for my wife to finish her shopping one evening, I stood in the bookstore and leafed through a lesser-known stage play that made this very point. It was bluntly titled *Sex*.[14] It is a simple play about a man walking down a path toward the city. On his way, he imagines the fun, the pleasure, the excitement he will enjoy once he arrives. On the way, however, he is approached by a young woman coming from the other direction, who lures him into a liaison. When the escapade is over, the man returns to the path and continues his journey toward the glamorous city. On arrival he discovers that the town is only a village, nothing spectacular at all. He has been deceived. His expectations have exceeded reality. As the scene ends, the reader is left to wonder if significance or meaning in life might not be limited to whatever pleasure we may experience along the way. It is a stirring symbol of hopelessness; the perfect description of people with nothing to look forward to. That they may have pleasure where there is no hope means only that the demons will play with mortals before devouring them.

> Rather than laughing until we hurt, we hurt until we laugh.

And how do we fight back? Most recently, our weapon of choice has been laughter. If you doubt that, simply turn on your television set and observe the proliferation of sitcoms, late-night comedians, and tasteless jokes. Stroll down the aisle of your local (even Christian) bookstore and note the number of books devoted to making you laugh. The highest compliment paid to speakers these days is that they are "funny." And witness the speed with which our society can create sick humor in the wake of a tragedy. When the space shuttle *Challenger* exploded, killing all seven passengers aboard, we were inundated with jokes about feeding the fish. When an airliner crashed in the gator-infested swamps of Florida, we heard jokes about airline food before even one body had been recovered. We use humor to cover despair the way a stranger uses laughter to cover nervousness. That is, rather than laughing until we hurt, we have hurt until we laugh. Our shock absorber has been shattered into nihilistic humor. And the deeper we hurt, the harder we laugh.

But in holiness, our laughter comes from joy, and our joy comes from a personality transplant. This happiness is not a mood or a smile on the face of a smart shopper who has just saved time and money. It is not a temperament or an optimistic, never-a-dull-moment attitude. It is more than blustering worship. In holiness, our soul has finally settled down with God, and he has placed his Spirit inside us. As with any transplant, the presence of Christ within the recipient causes natural inclinations toward things that were previously unfamiliar—in this case, joy. And this joy is not manufactured, but miraculous. That is, we are not put into joy, but joy is put into us—permanently—and here it stays, even in the worst of times. For holiness, and not heaven, is the hope of a Christian.

It has been said that the final test of any religion is in how it handles suffering. The Buddhist tries to eliminate it. The Christian Scientist denies it. The Muslim accepts it. Some religions inflict it. Only Christianity transforms it. Is this why Paul gloried in the Cross? Or why Martin Luther suggested we should "seek it like a treasure and to bring it about"?[15] For in suffering the heart is cleansed from any shallow and selfish aims. Since we are naturally turned inward upon ourselves, we usually seek to serve God for the pleasure it brings us rather than for the service we can offer to him. Suffering will fix that in a hurry. For in suffering, God withdraws and leaves us without the warm enthusiasm and the happy company we are used to. He does this, said John of the Cross, to determine whether we love God himself or only our feelings about God.[16] In holiness, wish for God to purify us and make us his children, with all the suffering that entails (see Heb. 12:10). So countless scriptures portray suffering not as an inconvenience to be tolerated while standing in line for heaven but as a means of being conformed to Christ's image (Rom. 8:29) or becoming like him in his death (Phil. 3:10).

When the Jewish writer Martin Buber complained to his friend that his illness was keeping him from writing, the friend replied, "How do you know that your suffering does not glorify God more than your sickness?"[17]

TOWARD HOME

Into every human heart God has wired these needs. For some, they are the appetite that invites them to communion with God. For others, they are the cravings that lead to every form of indulgence.

It is this way with all human needs. It is not power or things that we crave. It is significance and security. We only settle for power and things. But holiness—communion with God—will satisfy these hungers with humility and trust.

Of the five basic needs described above, some are more cheerful (trust, worship, and cleansing) while others are not (humility and suffering). Yet holiness encompasses them both.

And there is an inevitability to holiness for anyone who is truly converted. For in conversion, God suddenly gives us the capacity to do by nature things we have up to now only admired.

Now in order to help those people who, like Big Daddy Lipscomb, have gotten lost in their appetites, we will need a vision of Jesus that is clear and helpful. We must speak of his desires and inclinations since these are the fountain of his thoughts, actions, and destiny. We will need to speak of miracles, of God breaking in on him, and of hard discipline.

But first things first.

For now, where does conversion begin? What is the most fundamental difference between a sinner and a saint? Where does repentance get its power?

Three questions.

One answer.

LIFE RESPONSES

1. In what ways have you seen a desire for holiness exhibit itself in nonbelievers?

2. What are some of the unsatisfying ways in which you have tried to meet your need for significance.

3. What would you say to convince someone that God can meet his or her deepest needs in a way that sin cannot?

Chapter 2

A MIRACLE NAMED DESIRE
Conversion As a Change of Heart

In his *Preface to the Romans*, Martin Luther said that keeping the law of God means keeping the law even when there is no law to keep. Then he observed that we usually do the opposite.

> In your appearance and conduct, you observe the law, owing to your fear of punishment or hope of reward; yet you do nothing from free choice and out of love for the law, but unwillingly and under compulsion. Were there no law, you would rather do something else.[1]

Two hundred years later, that statement ripped through the self-righteous armor of John Wesley as he sat in stunned silence while someone read it at a prayer meeting. Here was Wesley—a preacher's son, a fellow at Oxford, a lecturer in Greek and philosophy, an ordained minister for ten years—suddenly smitten with the truth that he did not yet possess the essence of religion, but only the shell. Three years after this "heart warming" experience, Wesley described his previous condition:

> I did go thus far for many years, using diligence to eschew all evil and to have a conscience void of offence; redeeming the time; buying up every opportunity of doing good to all men; constantly and carefully using all the public and all the private means of grace . . . and God is my record, before Whom I stand, doing all this in sincerity, having a real design to serve God [and] a hearty desire to do His will in all things. . . . yet my own conscience beareth me witness . . . that all this time I was but *almost a Christian*.[2]

He's not alone. Luther's penetrating insight aptly summarizes the plight of many people in all stages of the Christian life whose morals are not really their own but are borrowed from someone else. Luther undresses the facade of many who occupy positions at every level of the church. The matter is never so much about what we do, but about whether or not we truly *want* to do it. This being true, people may sin without ever having *done* anything, and sinners may be converted even before they pray. This explains why Wesley could argue that "all sin is a transgression of the law . . . [but not] all transgression of the law is sin."[3] A person's desire is at least as important as the action that follows it. Without an evil or selfish desire, the sin itself is defanged.

But we must be cautious, for the opposite is also true. Our kindness is really disguised evil if it flows from a selfish heart. We may hoard our money even as we give it away, or we may kill our enemies without raising a hand against them—if only we *want* to. It is all about desire.

In this sense, it was not the forbidden fruit itself but the desire to be as gods that plunged Adam and Eve into their abyss. It was because the Pharisees desired to seem more righteous than they were that they were actually less righteous than they seemed (see Matt. 6:1–8, 16–18). It was the desire of a nameless tax collector that rendered him more righteous than the law-abiding Pharisee at his side (Luke 18:9–14). And it was the desire of people to be healed that led them to seek that healing in Jesus (see Mark 10:46–52).

IMAGINE THERE'S NO HEAVEN

Desire is not the only thing important to a genuine conversion, but it is the first thing. After desire, the rest is downhill. Right here is where those of us raised in the church often have our biggest struggle. For most of us had our behavior changed long before our desire was—if, in fact, it ever was at all. We grew up wanting the things our unchurched friends did, but such things were forbidden by the church so we managed to keep them between our ears. That is, we did with our minds what others were doing with their bodies, and so kept our reputations intact.

But what if heaven and hell suddenly vanished? Or what if God allowed us to do anything we wanted to do for the next twenty-four hours and promised never to mention it again? What might we do? How faithful would we be to our families? Our church? The law? That is Luther's horrifying quandary.

And so the real miracle of conversion is not that our sins can be forgiven, but that they can become undesirable to us. We can not only quit committing our sins, we can also quit liking them. The desire to be saved is the beginning of salvation, just as faith in Christ is the end of it. One creates the tension and the other releases it. Faith without desire results in dry intellect or routine liturgy. It is a castrated obedience that renders one "almost a Christian."

But desire without faith is shallow mysticism, an ethereal and haunting restlessness that cannot find its rest in God. It is always asking without receiving, seeking without finding, and knocking without having the door opened. It is, as I heard one man confess, "to live the questions of life without seeking their answers."

Of course, this is absurd. For just as education consists not only of being curious, but also of acquiring knowledge, so true spirituality consists not only of wanting to know Christ, but also of actually living up to what we have already attained (Phil. 3:10, 16). But now I am far ahead of myself.

For the moment, let us remember that in the Gospels, Jesus offers to us the good life—that inner place where faith and desire meet. This is the primary meaning of eternal life. It has less to do with the length of life than the quality of it. This is what it means to have "streams of living water [flowing] from within" us (John 7:38). This is having life "more abundantly" (John 10:10, KJV). This is the "rest for [our] souls" that Jesus promised (Matt. 11:29). It is the condition that enables us to obey the law of God because it is written on our hearts. It is the spirit of adoption. It is having the love of God as the ruling principle in our souls. And so it is much deeper and more radical and lasting than the fleeting "sinner's prayer" or casual profession of faith that we see so often. For conversion changes the heart and not the actions only.

Therefore, we may picture ourselves—or anyone else—in one of four conditions at any point in our lives. These conditions range from the very evil to the very good. Each person, whether sinner or saint, will find himself in one of them all the time. Two of them seem very similar, but only one is pointed toward heaven. Two others seem very far apart, but they are more closely linked than they appear. I have pictured each condition as a chair and placed it on a spectrum as follows:

| First Chair | Second Chair | Third Chair | Fourth Chair |

THE FOUR CHAIRS

However complicated our society has become, all people are still either saved or lost, for Christ or against him, headed for heaven or headed for hell. But from there it gets confusing. For the true children of heaven and sons of hell are not always as they seem on the surface.

For example, there are two kinds of sinners. There are those who act like sinners, and there are those who act like saints. One kind of sinner indulges an appetite while the other starves it, but both have the same appetite. One kind does whatever he wants while the other does what he thinks he should, but underneath they both want the same things. One fornicates while the other lusts, but both have committed adultery (see Matt. 5:28). One tells dirty jokes while the other merely laughs at them, but both enjoy bawdy humor. One perjures himself in a courtroom while the other slanders his enemies over lunch, yet both are guilty of bearing false witness. Yes, there are two ways to commit nearly every sin, and so sinners are not always what they seem. Some are proud of their brazenness while others rest in their apparent righteousness; some are straight forward, others self-righteous; some ignore the Cross of Christ while the others presume upon it but, both are its enemies. These, then, are the first two conditions. Let's look at each of them.

The First Chair

The person in the first chair represents those who do not want the good life of Christ and do not have it. These are evil, malicious, God-haters who oppose Christ and his followers. The Apostle Paul said "they are gossips, slanderers, God-haters, insolent, arrogant and boastful; they invent ways of doing evil; they disobey their parents [or authority]; they are senseless, faithless, heartless, ruthless" (Rom. 1:29–31).

Other than that, these are some pretty nice people.

This aptly describes people like Theodore Kaczynski, the Unabomber, who mailed bombs to his enemies in order to maim or kill them. Tragically, he succeeded several times before he was finally arrested, and when questioned, his only response was an icy-cold regret that he hadn't kill more.

This is Daniel Colwell, the thirty-seven-year-old introvert who brutally murdered two people with a knife then argued at his trial that the state should execute him or else he would do it again. This is Eric Harris and Dylan Klebold, the mass murderers of Columbine High School whose rampage one April morning left twelve students (eight of them affiliated with churches) and one teacher dead. It is Pol Pot, the twisted mastermind behind Cambodia's killing fields. These are they who burn crosses, who terrorize children, who admire virtue only in order to steal it.

But these are the poster children of the first condition. There are other, more anonymous, culprits whose crimes are hidden behind the doors of bedrooms and boardrooms. They are conniving and egotistic, or as Paul put it, they are "loaded down with sins and swayed by all kinds of evil desires" (2 Tim. 3:6).

Yet not everyone in the first chair is this malignant. Many are ordinary, even good citizens who earn their wages, love their families, honor the dead, and vote in November. These are teachers, coaches, police officers, engineers, secretaries, technicians, nurses, hardworking farmers. They raise their families and pay their debts. They live and let live. But they live for the long weekend. As consumers, they are motivated by the next pleasure or purchase. Which of us has not encountered the nice individual whose morals are impeccable and whose word is as gold but who is not much interested in our religion, thank you?

Once on a flight to Atlanta I happened to sit next to a young man who was quite talkative. After we exchanged a few courtesies, he told me about his job (he's a wine salesman), his girlfriend (they live together), his dream to retire early (by getting rich), his parents (they're devout Catholics), and his philosophy of life ("I think all religions are the same").

> Jesus offers the good life— where faith and desire meet.

Then it was my turn.

After a series of questions, he learned that I was a Christian and a preacher in an evangelical church. I told him that our church favors the biblical interpretation of John Wesley and that Wesley taught, among other things, that we can know we are the children of God.

"No kidding?" he asked. "And how's that?"

"Well, the Bible says that God's Spirit will bear witness with your spirit that you are a child of God."

"Whoa. You've lost me. Could you put that in layman's terms?"

"Sure! The Bible says that underneath all of your actions is a mind; that is, we *think* before we *do*. Underneath your mind is your spirit, and your spirit is the little rudder that determines the whole course of your life."

He nodded. I continued.

"Now your spirit can take one of only two directions," I said. "Either it is turned inward toward itself, or it is turned outward toward God and others. When your spirit is turned inward toward self, then everything you do is governed by your own best interests. What do you want to do with your life? Who should you marry? How should you spend your money and your time? What's most important in life, and what are you willing to sacrifice in order to get it? You decide all of these questions *by* yourself and *for* yourself. You choose a career, go to school, marry your lover, settle down and feather the nest. But when we are turned outward toward God, it means that all of these questions are decided by *him* and that we try to discover what he wants us to do."

"Wait a minute," he interrupted, "you don't need to go any further. I already know which one I am. I'm the first guy."

I was pleasantly shocked.

"Does that bother you?" I asked.

"No, not really," he shrugged; "not yet, anyway."

The plane jolted as we touched down. He thanked me for the conversation.

"You're the first person I've talked to about religion who didn't try to convert me," he said.

> Pagans cannot repent unless God, by grace, makes it possible.

And it's no wonder that others had tried. After all, he *did* ask how people could know for sure that they are children of God. As opportunities go, that was as good as it gets. But another look reveals that my inquisitor was not yet ready for conversion. He was a nice man. We could have served together in any civic organization. We might have belonged to the same club, played on the same team, elected the same mayor. But we are fundamentally different. He is a "good pagan," to borrow Luther's term, who does not desire the life of Christ because he does not think it is necessary. He does not accept my basic assumption that all people have gone astray. He does not fear hell or love Christ, even though he believes in both of them.

As nice as he was, he was firmly seated in the first chair. He did not desire the good life of Christ, and he did not have it. He was not ready for the gospel.

Traditionally, the tactic of evangelists has been to blast these happy pagans with a call to repent. But this is self-defeating since the failure to repent is what renders one a pagan in the first place. Those in the first condition cannot repent, or they would not be pagans. And this is not because they are always rebelling (though some are) but because they genuinely cannot see the need to repent. In this way the "god of this age has blinded [them] so that they cannot see the light of the gospel"

(2 Cor. 4:4). Perhaps this is why Paul said so little about repentance, mentioning it only about ten times, and even then seldom in first person.

To the Greeks on Mars Hill he said only that God "commands *all people everywhere* to repent" (Acts 17:30 emphasis added), which is a funny way to put it when you have the pagans in your sights. But this makes perfect sense when we understand that it is simply not within the capacity of pagans to repent unless, through an earlier grace, God has made it possible. No one knows he was sleeping until he is somewhat awake. And no sinner in the first condition will even try to repent until he has already begun to move out of that condition.

A few years ago, I stood in the hospital at the side of a woman preparing to die. Years ago she had married a righteous man and followed him to church every Sunday. But the line on Susan (not her real name) was that she had never claimed this religion as her own. She was kind, generous, intelligent, witty, and a friend to all of the ladies in the church. But she had never believed the gospel. And now time was running out. While her son paced in the waiting room down the hall, I had what I knew would be one of my last conversations with her.

And she had a dirty little secret.

Forty-two years ago, when she'd learned she was pregnant, she had conspired with a doctor to kill her baby.

"He gave me these big, dark pills and said they would terminate the pregnancy. So I took them. And they didn't work."

I couldn't believe what I was hearing.

"A few weeks later, when it was evident the pills were not going to work, I devised a homemade apparatus and sat in the bath tub trying to kill the baby myself."

"And did you?"

"No."

She fell silent. It was as though she was waiting for me to absolve her sin. But I could not.

"Why are you telling me this?"

She waited, and then slowly confessed, "Because the child that was born is now forty-two years old, and he is waiting for you in the room down the hall."

"Does he know this?"

"No! Do you think I should tell him?"

"Why do you want to tell him?" I asked, and I will never forget her answer.

"Because I don't want to die with that still on my conscience."

Forty-two years ago she wanted to be rid of him by means of abortion, and on this day she wanted to be rid of him by means of confession. She did not want this guilt hanging over her head.

"I don't think you should tell him," I said. "I think you want to confess today for the same reason you wanted to abort him forty-two years ago, because it is in your best interest to do so."

She frowned and looked away.

"Susan, I was hoping you would say you are sorry for what you did, that you wish you hadn't done it, and that you want to make it right."

"But Pastor," she said, "how do I make myself feel sorry for something I really don't feel sorry for?"

Susan has perfectly described the curse of those sitting in the first chair. I have witnessed to these people. I have counseled them while they nervously looked at their watches. I have argued with them while I drove them home because they were too drunk to drive. I have preached to them in funeral homes. I have prayed for them in nursing homes while they fumbled with the pages of a magazine they would not put down. I have prayed for the meal at their receptions and open houses. I have let them down gently when I could not baptize their infants.

But I cannot convert them. It isn't their time. For discontent is the first half of conversion, and they are not yet discontented. For now, they have nothing to confess. They are stuck in Susan's dilemma. Those in the first condition can only ask themselves why they have it so bad. They cannot repent and can only wonder why. They know that if they tried to repent, it would be a mockery. What is wrong with them that they should only serve themselves? Aside from the evil they are doing, they must wonder why they enjoy it so. Even to bad people, it does not seem normal so much as it does common to talk about people behind their backs, or to lie when the truth is so obvious, or to imagine a bloody payback for those who have done them wrong. Even those who do these things know inwardly that this behavior is not normal, or else they would trust each other, there would then be honor among thieves; but there is not.

So I counsel those in the first chair to go home and to be as good as they can for seven days. When the seven days are over, they must ask themselves how they did. Did they live the good life? Even on their best day, did they commit any sins? Did they think of self more than others? Did they break any laws? Did they wish they could? At once, their predicament becomes obvious. They cannot choose to do evil any more than a fish can choose to be wet. They are born in it, surrounded by it, and captive to it. They are, as Jesus put it, "slaves to sin" (John 8:34). Let this be their incentive to repent. With all of the evidence before them—they are worse than they thought, and they are not in control—let them take the risk of coming to God in broken humiliation. Let them confess not only their sins but also their powerlessness over their sins. Let them beg for mercy. Let them seek desire for change.

The Second Chair

The second chair is like the first, but it seems very different at first. Those who occupy it *do not want* the good life *but have* it. These are the good guys. They are law-abiding, church-attending preacher's kids (or their moral equivalent) who grow up in church and "get saved" early. Unlike those in the first chair, these people have never known life without Jesus. They were baptized into the Church. They sing in choirs, teach classes, chair committees, and even pastor churches. They know the Bible. Their friends are mostly churchgoers, and they are very uncomfortable around people from "the world." As children, they learned which behaviors were rewarded or punished; they learned their godly parents' opinions on every subject and gradually foisted these convictions onto God—with a verse or two to prove it. Now they keep these rules as though they were the eleventh commandment. They preach against lying but find other ways to avoid truth. They "brag about the law [but then] dishonor God by breaking the law" in subtle, sophisticated ways (Rom. 2:23). And they do this through desire.

They guard their reputations jealously. They hear a command from Jesus to do this or be that and they imagine others will hold them in high esteem if they obey. They wonder how far one can go into the world without "crossing the line." They develop trite answers to diffi-cult questions in order to insulate themselves against those dirty gray areas. What sins those in the first predicament commit with their bod-ies, those in the second predicament commit with their minds.

I grew up in the second chair. I still remember the trembling in my knees the first time I said a "dirty word." I thought the earth was going to open up and swallow me. I remember sitting on the gym floor as a third-grader with my face against my knees while the rest of my class learned to square-dance. In my church, dancing was forbidden as "worldly." My classmates were laughing and kicking up fun while I sat (by my own choice) motionless against the wall. The pleasures of sin are but for a season, I told myself. My classmates would pay for this in the next life, and we would see who got the last laugh.

I remember the agony with which I decided to attend my first movie in a theatre, *Willy Wonka and the Chocolate Factory.* What if Jesus came back during the show? Would he take me to heaven and leave the boy sitting next to me? Why should he? We were both doing the same thing.

Like my friends in the same predicament, I could not play ball on Sunday, or even leave the yard (until I was older). I could not take without asking, eat without praying, kiss without telling, nor earn without tithing. I could not watch Batman (he wore black!) or movies about ghosts. In fact, I could not watch more than two hours of television per day, and *none* on Sundays. I was not a sinner because I did not do what sinners did.

But I wanted to.

So for years I learned to "repent" of the crimes I committed without ever repenting of *the desires* that led to them. With a truncated morality, I believed that certain things were wrong simply because the Bible said they were wrong. It did not much matter to me that such things were out of character with Jesus, whom I said lived in me. It was more important that they were strictly forbidden in Scripture.

And so for those of us born in this predicament—who do not want the good life, but have it anyway—repentance comes very hard, for we cannot always discern between guilt and godly sorrow. Both feel the same since God is our parental hangover.

I remember the day this dawned on Justin. He was a young man who had attended church for over a year when he responded to an altar call at the end of a service. By the time I got to him, he had met with a couple others and was convinced that he needed to repent and "accept Christ" into his life.

"Why do you want to do that?" I asked.

"Well, I've been having this problem with . . . uh, gambling and . . . well, I just don't know what else to do. I really think I ought to confess it," he said.

"Why do you want to confess it?" I asked.

He said he wanted God to take his sins away. I was still not convinced.

"Justin, I am going to define two categories for you, and I would like you to put yourself into one of them. The first is *attrition*, which means that you feel very sorry for your sins because you know they are ruining your life and keeping you from heaven. In addition to this, you know that the Bible and the church are against these things, and so you feel guilty when you do them. The other is *contrition*, which means that you feel sorry for your sins because you know they grieve the heart of God. It means that even if the church and the Bible did not forbid such things, and if they did not ruin your life, you would confess them anyway because you truly desire to be rid of the sins themselves, not merely the guilt incurred by them."

"I understand," said Justin, "and I am closer to attrition."

It was not what I wanted to hear, but it was the truth.

"I'm sorry, Justin." I stammered for a better way to say it. "But on this day, you cannot be saved."

Justin was smitten with guilt but confused it for godly sorrow. He was not sorry for gambling; he was sorry it was wrong. Failing to understand this distinction, we sometimes baptize unbelief by trying to convert it too soon, without allowing it to be interrogated. It is as though we are afraid we might talk our prospects out of conversion. But in fact, we ought to fear that we may talk them *into* it by minimizing the radical depth of repentance. They may repent only because they are conditioned to do so after each sin.

Many times I have debated with seasoned Christians who wondered whether they would go to heaven if they died before they had time to confess their last sin. I have seen them read the Scriptures with scientific precision to determine whether some behavior was or was not forbidden. In my opinion, they betray the serious misunderstanding that sin is only a transgression of the law. In reality it is more fundamental and more personal than that.

So the question confronting those in the second chair is whether or not they would keep the law even if there were no law to keep. If they were granted a single day to do whatever they pleased with no need to fear the wrath of God, what would they do? If it were not wrong to neglect the reading of Scripture, would they read it simply to know the mind of Christ? Do their sins truly bother them, or do they hate to love them? Do they truly love their enemies, or is it only that they are supposed to?

"What do you want?" I asked a frustrated youth plagued by doubts over his faltering faith.

"I want to want," he said.

It is the best answer I have heard from anyone in the second chair. They have lived around the trappings of the good life long enough to truly admire them, only they cannot understand why it is so difficult to *want* them. They are stuck between boredom with the good life and shame for not truly living it.

But let them be honest about their condition, first to themselves and then to God. Let them dare to tell God what he already knows. Let them keep the law, for now because they must, and wait for the miracle of desire. God willing, they will pass through this season of holy discontent and will emerge into a bright new day.

The Third Chair

The third chair has something in common with both the first and the second, but it is really far from each of them. Those in the third chair want the good life, but they don't have it. They have had a fundamental change in desire that does not always show itself on the surface. These people have a natural love for the Word of God and a desire to be with his people (the Church). They have an aversion to sin and try to avoid it, even as people try to avoid a virus but sometimes get it. Their concept of sin is shaped by the holiness and fatherhood of God, and so their repentance is more frequent, more meaningful, and more intimate.

The Apostle Paul described this condition perfectly when he admitted: "I have the desire to do what is good, but I cannot carry it out. For what I do is *not* the good I want to do; no, the evil I do not want to do—this I keep on doing," (Rom. 7:18–19 emphasis added). While Paul has been the target of many sermons because of his candid remarks, we must give him his due. At least the good apostle *wanted* to do good.

"In my inner being I delight in God's law," he said of himself. This one desire easily puts him among the most righteous 10 percent of all church members today. For Paul, who grew up self-righteous (see Phil. 3:4–6), had been converted. And right here is the fundamental point: the transition from the second chair to the third is the magic of conversion. This is the reason for the gap between the two.

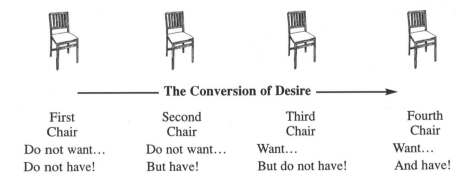

——————— **The Conversion of Desire** ———————➤

First Chair	Second Chair	Third Chair	Fourth Chair
Do not want...	Do not want...	Want...	Want...
Do not have!	But have!	But do not have!	And have!

Of course, this change in desire is at first visible only to the eyes of Jesus. He saw it in the sinful woman at his feet (Luke 7), in the paralytic lowered through the roof (Mark 2), in Zacchaeus sitting in the tree

(Luke 19), in blind Bartimaeus as he shouted from the roadside (Mark 10). This is why all of them were "saved," in one way or another. It is why one Pharisee who questioned Jesus was "not far from the kingdom of God" (Mark 12:34), and why the rest of the Pharisees were.

Unfortunately, it is easier to measure people by their actions than by their motives, so this will always be the practice of those in the church. They want to know if we are tithing and attending. They want to know if we have said the sinner's prayer or are still using dirty words when we get angry. They wonder if our taste for music has changed to become— well, more like theirs. They will have us wear our ties and wipe our mouths. Right here I am thinking of the mother who scolds her child after he has been rude to a friend, "Now Junior, you tell him you're sorry!" She wants to teach him manners, but she is teaching him to lie— to say what he does not mean. Instead, she ought to convince him of the badness of his actions or that Jesus wants him to behave differently. Convinced of these notions, Junior will one day apologize on his own.

And so when a person has jumped from the second to the third chair, he has been changed on the inside. Without any visible evidence, his inner convictions have been turned around. He now sees God, himself, and the world through a different lens. This is what it means to repent. And this is why repentance is so difficult yet so effective in making people new.

In repentance, a person's vision of God changes from apathy (as in the first chair) or fear (as in the second chair) to holiness and omnipresence. He learns to see God in everything. His vision of himself shifts from pride (as in the first chair) or paranoia (as in the second chair) to confidence and humility. And his vision of the world turns from consumption (as in the first chair) or competition (as in the second chair) to genuine love and compassion. And these virtues are not reserved for some later time in the Christian life when the person is safely insulated against the real world; they are for *now*. They grow in varying degrees, but they are all partly present in the life of every convert—or what, exactly, got converted? From what was he saved? Where was the real miracle? And whose spirit does he now have? From Paul we learn that "if anyone does not have the Spirit of Christ, he does not belong to Christ" (Rom. 8:9). Presumably, there are no exceptions to this.

The Fourth Chair

The people in the fourth chair is similar to those in the third, but have something more. The fourth chair is occupied by those who desire the good life and have it. In this condition "the righteous requirements of the law [have been] fully met in us, who do not live according to the sinful nature but according to the Spirit" (Rom. 8:4). By faith, we are learning to "put to death the misdeeds of the body" (8:13). The fourth chair describes those who have entered into the life they began to want at conversion. In just this way, the fourth chair is not an extra measure of grace or a second miracle independent from the first. Rather it is an extension of the first miracle. It is more of the same. It is not something else. Like Wesley, I believe our sanctification may come gradually or all at once, but it is always the completion of a work Christ began in us at conversion. The water of life that Jesus offers the sinner "will become in him a spring of water welling up to eternal life" (John 4:14). It is a not a different water. The trickle of grace that saved him has become a mighty river. To come to Jesus and drink is to believe in him, and for those who do, "streams of living water will flow from within" them (John 7:38). The drinking fountain of grace will become a geyser.

Paul makes the same connection more subtly by mentioning the third and the fourth conditions in the same breath. (Emphasis added in each case.)

> Christ Jesus . . . has become for us wisdom from God—that is, our *righteousness* [and] *holiness* and redemption (1 Cor. 1:30).

> But you were washed, you were *sanctified*, you were *justified* in the name of the Lord Jesus Christ and by the Spirit of our God (1 Cor. 6:11).

> Put on the new self, created to be like God in true *righteousness* and *holiness* (Eph. 4:24).

> He [God] has reconciled you by Christ's physical body through death to present you *holy in his sight*, without blemish and *free from accusation*" (Col. 1:22).

> For God did not *call us* to be impure but to *live a holy life*. Therefore he who rejects this instruction does not reject man, but God, who gives you his Holy Spirit (1 Thess. 4:7–8).

In classical theology, our righteousness and our sanctification are separate but related acts. *Righteousness* (or justification) is that moment in which we are "made right" in the eyes of God; we enter into a new relationship with him and begin to walk before him. *Sanctification* (or holiness) is the life that follows. It is the gradual, then final, setting apart of God's people for his private use. He does not mean to say that holiness is the second work of a different grace, but a second helping of the first. Even when it is distinct, it is similar. Those who have entered into the fourth chair no longer commit the sins they abhor and not because they only quit abhorring them but because they really quit them. This is to be "created . . . like God in *true* righteousness and holiness" (Eph. 4:24 emphasis added). So in the third chair, God *trans*forms our desire. In the fourth chair, he *con*forms it. In the third chair, we desire to be like Christ. In the fourth chair, we are like Christ.

Those in the fourth chair think differently. They play to an audience of One, that is, they do everything in the name of Christ. They embrace suffering when they would normally avoid it. Their joy is contagious; their honesty disarming; their simplicity profound; their love consistent; their obedience radical; their passion intense; their hope unswerving; their path less traveled. They are increasingly drawn into a jealous and private obsession with Christ that none—including their spouses—can fully appreciate.

But their predominant characteristic is love—first for God and then for those least like themselves. This is their peculiar mark. Those in the fourth chair are drawn by empathy and compassion toward people in the first chair. And why not? Those in both chairs are the logical conclusion of their inward convictions. They are different in kind but alike in degree. One is turned inward toward self (the first chair), so his usefulness and virtue disintegrate. The other is turned outward toward God (the fourth chair), so his usefulness and virtue are multiplied a hundred times. What neither of these people can understand is the transient apathy of those in the middle two chairs. Like Jesus, they would that those in the middle were either hot or cold, but since they are not, those in the first and fourth chairs will nearly always migrate to each other or to others of their own kind.

THE PECULIAR AND OFFENSIVE MARK OF THE GOOD LIFE

In 1999, after Eric Harris and Dylan Klebold shot up Colorado's Columbine High School leaving thirteen dead before turning the guns on themselves, an Illinois carpenter named Greg Zanis drove all night to construct fifteen wooden crosses on a hill just outside the school. Each cross bore the name of a fallen student, and there in the lineup was also a cross for Harris and one for Klebold. It was not to be. Soon after they were planted, one angry father, whose son had been slain just outside the cafeteria, mounted the hill and posted a sign on each of the killer's crosses: "Murderers burn in hell!"

"We don't build a monument to Adolf Hitler and put it in a Holocaust museum," he said on the evening news, "and it's not going to happen here." Later he tore down the two killer's crosses, chopped them up and threw them into a Dumpster.[4]

It does not seem fair that those who hate Christ should be honored alongside the Christians they killed out of hatred. Yet the murderers and their victims are more similar than they first appear. The former were willing to kill for the gospel while the latter were willing to die for it. Both were fully convinced of the things they believed, and for one brief, tragic and horrific moment they met in the hall at Columbine. It was not the first time. They had met before on Golgotha where the best of men died between two others who were as far removed—yet as similar—as were the martyrs and the murderers at Columbine. Very appropriately, God placed the dying Messiah between two thieves—one who wanted Christ for himself ("Save yourself and us," Luke 23:39), and another who wanted only to be with Christ ("remember me when you come in your kingdom," Luke 23:42). Of course the Christ in the middle loved them both, but only one was going to heaven.

> Jesus went into the thick of this world without becoming part of it.

So I counsel those in the fourth chair to stay with the sinners, to get out of the temple; for Jesus did "not come to call the righteous, but sinners to repentance" (Luke 5:32). Those in the fourth chair need to follow Jesus into the soup kitchens and men's leagues and pool halls of their city. One pastor has taken this notion literally and made the streets of Chicago his sanctuary. Mark Van Houten meets daily with the homeless addicts and hookers on the Uptown streets and refers to this as his "reasonable service."

"To many Christians," he writes, "bars represent the antithesis of the Church, [but] what they don't realize is that by deciding not to set foot in a bar they make it easier for the unbeliever to reach a similar resolve—not to set foot in a church."[5] He has a point. So he has told prostitutes to use condoms and taught users how to clean their needles in order to spare them the curse of AIDS. And right here is an important distinction between those in the fourth chair and their counterfeit friends in the second chair. It is precisely here that the two have their falling out, for those in the second chair are certain that AIDS is the curse of God and that any attempt to spare hookers and users of their damnation is to play God themselves.

"Let them have their hell hole," one such person told me recently. "They deserve everything they get."

But if we would really play God, we would follow Jesus into the thick of this world without becoming part of it. We would follow Christ, as one writer put it,

> to where the hungry sit on the ground with distended stomachs . . .
> to where old people are forgotten and young people brutalized, where
> innocent villagers have their legs smashed with clubs and innocent
> passersby get blown up in car bombs. "Follow me," [Christ] says, to
> where the rich buy unhappiness in expensive wrapping-paper, to where
> the poor people fight for the crumbs that fall by accident. . . . "follow
> me" to the corridors of power and the alleyways of despair, to the
> married people who have forgotten how to love and the unmarried
> people who long for a chance to learn how, to the businessman and
> prostitute, the camel driver and taxi driver, the security force officers
> and the little boys throwing stones at them; tell them that I died for
> them; tell them that I am alive for them; tell them that there is a new
> creation; tell them that there is a new celebration; tell them that there is
> a God who made them and yearns for them, and that if they find me they
> will find Him."[6]

This is not comfortable for those in the second chair, who like to measure their holiness by the distance it has put between themselves and those who have made bad decisions. So when the person in the fourth chair moves next to the one in the first chair he is criticized as "liberal" or "compromising" by those in the second chair, who have not budged an inch. In just this way Christ found himself caught between the sinners and the Pharisees. One of the many ironies of the Bible and in life is that the holiest people among us are not so labeled in the very place (the Church) where they should most be welcome. It is as though genius is not recognized by the intelligent, but rather by the idiots among us. This is not simply because the intelligent are embarrassed by the genius. It is more likely that the genius is intelligent in a different way, so that those who measure brilliance in the traditional manner will never see it in the truly gifted. The problem of those in the second chair is not that they possess less righteousness than those in the fourth chair, but that they possess a *different* righteousness. This is why Paul would pray to "be found in [Christ], not having a righteousness of my own *that comes from the law*, but that which . . . comes from God and is by faith" (Phil. 3:9 emphasis added).

A MUTUAL DISCONTENT

But there are other observations that need to be made about the four chairs, or types of people, mentioned above. One is that those in the first and second chairs often eyeball each other and covet what the other endures. They share a mutual discontent. The rebel in the first chair often wants to be accepted by the body politic. He wishes that nice people would say nice things about him, so occasionally he will straighten his tie and polish his act to curry the favor of others, but he quickly returns to his darker side when the others have gone home. Occasionally, even a bad person will confess to a priest or donate money to charity, but he will always do so out of interest for himself and contrary to his true character. When you scratch him, you'll find these real interests just below the surface.

On the other hand, the churchman in the second chair secretly desires to be free from his pious and stuffy constraints and really enjoy himself. So he waits until he is far away from pressure and accountability then he does what he pleases. Sometimes he even shocks the rebel with this flare for evil. That is, even wicked people are disappointed when their president curries the sexual favors of a White House intern. Even sinners are offended when a pastor in their community is caught in a tryst. Of course, they would not be surprised by this if they could read the private thoughts of their pious leaders. When he has sinned, the religious person in the second predicament will convince himself that he really loves God, but that he is a victim of "the world, the flesh and the devil." But the Spirit is just as sure that a person is "tempted when, by *his own* evil desire, he is dragged away and enticed" (James 1:14 emphasis added). This is another way of saying he is not thoroughly converted.

THE ORIGIN OF DESIRE

Thus, another observation is that desire is the magic of conversion. In other words, justification is not merely the changing of labels. It is not as though God lies to himself by labeling that which is evil as good.[7] In fact, God actually creates his righteousness inside the believer by changing the believer's desire. This is the line between Wesley and Luther. A holiness writer of the last century, Daniel Steele, has described it as a change in gravitational pull.[8] Just as a rocket will resist the pull of the earth's gravitational force and then suddenly encounter the gravitational pull of the moon toward which it is headed, so the believer in the second predicament will always feel himself pulled toward the sin he enjoys (but

52

tries to resist) until that time when his desire is changed. Suddenly, he will feel himself pulled naturally toward the good life he has come to enjoy and away from the old life he now abhors. This new love of Christ and repulsion from sin is as miraculous as it is sudden. It feels natural. But it is an act of God. More rules and more talk about the good life cannot make this miracle happen. That would be like trying to create the child by going into the womb after it. Instead, the convert is conceived by grace. The change is fundamental and radical. But it is inward and unseen. It has consequences, but it must not to be confused with those consequences. For this reason, when people are truly converted they will skip one chair in their movement toward the fourth.

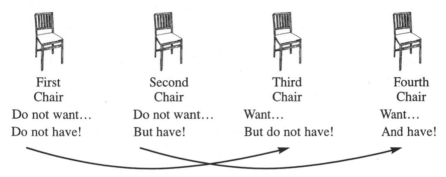

First Chair	Second Chair	Third Chair	Fourth Chair
Do not want... Do not have!	Do not want... But have!	Want... But do not have!	Want... And have!

Once they are smitten with grace, those in the first chair (rebels) will generally not bother with the second chair, but move directly to the third. Why should they settle for the shell of religion (actions only) when they can have the essence of it (changed desires)? Likewise, those in the second chair, who are trapped in the rules and routines of the good life without truly desiring it, are usually converted into the fourth chair, since the only part missing from their cosmetic holiness is the desire for it. Once converted they have a soul to match their otherwise perfect body of practice, and the new person is finally complete. But in every case, whether he begins in the first chair or the second, a genuine conversion transplants into the believer a sudden, holy desire to follow the living Christ until that time at which Christ himself occupies the person.[9]

Augustine prayed that God would give us whatever he willed— which is our conversion—and then that God would will whatever he wished—which is our sanctification. Augustine is right, so I have observed that many who seek sanctification in my church really need to be converted. Is it the same in yours?

And speaking of conversion, those in the first chair usually experience dramatic conversions with stirring testimonies, while those in the second chair move through subtle, less interesting moments. Of course, those in both chairs need to be saved, but only those in the first chair think so. Those in the second believe they already are, which makes their genuine conversion more difficult and less likely. The kind of faith that will save them is the wild and painful belief that nothing they have done up to now will matter in the end. All sinners must come to believe they have grace in their future. So those in the second chair must believe they have sin, real sin, in their past. For this reason, we must be willing to label self-righteousness as sin. We should grieve over those who have turned the abundant life into a marathon of misery. We must repent of our tendency to turn grace into law by measuring our spirituality according to rules kept, disciplines practiced, and sins avoided, or according to reputation alone. Surely this would awaken a cry for conversion among those who are already "born again."

THE SECRET OF AN UNDIVIDED HEART

Finally, we must offer hope and advice to those who are stuck in the second chair. There are so many of them, and some of them feel as abandoned as they do sorry for their awful predicament. As the young man said to me, they want to want but they cannot. What are they to do? Should they try harder, or quit altogether?

I am thinking of the student at one university who confessed to me that he really loved God and wanted to serve him but that he also liked women and liked to party. What should he do, he wanted to know.

"The desire you have has come from God," I told him. "Don't squander it. The decision to follow Christ with all of your heart is not like a surgery you can decide to have later. You must honor what measure of grace God has given you today."

"But how?" he protested. "I still want to party."

And now he speaks for most of us. We really *do* want the good life, but we are not quite finished with the bad. Would to God it were easier than this.

I have learned that the way out of the wilderness begins with David's simple prayer for an undivided heart (Ps. 86:11). It is the promise of the prophet (Ezek. 11:19) and the prayer of an apostle (1 Cor. 7:35). Is this the secret of those in the fourth chair? If it is, our quest for holiness does not end on the same day it begins. We cannot be easily satisfied by a single prayer of consecration. We cannot feed ourselves with books about holiness—including this one—and pretend that this alone will fill us. No, our filling results from a perpetual hunger and thirst for righteousness. This is the secret of moving toward the fourth chair. Our problem is not that we do not desire the good life, but that we do not desire it for long. Too often, we are done with it the moment we rise from prayer. We are on to other things, and it is not that the good life is unimportant, but that other things are important too. And so we struggle with a divided heart. There are, then, two sides to the spiritual quest. There is that which we desire, and that for which we will settle.

Has it occurred to you that most of God's blessings lie within reach for the person with an undivided heart, who will not waver nor wander until he has gotten what he came for? Let him read his Bible with renewed hunger. Let him worship with others who share his passions. Let him continue to confess sins, first to God and then to a few trusted friends. Let him pray, and while he is praying let him ask God for an undivided, undistracted, and unswerving heart. For once God has given him this, the Christian will possess all things (Ps. 37:4–5).

And that is the miracle of conversion.

But for now, we should begin where the process begins. It does not begin with a turning from sin, but rather with a turning to Christ so that the disciple is preoccupied with Jesus Christ. That is, we are not made holy in the way that monks or the Amish are holy. It is not that we are peculiar or old-fashioned or separate from the world, but that we are at first fascinated with and later fixed on Christ. For Christ is not merely the author and finisher of our faith, he is the very center of it as well.

But here again, I have gone ahead of myself.

LIFE RESPONSES

1. How would you live your life if there were no heaven and no hell?

2. Do you agree that God not only forgives sin, but also changes the heart of the sinner? Has that been your experience?

3. In which of the four chairs do you see yourself?

Chapter 3

THE BLACK HOLE
The Inevitable Call of Holiness

A black hole is a tornado in space.
Think of it as a massive cyclone of meteorites and gasses whirling in orbit around a center that is so compelling and so dense that not even light can pass through it. The layers of meteorites (called accretion disks) that orbit the black hole grow more dense as they are drawn toward its center, where the compelling force of the black hole becomes stronger and stronger until, finally, there is no escape. It consumes everything within its vast reach.

Now Jesus is a black hole. And just as a meteorite may orbit a black hole, compelled by it without yet being consumed, so we who love Christ may have once arrived, yet are always arriving. We are always under his influence, pulled into greater depths that seem very different from where we once were, yet still far from Christ himself. We are somewhere between the *already* and the *not yet*. Here, labels are less important than experience; what you call yourself means less than where you are, and where you are is not as important as where you are headed. And from the stagnant inertia of this drifting around may God spare us all.

As a young man, I was trained to read the Gospels in the traditional way. I saw the Christian life as continuum marked by a series of lines that helped determine where I was on the journey toward heaven. When I was growing up, there were two kinds of people: those who said there were two kinds of people, and everyone else. And I was not like everyone else. For in my mind people were always *either/or*. They were either saved or unsaved, Christians or sinners, conservative or liberal, sanctified or carnal. These definitions survived quite nicely when the day was simpler. But in today's complicated society, with its

Pandora's-box questions and sophisticated answers, it is neither efficient nor right for me to reduce all of life into two categories. Of course, there are still those who are going to heaven and those who are going to hell; there is still a moment (instantaneous, not spontaneous) wherein one stops going to hell and starts going to heaven; but there is more— much more—to be said about those who are going to heaven. Some are sanctified, others are not. Some are near the black hole and others are farther away. But between them lies a vast and gradually thickening field of intensity in which one's spirituality is measured in degrees rather than in lines. The one-dollar term here is progressive sanctification. And this does not refer to an interim period of self-fulfilling prophecy between salvation and full surrender. Rather, progressive sanctification is a hard incline. It is the subjective side of holiness.

Progressive sanctification is a hard incline.

The Reformed writer Alister McGrath has noted there are two ways to study theology, just as there are two ways to study the ocean. One is from the top of a map, and the other is from under a sail. One is objective and the other subjective.[1] Likewise, one may examine his own sanctification in two ways, from the top and from the below. We may say, objectively speaking, that "Christ suffered . . . to make his people holy," and so we *are* holy. We may reck-lessly abandon all of ourselves that we know into all of Christ that we understand. We may say, by faith, that every known sin is confessed and that God has cleansed us from all unrighteousness. We may claim to be holy without taking credit for it, and this does not (as some suggest) indi-cate pride.

But that is a view from the top. It is a different story from below. From here, holiness is more subjective. There are some who have thrown all that they have into Christ yet will not venture to call them-selves "sanctified," and not because they harbor some hidden sin but because they are harder on themselves than we are. Their expectations are higher, their definitions more stringent than ours, even though we are the ones dancing in the Spirit. These cautious saints do not want to minimize the power of the cross to cleanse us from *all* unrighteousness, and so they do not deny that sanctification must be possible. But because they have viewed holiness as perfect love rather than absolute purity, the target is always moving.

"I do not love Jesus as I ought," they tell me. And are they wrong? Isn't there more to sanctification than not sinning? So because of the growing disparity between what they want and what they have, they will not profess the holiness I am sure they possess. Perhaps this is why the holiest among us seldom admit to their holiness. They appear to be always on the hunt for selfish ambition, and always looking in places the rest of us forget to check. Because this is true, the person who professes sanctification may be no more holy than the one who does not. It is only that each has viewed the same grace through a different lens.[2]

So here is the problem with the concept of holiness today. In every congregation, within every denomination, there are people who should claim holiness but do not, and there are others who do claim it but *should* not. There are some who emphasize the power of sin. There are others who emphasize the power of the Cross. To me, the difference is often (though not always) in whether we are speaking objectively or subjectively about the same experience. One is our hunger and thirst for righteousness (subjective), and the other is the filling (objective). In one, I have all of God; in the other, he does not yet have all of me. The one relabels our sins; the other agonizes over them. One genuinely loves the Lord; the other believes it does not love him enough. And the trouble with our modern concept of holiness is that it has too much of the one, and not enough of the other.

Everett Cattell, a holiness writer of the last generation, has captured the tension well:

> The claiming of victory needs to be coupled with a deep understanding that the grace of God is constantly cleansing our souls of [our] inadvertent wrongs; and just as there is no specific consciousness of committing these wrongs, so there is no specific awareness of the cleansing. But that does not mean that either the wrongs or the cleansing are not there. . . .
> Our appreciation of grace and our humility of spirit should deepen as we realize how much God is having to do for us all the while we *feel* free from sin.[3]

So when we speak of progressive sanctification we are speaking of the subjective side of holiness. We are not thinking of an interlude between two works of grace. We are not speaking of a warm-up to holiness. We are speaking of holiness itself, only we are speaking of it differently. When we speak of progressive sanctification, we are not describing our cleansing in the past, but our cleansing in the present and future. We focus not on our good works, but on God's grace. We are not defining sanctification only as cleansing from sin (which is negative), but also as a present and growing fondness for Christ (which is positive).

The late professor Elton Trueblood observed that whenever he looked at himself, he marveled over how far he had come; but whenever he looked at Christ he was humbled by the distance between them. This very tension between pride and humility, between contentment and desire, is the proving ground of progressive sanctification. Here is where we learn to be hard on ourselves, easy on others, and honest with God. Here is where we learn to see what only the trained eye can. Here Christ bids us to follow him long after we have carried his Cross. Here is where our love matures and takes on hard consequences. If we do this right, we will never get over it. And this is why progressive sanctification *follows* a spiritual crisis as well as precedes one.

THE PROBLEM WITH LINES

It appears we have based our doctrine of holiness more on the writings of Paul than on the teachings of Jesus. It is Paul who speaks of Christianity as a series of categories with lines over which one must cross. According to Paul, we were once ungodly sinners but "have now been justified by his blood . . . [and] saved from God's wrath" (Rom. 5:9). This tireless apostle, who never forgot his own conversion, once told the Ephesians to "put off your old self . . . to be made new . . . and to put on the new self" (Eph. 4:22–24). And note the sharp definitions a chapter later: "once you were . . . now you are . . . [so] live as . . ." (Eph. 5:8).

To the Corinthians it was the same message: "If anyone is in Christ . . . the old has gone, the new has come!" (2 Cor. 5:17).

And to the Colossians: "Once you were alienated. . . . But now he has reconciled you" (Col. 1:21–22). To Paul, salvation is either in or out, fair or foul, heaven or hell. The only exception is a wide median down the center called *yet carnal* which, traditionally speaking, includes young Christians still in the incubator.

Some have noticed that even the allegories of Paul lend themselves to lines and categories. To Paul, salvation is described as passing from death to life, and from darkness to light. People are said to be under God's wrath one moment and children of God the next. The self is crucified (not strangled), then buried, and resurrected into the newness of life. And all of this is the language of lines that divides people between the haves and the have-nots. We become eager for a second work of grace, even as we once were eager for the first. By this reasoning, those who do not fit neatly into either category are labeled *yet carnal*.

A Theology of Lines or Categories

Now it is not surprising that the good holiness folk of the last generation spoke very frequently about the meaning of carnality, since they learned to define holiness through the writings of Paul. I have many of their books in my library, and the language in all of them is similar. The sinful nature is presumed still present in every new believer, and this nature is variously described as a tumor, a blood disease, the Devil, leprosy, or the old man. One writer conveniently separated *purity* from *maturity*. Another divided "excusable sins" (he listed anger, strife, and envy) from "inexcusable sins" (adultery, fornication, and uncleanness). Yet another admitted that "in our best estate, there is something of the devil in us." To these writers, when one is entirely sanctified this nature is surgically removed, or "eradicated," and from then on, to sin would be very unlikely, though always possible.[4]

Now if sanctification is a line that one crosses, then the actual moment of sanctification will be not only clear, but often dramatic. It makes for good testimonies. And those of us who grew up in the church have heard a good many of these testimonies and have wondered about our own conversions, which seemed less dramatic. We second-generation Christians love Jesus completely, but we cannot always remember when that came to be. Our testimonies are less convincing to everyone, including ourselves. I know of many raised in the church who doubt even their salvation. Their conviction about their experience of entire sanctification (though they still believe in the doctrine) is even more shaky. When we prod them by asking, Do you have the assurance that you have been entirely sanctified? they invariably resort to telling us about the time they consecrated everything to Jesus at an altar of prayer.[5] Usually, this refers to the time they got serious about their hobby of religion. They took a radical step toward ordination or membership. They crossed a line. Now we can count them among the sanctified. And while this approach to holiness plays very well inside the epistles of Paul, it does not fit well with the Gospels. And it has caused certain side effects that continue to have a devastating effect on the body of Christ.

Laziness

First, the "in or out" language has caused some to rest on their laurels once they were certain they were "in." They are like people who let their appearance and etiquette go to pieces once they get married. All of us have seen the proverbial couch potato who used to do everything for his dear lovely wife but now only flattens the cushions on his cheap velvet sofa while clicking the remote control and belching into thin air. For him, dating is better than marriage, and love is the thrill of the chase. Of course Paul did not intend for us to stop pursuing what we have already apprehended in Christ. It was Paul who told us we were "created in Christ Jesus *to do good works*" (Eph. 2:10 emphasis added). It was he who warned us to "live as children of light" (Eph. 5:8) because, after all, we were "created to be like God in true righteousness and holiness" (Eph. 4:24). And besides, we will be "reconciled and free from accusation *if [we] continue in [our] faith*" (Col. 1:22–23 emphasis added).[6]

It is possible that many who continue to sin freely after their salvation experience were never truly saved in the first place. But there may be more to it than that. It is possible that they were converted to a gospel of lines and not to a growing obsession with Christ. In that case, the convert never moves toward Christ; he merely shifts categories. He steps over the line. And of course, holiness is a pretty hard sell to someone who believes he already has enough of what it takes to get to heaven.

License

The second result of a theology of holiness based solely on Paul is that the category *yet carnal* has become a form of diplomatic immunity for those who claim to be saved, allowing them to do anything they please. In the past couple of years, I have heard or read about "Christians" who peddle drugs, beat spouses, steal whatever they get their hands on, and chase women. Of course, in today's language there is always a perfectly good, psychological explanation for all of this. And until these frustrated, defeated "Christians" can get all the bugs worked out, we are obliged to consider them "saints" who are "yet carnal."

But Paul never intended his first letter to the Corinthians to open a bypass around the serious call of holiness. That is, Paul was not creating a new category when he scolded the Corinthians for being "mere infants in Christ" (1 Cor. 3:1). Instead, he was scolding them the way a mother scolds her rowdy children in the back seat of the car.

"Stop it! You're acting like animals."

The angry mother has not created a new category somewhere between the human and the animal. She has not said that her children are animals on their way to becoming humans. She has used the word *animal* as an adjective rather than a noun. Even so, Paul is not giving credence to tumors, blood diseases, or the "old man" living inside the new believer. He has said only that good people can sometimes behave like bad ones, and that younger believers will do this even more often. But this is a far cry from labeling us "carnal." For even though we may do carnal things, we are still spiritual people, since every believer has the Spirit of Christ or he is not a believer at all (Rom. 8:9). And everyone who has the Spirit of Christ will one day conform to the image of Christ since "God's seed remains in him," that is, since "he has been born of God" (1 John 3:9).

Not long ago I watched a television documentary on the medical miracle of organ transplantation. Here were thousands of people who had no hope of living until someone else died and provided them with a new heart, or kidney, or pancreas. They received an unexpected, undeserved lease on life. But several of these recipients got something else, something they did not expect—a gradual craving for foods they once disliked. One woman began craving coffee, and another grew to like pickles, where before neither person could stomach these things.

In just this way, God has placed his Spirit—his DNA—inside us and programmed us to become like Christ: to like what he likes, to hate what he hates. We ourselves can hasten the process, but there is always an inevitability to holiness because it is programmed into us at the moment we are saved. The gradual, often imperceptible, changes we undergo through the years are real and certain. But they are not measured by the week, the month, or the crisis. And they are not measured by lines. They are measured by degrees and by their movement toward Christ.

Isolation

A third negative consequence of defining our spirituality by lines is that such lines subliminally separate us from those we are supposed to reach with the gospel. Believing that people are either sanctified or carnal, we treat them as such, and this creates categories that put us forever on the other side from them, to whom we are still more similar (even after our conversion) than we are different. In the theology of lines, evangelism is a way of holding another person hostage to our beliefs, a way of forcing him or her to catch up to us. In the theology of lines, holiness is not measured by our fascination with Christ but by our distance from the world. It is not our virtue but our peculiarity that defines us. I am not suggesting that we should mimic the world. But I wonder if we have not made ourselves peculiar beyond usefulness. I wonder if we have not focused on ways we are different rather than on ways we are similar to others in the same circles. I wonder if, in order to appreciate our distance from the world, we have not turned our backs on Christ.

The Jewish philosopher Martin Buber told the story of a peasant who sat drinking with other peasants.

> For a long time, he was silent as all the rest, but when he was moved by the wine, he asked one of the men seated beside him, "tell me, do you love me or don't you love me?" The other man replied: "I love you very much." But the first peasant replied: "You say that you love me, but you do not know what I need. If you really loved me, you would know." The other had not a word to say to this, and the peasant who had put the question fell silent again.

"But I understood," wrote Buber. "To know the needs of men and to bear the burden of their sorrow—*that* is the true love of men."[7] The theology of lines is not concerned with the needs of people or the burden of their sorrow. It is concerned with winning them over. It seeks only to bring the sinner across the line. It cannot love him just as well on either side.

So a theology of lines creates a climate within us that is not conducive to scriptural holiness. For holiness is more (in fact, it is other) than a second work of grace. It is a black hole into which we pour ourselves. It is loving the Lord our God with *all* our heart, soul, mind, and strength. It is loving our neighbor as much as we love ourselves. It is being preoccupied with Jesus. And on the day our labels hinder this preoccupation, we should be done with them.

THE FIRST DISCIPLES

That was the pattern of Christ's first disciples. The lines that divided them were often blurred, but the disciples seemed to center around the call. This means that the word *disciple* is usually used as a noun and seldom as a verb.[8] It is not something we *do*. It is something we *are*. Jesus does not disciple those he calls. He calls disciples, who in turn follow him for the sake of the call. As Deitrich Bonhoeffer put it, "he bids us come and die," and we do so because we are consumed by the One who calls us. There are no neatly lined contrasts between justification and sanctification. To be sure, there is a standard and the very real promise that we will reach it. But there is no formula for getting there. The disciple simply studies, then imitates the life of the person with whom he is preoccupied. To be a disciple is to have one's interest arrested by another: to observe him, to walk with him, and, ultimately, to follow him. Discipleship is less a decision (I have decided to follow Jesus) than a response. That is, people are not called because they follow Jesus; rather, they follow Jesus because they are called. It is not a program (Have you been discipled?) but a pursuit.

Look over the Gospels again, and you will see this very important sequence emerge. You will watch Jesus apprehend a person and pull him closer to the center with almost irresistible force. Gradually, Christ will transplant into the young disciple a compelling desire to follow him, until the disciple has nothing but Christ to follow. The disciple does not think about lines. He thinks about a Person. He is not running from his sins, which are on the periphery. He is drawn by the Personality in the center. That is, Jesus has a tremendous influence over the disciple that increases exponentially as he gets nearer to Jesus. From here, there is almost no escape and very little satisfaction. The disciple loses track of time and distance. Distractions grow pale. He does not bother with terms like *Spirit filled* or *entirely sanctified,* even though such categories exist. He is the perpetual student of God who never looks back at the degrees he has already mastered. He is more concerned about learning what he still needs to know.

INTO THE ORBIT

It surprises some to learn that the Gospels do not begin with the calling of the Twelve, but with the ministry of Jesus to the general public. Long before there were apostles at his side, Jesus moved from village to village, healing the sick and preaching in synagogues (see Matt. 4:17; Luke 4:15–21). According to the Gospels, it was only after he preached to the masses that Jesus called the Twelve. More than this, he did not call the Twelve to be disciples, in the formal sense of the word, but to follow him. It was the same with all of his disciples—and there were many more than twelve.

Luke does the best job of pointing this out. According to this careful historian (Luke 1:3), Jesus was preaching to a crowd of people on the day he called the fishermen Peter, James, and John. One cannot read this account (Luke 5:1–11) without wondering if there is a symbolic distinction here between those on shore, who are listening to Jesus, and those in the boat, who are helping him. For it is those in the boat who are later numbered among the twelve.

This is the way it has always been with Jesus. He is a decision point. He is a fork in the road. He is either making disciples of people or he is abandoning them to the crowd. He either draws them closer or pushes them away, but he never leaves people in the same, comfortable position as before they met him. The professor who visited Jesus at night (John 3), the woman at the well (John 4), the crowd that gathered for miracles (John 6:24), the Pharisees who waited outside the door (John 7), and even Jesus' own family—none of them could listen to him one moment and forget about him the next. His words were like bolts of lightning. Those who didn't get hit by them, were talking about it afterwards. The people were amazed (Matt. 7:38). His family thought he was crazy (Mark 3:21). A Sadducee marveled (John 3:7). A woman wept at his feet while a Pharisee stewed in the corner (Luke 7:38–39). Demons fled from him (Mark 1:23–24), and Pharisees wanted to kill him (Matt. 12:14). But the one thing nobody did was change the subject.

It is still this way. For Jesus does not merely testify to the truth; he *is* the truth. And truth, by its very nature, will either convert a person or ruin him.

Nowadays, people stumble numbly into their church pews and face the front. They encounter the living Christ in Scripture and sacrament, then move quietly to their cars. Nothing has happened today, they presume. But it has. For if the truth they encountered did not make them better, they are already worse. No discussion about the claims of Christ can ever be tabled for another day. For that moment, obedience will gradually become harder or easier based on one's response to Christ. His effect on the individual is immediate, either drawing him out of his hole or driving him deeper into it.

For those who will listen, the call of Jesus soon compels them to turn in his direction. That, I believe is conversion. It is an inner turning toward Christ, who has confronted us. It is not an understanding of certain concepts. It is not a baptism or a prayer or even a level of comprehension. It is, quite literally, the turning of our inclinations and interests. This is why the Pharisees (who said they could see) were blind, and the blind man (who said he was blind) could see (John 9:39–41). Clearly, the Pharisees were closer to God in their knowledge, but their backs were turned to Christ so they could compare themselves to the "sinners" behind them. On the other hand, the blind man and his ungodly friends (prostitutes, tax collectors, and Gentiles) were far from God in their ignorance, but their faces were turned to what little of Christ they knew—and they were saved! Even in their paganism they had a righteousness that exceeded that of the Scribes and Pharisees.

These "sinners" had entered the orbit of Christ. Their hearts were open to respond to the message (Acts 16:14). They would listen to the Father and move toward the Son (John 6:45), and the Father would get the credit while the Son received the glory (John 5:22–23). They had become Christ's disciples.

According to Luke, there were many of these disciples, and the degree of their intensity and devotion varied. Think of discipleship as a series of concentric circles. There was the multitude that listened to Jesus (Luke 6:17); that's one circle. There was the crowd of disciples who followed him (6:13); that's a circle within the first. Then there was the circle of seventy-two (Luke 10). There was the cadre of twelve (Luke 6:13). And there was the inner circle of three—Peter, James, and John—who were granted access and time with Christ apart from the others (see 8:51; 9:28; Mark 14:33). In the beginning, there was no pecking order (that would come later, among the Twelve), nor was there any comprehension that one was farther along than an other. There was only a clear and simple devotion to the One who had called them.

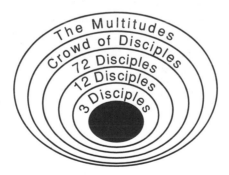

Followers

With the advantage of hindsight, we are able to see some differences between one disciple and another.[9] And each has its progeny today.

Some disciples were *followers,* or learners. These were marked by their unusual interest in what Jesus had to say and, especially, by what he could do. Some of these were secret disciples who "believed in him . . . [but] would not confess their faith" (John 12:42). At one time, Joseph of Arimathea was one of these (John 19:38). Most of them were driven by forces somewhere between infatuation and responsibility. It was intrigue, not curiosity, that kept them coming back. The woman at the well was thunderstruck by "a man who told me everything I ever did" (John 4:29), and if she ever progressed beyond this, we are not told of it. The demoniac and the blind man were cured of their maladies, so they followed at a distance. Even today these followers at the periphery will eat what Jesus prepares, whether sermons or miracles. They will speak to him when they get the chance. They will even mourn as he goes to the Cross every Good Friday—but they are not prepared to follow him there.

Judas Iscariot was one of these, one moment praying with the Twelve and the next dipping his fingers into the till; now kissing his master, now counting his money. He is very sorry it must end like this. He weeps (won't somebody stop me?) and wants to give the money back. His closest friends are among the chosen. But he himself is always among the crowd.

The most revealing characteristic of these disciples is that they always leave after they get what they came for. That's because it is always their need that motivates them. The gospel has arrested their attention and they will thus pursue the gospel for as long as their attention lasts. And once it begins to fizzle they will not come forward with any brave announcements or dangerous heresies. They will never officially backslide. They will just stop showing up. They will resign their positions at church or ignore them. They will put longer spaces between their disciplines and greater distance between themselves and the people of God. But the grace of God will not leave them here, at least not comfortably. Christ will prod them and pull them inward with a current so strong that they must ruin themselves (and some do) to escape it.

Adherents

Other disciples are *adherents,* or supporters. These are they who are eager to progress in their commitment to Christ. Too often, they are not called; they call themselves. This is the fundamental failure of many would-be disciples in our own day.

"I will follow you wherever you go," says one.

"I'll follow you," says another, "but first let me go back and say good-bye to my family."

"What must I do to inherit eternal life?" asks a third.

In each instance, the would-be disciple gives himself a call that Christ has not given him. He believes in the Bible and tries to govern his life by it. His values and his tithes are all in order. His assurance is blessed. His witness is bold. He is capable of profound sacrifice. Yet he is challenged each Sunday by sermons that call him closer to One he has already apprehended. He is graciously offended by the jagged sayings of Jesus. He is drawn toward a life he fears, charmed by the things that will bite him. If he can only grasp the meaning of his call, if he can understand how his suffering—and not his happiness—will glorify God (John 21:19; Acts 9:16), he will move into the current of grace that pulls him steadily into the bottomless hole of Jesus. But he can never seem to grasp it, so he is held in orbit, never moving closer to Christ but never moving away.

Shadows

A third group of disciples is *catechumens*, or shadows. These are they who are alone with God often and long. While the seventy-two and the Twelve were both given the same orders "to preach the kingdom of God and to heal the sick" (Luke 9:2; 10:9), only the Twelve were chosen "that they might be with him" (Mark 3:14). Only the Twelve were invited to "come with me by yourselves to a quiet place" (Mark 6:31). Only the Twelve left everything to follow him (Mark 10:28). Other disciples could turn and leave if things didn't work out, but the Twelve had burned their bridges. They were stuck with Jesus (John 6:68). Those who are nearest to the black hole usually abandon everything but the pursuit of God. Every part of their lives—their marriages, their careers, their goals, their laughter, their definition of success—is pulled into the wake of one holy passion that is fueled by a growing obsession with Christ. And this does not happen because they want it to. It happens because they can't help it. Or what does it mean to fall in love?

Questions from the Center

If we have this model of holiness in mind, the questions that drive our evangelism, discipleship, holiness, and even church administration will be fundamentally different than they were under a theology of lines. I say "questions" because it is always the questions we ask that control our direction. For our questions are always driven by our interests, and our interests are fueled by those things that are most important to us. This is why I will sometimes ask ministerial candidates to tell me about the problems they are trying to solve in their churches or to describe their last "really great idea." I am not trying to plunder it for myself. I want only to know what questions are consuming them. If the candidate devises a solution to a question that does not really consume him (say, what is conversion? or, how are the heathens converted?) then he will not likely consider it one of his greatest ideas. But when he has landed upon the perfect solution for what is to him the biggest problem (probably how to assimilate inactive members), I will discover both how he thinks and what he thinks about.

So since every person's pursuit is a result of the questions which consume him, what would be our questions if Christ were at the center of our lives? How does this new paradigm affect our mission and our holiness?

Evangelism: To Whom Do We Call the Lost?

To some degree, the Church exists for those who will never go near it. There are lost sheep in any society, and if we do not make it a priority to reach them we will have severed the body of Christ from its Head, for Christ came "to call . . . sinners to repentance" (Luke 5:32) and "to save what was lost" (Luke 19:10). While evangelism is not our only purpose, it must be one of our primary objectives if we are to love Christ as we must and love sinners as we ought. But to whom are we calling the lost? To what are our converts being converted? Is our message focused on Christ as he is, and not on Christ as we think people want him to be? That is the question of evangelism. For if Christ is the center around whom all believers orbit, then *he* is the one to whom we must call sinners—and not to something else.

Our failure to do that was evident to me one Sunday morning after I concluded my message and met with a few at the altar to pray. One woman, a visitor to that service, described herself as a Christian but then asked, "Now who is this Christ you're talking about?" She had heard of God and said that she loved him. But she had never heard of Christ.

"Excuse me," I stammered, "but did you say you were a Christian?"

"Oh, yes, I've been a Christian for many years," she promised me.

Are there really "Christians" who do not follow Christ, I wondered

70

then. And I wonder still.[10] For anytime we invite people to say a prayer, join a church, receive a sacrament, sign a pledge, recite a confession, or do just about anything else with which we have confused conversion in the past forty years, we have peddled to them something other than Christ. For Christ cannot be peddled, packaged, or accepted. He can only be trusted and served.

Recently I attended a funeral for a woman who was noticeably distant from the Church, conspicuously silent about God and religion, illiterate of Scripture, difficult to live with, and concerned mostly with herself. Other than that she was a fine Christian. So we were promised by the nice preacher that she was now "with the Lord because one day she decided to accept Jesus as her Savior." He said he did not know what prompted her to make this decision, and that it didn't really matter. What mattered is that she had taken that "very simple step" for which she was now reaping the benefits.

Elsewhere, a friend of mind was called to the side of an ailing man some years ago and challenged by a family member to confront him with the gospel. But when he did, the man—then dying with emphysema— motioned for someone to fetch his only Bible. Moments later they returned with an old Gideons New Testament that the man had received years ago while serving in the army,

> We are still making "Christians" out of people who never met Jesus.

and, sure enough, there inside the cover was his signature under the title *My Decision to Receive Christ As My Savior*. That settled that, he thought, and all of his family with him.

Apparently it was not important whether or not these "Christians" ever resembled the character of the Christ they claimed to follow. It did not matter what these dying souls pursued in life, nor what were their passions, their conversations, their spending habits, their routines, their personalities. What mattered most to the old veteran and the young preacher alike was that each "convert" had, at *one time* in the past, "accepted" Christ as Savior.

Today, our methods have changed, but we are still making "Christians" out of people who have never met Christ. Some busy pastors are building "Christian" haunted houses while others are staging dramas about hell's flames from the platforms of their church. One evangelistic entrepreneur visited his local pharmacy and slipped religious tracts inside the pages of the pornographic magazines down aisle six. To Andrew Meekens of the Evangelical Church of Ethiopia goes the award for the most resourceful effort. After the ill-fated airplane he was aboard ran out of fuel over the mountains and the pilot had announced a crash landing, Pastor Meekens stood up and "presented the gospel of Jesus Christ, and invited people to respond." Not surprisingly, some of the passengers (about twenty) did, which was good, since many did not survive the crash. Nearly as far out is the thirty-five-minute video that uses "state of the art 3-D computer animation and dramatic reenactments to logically show the only way to get to heaven."[11]

If that's not enough, I can subscribe to a service that gives me the name and addresses of everyone moving into my community. According to the advertisement, there are "fifteen to thirty good soul-winning prospects every day," and my investment will "result in increased membership."

Conversion changes the way one feels about Jesus.

But if Christ is the center to whom we must call the lost, we ought to stop and examine the questions that drive our evangelism. Is evangelism a matter of increased membership? Is it church growth? Are we peddling happiness, an aesthetic ability to cope? Do we promise our converts meaning, or belonging, or heaven? "After a week like yours, you need a church like ours," says the ad for a church in the Yellow Pages. Another begs, "Come, let us love you."

Of course, we may use all of these, but if Jesus is the center, then we must call people to confront the Christ who has confronted them. We must ask them to be caught up into the death and life of Christ. We must tell them to follow him (Luke 9:23), to imitate him (1 Cor. 11:1), to think like him (Phil. 2:5), to learn from him (Matt. 11:29), to love him with all of their mind, soul, and body, (Mark 12:30). We must call them to recklessly throw all of themselves that they know into all of Christ that they understand.[12] Any tactic, program, or personality that obscures the sinner's view of Christ, any presentation of the gospel that minimizes (even if it mentions) what Christ has done in deference to what benefits he will provide, any sinner's prayer that does not confer upon Christ the prominence and glory he is given from heaven, any repentance that does not grasp how serious and personal man's sin against God is, in the end, counterproductive to the real gospel. If conversion does anything for a person, it changes the way he feels about Jesus.

Discipleship: How Should We Imitate Christ?

Next to evangelism, discipleship is the buzzword in all conscientious churches these days. There are details in everyone's life which the gospel confronts, and these need to be heard and processed by experienced mentors in the church. This is discipleship. But again, if Christ is at the center of our lives—and churches—then the questions here must reflect that. We will be concerned with something more than the question of how to modify behavior—that is, to quit this sin or begin that discipline. We will wonder how to replicate the life of Christ in the life of the new believer. How do we retrain the young disciple's mind to think differently? How do we teach him to represent Christ in every situation of his life? Of course, this goes far beyond the traditional seven or twelve discipleship lessons, or the "new members" class that meets in the corner of many churches, or the spiritual gifts test we are so eager to apply. Once again, when we change the questions, we tinker with the methods as well.

Most of modern discipleship is about either leadership or membership. When we disciple leaders we are concerned primarily with turning spectators into donors or participants. We are enthralled with our vision; we are planning our work and working our plan. We have five- and ten-year goals, and practice the seven characteristics of highly effective Christians. Very nobly, we set out to make pastors, missionaries, or deacons out of ordinary people. That is, we want them to *produce,* not just consume, when they attend each Sunday. And while this wish is not wrong, our obsession with it might be, since one need not truly love Christ in order to do any of these things. It is as possible as ever even to be ordained without ever loving Christ. The church is rife with preachers who study only in order to preach, missionaries whose primary motive is pity, and deacons whose devotional life has grown cold.

Too often, when we disciple members we are concerned primarily with behavior modification. Are they good enough to join our church? Have they broken old habits? Have they made new friends among us? Once the new believer's lifestyle is consistent with our standards (read "membership commitments"), we are ready to have them join. Even if the discipleship process is not finished by that time, it has already been viewed (by the new believer and the church) as mostly effective. This is because the question that drives modern discipleship is in how to bring the believer into the graces of the church. It is an almost Catholic view of grace.[13]

But as we examine the discipleship writings and practices of Christians of a thousand years ago, we find a very different process at work. The writings of the mystics are replete with references to loving Christ, the Person, and so their practice of discipleship was generally less methodical and more related to virtue than to discipline. Bernard of Clairveaux's four stages of love—in which the disciple progresses from loving self to loving God is one example of this.[14] Saint Bonaventure's threefold way— the believer's progress from flesh to mind to spirit, causing a reorientation of the believer—is another.[15] John of the Cross's classic inquiry into the seven deadly sins (as found in the new believer) is still another.[16] Teresa of Avila's interior castle is yet another.[17] The desert fathers spoke of three conversions—the conversion of meaning, of betrayal, and of loneliness— as the pattern of discipleship. In each conversion, the disciple was confronted and defined by a spiritual crisis, and discipleship was largely a matter of supporting a believer who was hard on the anvil of experience.[18]

While modern discipleship speaks mostly of lessons or disciplines, our forefathers talked about virtues or seasons in a young believer's life. They focused on reenacting the life of Christ in the life of his followers, thus suffering and sacrifice were honored among them.

Even so, if Christ is the center, we must ask ourselves and our church committees to clearly define the virtues a disciple should possess and to build an infrastructure into our churches that supports their acquisition. We must make love of Christ the measure of leadership and motivate our deacons and teachers to know Jesus as well as they presently know church polity. We must become conversant in the Gospels by encouraging our people to read them regularly, or even by preaching through them ourselves. We must introduce ourselves to the people, whether dead or alive, who have been nearest to the center (Christ) and study their patterns and their passion. We must provide a wider network of opportunities for people to learn Christ and to live him, in soup kitchens, mission fields, silent retreats, or troubled homes. We must learn to identify our struggles with those of Christ so that our suffering becomes an imitation of his and our devotion to the Father rivals that of Christ. We must learn to make decisions by using the mind, disposition, and imagination of Christ. We must become *Christians*.

Sanctification: What Is the Way Through the Woods?

To be sure, most of the clamor about sanctification today is academic. We risk missing the grace of God in the explanation of it. To borrow an analogy from Rudyard Kipling, a lot of trees and brush have grown over the path that used to mark the way from here to holiness, "and now you would never know there was once a way through the woods."[19]

But there was, and there still is. There are a few things we know for sure, and these certainties form something of a compass for those of us still lost in the woods of wonder, love, and grace.

Direction Versus Proximity. The first certainty is that discipleship is more about direction than proximity. As we have seen, this explains how the blind man, who knew nothing of Jesus, could be numbered among the disciples, while the Pharisees, who knew everything about Jesus, could not. It explains how the women at the Cross who stood at a distance (Luke 23:49) were closer than the soldiers who gambled at his feet (Matt. 27:35–36). It is all about direction.

Apply this notion to a discussion of church membership and you will make a painful discovery indeed. You will see that pagans may be saved in ways that church members are not. This idea transforms our definition of spirituality. True disciples, then, are not those who have waited in line for their position on the church board or platform. And they are not necessarily the deacons we elect to govern us. Instead, they are the candid, often simple, followers of Jesus who have not yet learned our God talk. They do not know as much as their teachers, but they have followed what little they know. Read the Gospels again. Are these not the people to whom the kingdom of God is given (Matt. 21:43)?

> Discipleship is more about direction than proximity.

Discontent Driven by Proximity. A second certainty is that those who are facing Christ, with whatever level of comprehension they have, experience a growing discontent that is in direct proportion to their proximity to him. For them, sanctification is not a neatly defined category. These men and women endure daily the paradox of the fourth beatitude, in which Jesus promises to fill those who are hungry while he blesses the hungry who are not filled. These people are filled with hunger, and it is good. For if Jesus ever finally filled the hunger he blesses, his filling would be a curse. In this sense, their holiness is a passing from unconscious hunger to conscious hunger.

Response, Not Initiation. And how does one progress? This is the third certainty: The disciple always responds to and never initiates the next step in his progress. Like Peter, every disciple is called to follow Christ at the beginning of his life (Mark 1:17), at the end (John 21:22), and in between as well (Matt. 16:24; 19:27).

"Three times Peter gives the same proclamation that Christ is his Lord and God," says Bonhoeffer, " [and] three times it is the same grace of Christ which calls to him, 'follow me.'"

75

It is the same with other disciples. Matthew is collecting his taxes, James and John are mending their nets, Philip is running his business from under the tree. All of them are busy in the moment Christ calls, and all are called *before* they come to Jesus. In every instance, Christ interrupts the individual, and the individual is asked to take up the agenda of Christ. Philip, Andrew, and Matthew are told to follow him. Peter, James, and John are told to fish for men. No disciple follows Jesus merely because he wants to go to heaven (If you died tonight, do you have the assurance? . . .). In the Gospels, no disciple is down on his luck or contemplating the fires of hell before he signs on the dotted line. No disciple has heard the plan of salvation from another. None have gone to the altar, and it is not because these things are wrong but because these things, in themselves, cannot produce disciples.

> There is no disciple who is not interested in the agenda of Jesus Christ.

Instead, people become disciples because they are taken up with the call. In other words, a disciple's response is always an echo of the voice of God from the other side of the chasm. The disciple is to Christ what a print is to the original, what a song is to the singer, what an answer is to a question. To move forward in the Christian life without this perpetual call is like clapping with one hand. The disciple is made by the call, and the call is fulfilled in the disciple.

And what is the call? It is the agenda and emotion of Christ. Not surprisingly, Jesus' own calling of the Twelve comes on the heels of his prayer for God to "send out workers into his harvest field" (Matt. 9:38). Is it by accident that Matthew records the sequence as follows? (a) Jesus preaches the kingdom and heals the sick, 9:35; (b) Jesus sees the crowd and is moved with compassion, 9:36; (c) Jesus tells his disciples to pray that God will send workers into his harvest field, 9:38; (d) Jesus calls the Twelve and commissions them to preach the kingdom and heal the sick, 10:1, 7. It is as though the apostles were the answer to the prayer.

We still are.

These are profound—and perhaps disturbing—discoveries for those content with lines and labels. There is no such thing as a disciple who is not much interested in the agenda of Christ. For the authority of Jesus is the kingdom of God. To separate Jesus from the coming of his kingdom (inward or outward) is to preach "the name of Jesus simply as the one who brings salvation without involving one in costly actions at the points in public life where the power of Satan is contradicting the rule of God."[20]

Historically, the church has always seen itself as the feet and hands of Christ. It was the church, and not the government or the Red Cross, that first founded hospitals, schools, nursing homes, and recovery programs. It was the church that taught illiterate people to read, forced the motion picture industry to rate its movies, built aqueducts to bring fresh water into the cities, brought down the tyranny of slavery, liberated women, and makes people free today. C. S. Lewis was right when he said that it is precisely those people who think the most of the next world that do the most for this one.

I remember the story of an American soldier patrolling the streets of a German village some time after an Allied bombing raid had destroyed nearly everything in it. There in the middle of the wreckage, the soldier noticed a German child, all alone, his confused face marked with scrapes from the charred debris. Without saying a word, the soldier gently tugged on the child's arm and motioned for him to follow. Together they walked to one of the few buildings still standing, and the soldier ordered an ice-cream cone, then handed it to the child. Very slowly, the boy took the ice cream and ate it, never once taking his eyes off the soldier.

"Mister?" said the boy in broken English, "Are you Jesus?"

I believe that at that moment, and for that child, he was. He had taken up the agenda of Christ. Of course discipleship is more than this, but it is never less.

Again, there is no such thing as a disciple who is not much interested in the agenda of Christ. And there is no such thing as a disciple whom Christ has not himself confronted. There are no disciples who grew up in the church and continued to support the faith of their fathers without ever having had defining moments themselves. And the call to follow Christ is perpetual. It comes again and again throughout our lives, not just at the beginning. Christ's first and last command to every person is "follow me," and there is no progress without it.

It is important, then, that we remain sensitive to the call that God places upon us. What does he ask us to do? What must we forsake? How shall we love him? What will it take to enter the life of Jesus, and what will it take to have Jesus enter us?

Ultimatum and Sacrifice. There is a fourth certainty. According to the Gospels, every step forward in the disciple's life is preceded by an ultimatum, usually in the form of sacrifice. There is always something more, something else he must do or stop doing, if he going to remain Christ's disciple. These are the new shibboleths, and they all have two things in common. First, they separate the individual from his previous existence, and second, they make him even more dependent on Christ. They come in the form of demands that seem impossible, as though they were meant to scare the young disciple away. That is because Christ is preaching for the gospel and against it, all at once. He is guarding the gate with barbed wire.

One disciple wants to bury his father and is told to "let the dead bury their own dead" (Matt. 8:22), which is a pretty cold thing to say. Another is told to "hate his father and mother, his wife and children" and, after that, to "give up everything he has" (Luke 14:26, 33). Every disciple must "deny himself and take up his cross" and finally "lose his life" for Christ's sake (Matt. 16:24–25). And if *this* isn't frightening enough, he must eat Christ's flesh and drink his blood (John 6:53). In Jesus' day, it was this last shibboleth that cured the curiosity of many would-be disciples. So painful, so utterly extreme are these caustic remarks of Christ that, even in the church, we dumb them down until they are little more than bland descriptions of our new church order. We have put the sayings to bed in order to live peaceably with the jagged conditions that were meant to draw us deeper into the cult of Jesus.

The disciple who hears these things and agonizes over them will always be somewhere between God and the Devil. Once the hard sayings of Jesus have made their claim on his life, he will never be the same. If he compromises, he will be hounded by God until he obeys. And if he obeys, he will tormented by the Devil until he compromises. No ordinary person would wish this upon himself, but then, discipleship is never an ordinary person's idea.

Movement to the Minority. That brings us to a final certainty: entering true holiness will always move the disciple into the minority. That is, disciples move against the friction of society. They are countercultural. Nonconformist. Extreme. Fanatical. Otherworldly. They have their own agenda. And in today's society, that can mean treason or pacifism. For the moment a person becomes truly dangerous is the moment he begins to act according to his convictions. Of course, he will be bitterly opposed by those who are passionate about their own beliefs, but ultimately, it will be the moderates—those in the middle—who do him in. Or as Caesar put it, "You too, Brutus?"

The only way for a multicultural, salad-bowl society like ours to get along is for none of us to take our religion very seriously. That is, we must not pursue our beliefs beyond their capacity to make us nice. For if we do, we will no longer fit in. We will seem to threaten the almighty "more perfect union and . . . domestic tranquility." Of course we are free to believe anything we like. We may tithe and even get tax credit for it. We are free to wear WWJD bracelets in broad daylight. But if we take things too seriously—even in North America—we will be tried for insanity or insurrection. That is true within the church and the family as well. I have seen entire congregations blush because their pastor's name appeared at the end of a newspaper editorial criticizing liberalism. Presumably, this kind of behavior is not good for the overall reputation of the church. Mothers want their children to be nice Christians. Employers want their workers to be religious. The government wants its citizens to have faith. And this is not because these things are right in themselves. No, they want these things for the same reason that wild and irresponsible men want to date women from the church. It is because of religion's capacity to make people nice or tame or ambitious or patriotic.

Like Mrs. Zebedee, we want our children close to Jesus, yet not so close as to drink his cup (Matt. 20:22). We want our families to pray for missionaries, but not to become them; to honor the martyrs, but not mimic them; to tithe, but not sell all they have and give to the poor.

So the dominant virtue in most homes and most churches is moderation. There will always be tremendous pressure placed upon the disciple to back away from the convictions of a *catechumen*, toward the more moderate sympathies of a *follower*.

As it was with Jesus, the disciple's loyalty to others will go standing outside, waiting its turn, while a new and different Kingdom from within pulls him toward the will of the Father (see Matt. 12:47, 50).

THE VESTIBULE OF HEAVEN

I remember coming home from a minister's conference one afternoon, tired and worn out from the competition I felt existed between people of the same faith. Whose church was bigger? Who got elected? Who was naughty and who was nice? Every minister knows this competitive spirit. And I was tired of it. I was digging in my heels, even considering resigning my church in order to give other, more competitive ministers my place at the table. It was by providence, I am sure, that I happened to visit a couple from my church that afternoon. As I knocked on the door, the woman motioned for me to come in while she finished her conversation on the phone. Still frustrated, I paced back and forth in the living room while she talked in the kitchen.

I was not prepared for what I would find. For there on the sofa was a small copy of a pamphlet written by G. D. Watson, a Methodist minister of the last generation. It read:

> If God has called you to be really like Jesus, He will draw you to a life of crucifixion and humility, and put upon you such demands of obedience, that you will not be able to follow other people or measure yourself by other Christians, and in many ways, He will seem to let other good people do things which He will not let you do. Other Christians and ministers who seem very religious and useful may push themselves, pull wires, and work schemes to carry out their plans, but *you* cannot do it; and if you attempt it, you will meet with such failure and rebuke as to make you sorely penitent. . . . The Lord may let others be honored and put forward, and keep you hidden in obscurity. . . . He may let others be great, but keep you small. He may let others do a work for Him and get the credit for it, but He will make you work and toil on without knowing how much you are doing; and then, to make your work still more precious, He may let others get the credit for the work which you have done, and thus make your reward ten times greater when Jesus comes. The Holy Spirit may put a strict watch over you, with a jealous love, and will rebuke you for little words or feelings, or for wasting your time, which other Christians never seem distressed over. So make up your mind that God is an infinite Sovereign who has the right to do as He pleases with His own. . . . Settle it forever that you are to deal directly with the Holy Spirit, and that He is to have the privilege of tying your tongue, or chaining your hand, or closing your eyes, in ways that He does not seem to use with others. And when you are so possessed with the living God that you are, in your secret heart, pleased and delighted over this peculiar, personal, private, jealous guardianship and management of the Holy Spirit over your life, you will have found the vestibule of heaven.[21]

Think of it! The black hole of Jesus is the vestibule of heaven. And speaking of heaven, I can think of no reason to expect our love for Jesus in heaven to be suddenly stronger than our love for him on earth. What if heaven is not all we imagined? What if our sins are forgiven, our minds informed, our bodies perfected, our tears wiped away—but our level of love is frozen wherever it was the day we left the earth? What if we pick up in heaven exactly where we left off on earth? What then? Is there any reason to suppose that those whose love for Christ was lukewarm on earth will suddenly love him passionately in heaven? If disciples are preoccupied with boats, houses, and stock markets on the earth, how do we know they will not be preoccupied with streets of gold and jeweled crowns in heaven—if those disciples are in heaven at all?

Put another way, there is more—always more—to holiness than that which we already possess. For it is faith, and not heaven, that is the substance of things hoped for and the evidence of things not seen. We should not, then, be comfortable on earth with any love for Jesus other than that which will seem ordinary in heaven. For holiness *is* the love of Jesus.

And Jesus is a black hole.

LIFE RESPONSES

1. What is the difference between a religion based on *categories* and a religion based on *direction?* Which one most closely describes your church? Your own faith?

2. Of the three types of disciples identified in this chapter—followers, adherents, and shadows—which type are you?

3. If Jesus were truly made the center of your life, what would change?

PART II
WHEN I FALL IN LOVE
The Dramatic Consequence of Loving God

I t is not possible to understand Jesus apart from his heart of love. Yet while the Gospels are filled with instances in which Jesus loved people, they record only three occasions when people were said to love him. The following chapters explore what happens when Christ's love is truly present in our hearts. How do we know that we love him? What will be the intensity of our love? What will be the result?

Just three people are said to have loved Christ. Here are their stories.

Chapter 4

THE POWER OF LOVE
Spending Self for Christ

In any relationship, there is a distinct turning point whenever one of us says, "I love you."

Once given, we can never take it back.

The moment we utter those words, we pass through a set of doors that lock from the inside. From there, we will pick up speed. We will lose control, which is why we speak of "falling" in love. In a single moment we have grabbed hold of the whirlwind, and the whirlwind has taken over. Suddenly, we have intentions for this relationship, which was previously headed nowhere. We are no longer a part of the crowd. We receive less from others and give less in return. We belong to each other now. We will go hide in our love, or what is a honeymoon?

Love is an all-consuming passion. This is why ex-lovers make lousy friends. Having given their souls to each other, they have spoiled every other, more shallow, level of friendship. They can make their peace, or they can bail out. But they can never go back. They are now in love. Disney called this twitterpation, that fine line between attraction and obsession. This is where most marriages begin, and it is for want of this that many end. It is here, where each person gives himself entirely over to the other, that modern people come closest to seeing their souls. They betray the fact that the image of God (imago dei) is still embedded in their conscience, for God is first a Person. Even the worst sort of people want their lover to put the past behind, to hold and to be held, to need and to be needed, to know and to be fully known.

For any mortal, that is as good as it gets.

When we find love, we think we have found our reason for living. And we could be right, if we will only get our lover right. For we are each created in order that God (and not just someone else) may discover us, and that we may discover him in return and find our greatest glory and joy in him. He wants us to jump into him and splash around; to frolic, with reverence, in his good pleasure. He wants us to hold him and to be held, to need him and to be needed, to know him and to be fully known. I suspect this is what attracts us to worship.

So a person's religion has taken a new turn whenever he can say and mean, "I love you, Lord!"

Conversion Without Love

Unfortunately, many came into the Christian life before they developed a genuine love for God.

If they were sinners before their conversion, they were probably told about their sin and made to feel guilty, then offered something of a reprieve, which we call salvation. If their conversion began the way of most in the last fifty years, its terms were bartered along the wire of a four- or five-step plan, culminating with a prayer that was intended to be the open sesame to their new life.

If they were religious before conversion—that is, they "grew up born again"—they already knew the expectations (and there were many) of both their parents and the church. If they conformed to these expectations, they were patted on the head and sometimes allowed to choose a prize from the treasure chest, traditionally reserved for those who occupied the "quiet chair." Their parents got a proud and sterling reputation, and they themselves were used as the standard for all good children to follow. In short, things went better for them whenever they conformed. And one of the earliest expectations thrust upon these children of the Sunday school was that they should invite Jesus into their hearts.

In either scenario, God was a force to be reckoned with. He had incredibly high standards, a vengeful wrath, and eyes in the back of his head. He offered mercy to those who deserved it and grace to those who promised to pay it back.

Later on, when these good Christians were bothered by a sin that would not go away (I did it again, Lord), or they felt the chafe of a dry, arid soul, they were invited (yea, commanded) to settle the tension with another dose of grace. Now they were sanctified.

But look again over each scenario and you will find the virtue of love conspicuously absent.

In the first scenario, we progressed as follows:

Awareness of Sin	→	Guilty Conscience	→	Repentance for Angering God	→	Salvation as Relief

In the second scenario, we moved this way:

Awareness of Unyielding Expectations	→	Sense of Duty to Conform	→	Repentance for Having Failed	→	Salvation as Acceptance by Leaders

I am not trying here to be critical of either scenario, and even less to undermine the sincere faith of some who fit either of the two patterns. I merely suggest that each sequence is strangely devoid of love, which is the very heart of God and the summit of all Christian experience. And I suggest that, perhaps, the reason so many do not experience love for God after conversion is that they were never exposed to it before conversion.

Guilt Versus Godly Sorrow

In both scenarios, the great need is for the traveler to comprehend how great, how deep, how undeserved, how safe, and how satisfying is the love of God. Or at least, to comprehend more of it. This, I think, is the difference between guilt and godly sorrow, between a religion based on love and a religion based on duty. And if I understand the term, only godly sorrow can lead to true repentance, for repentance is not the temporary grief we feel for having broken a faceless law. It is the deep and abiding ache that results from having cut ourselves off from God, in whom love and holiness embrace. Guilt brings regret. The love of God brings godly sorrow. So guilt makes us sorry we did something wrong, and godly sorrow makes us sorry because we did it *to him*.

Most of us will find that our Christianity is the product of one emotion or the other. But how do we tell the difference? Here are some questions to help us discern.

Is my devotional life a joy or a duty? Do I ever get sidetracked, or do I stick to the little devotional and thought-for-the-day calendars? A common characteristic among those who love God is that the Bible never wears them out. They do not suffer from what C. S. Lewis calls "the horror of the same old thing"—a dull and tired familiarity with the passage they are about to read.[1] One God-lover gets up before dawn to wade through a chapter in the Gospels and pray. Another pastes verses on the dash of his truck so he can learn them on the way to work. Another has undertaken the daunting task of writing her own paraphrase to the New Testament. For them, the Scriptures are not a cold countertop before which they stand, but a soft, wide chair into which they regularly fall.

Can I spend an hour with God without having him correct me on this or that virtue? Here is another diagnostic question. Typically, those whose religion is based on duty cannot, nor can they imagine why God would even want to squander a perfect opportunity like this. Why would he simply hold his children when he could straighten them up? But lovers of God know they will always have tomorrow to work on virtue, so tonight they enjoy the quiet evening alone with God.

When I sin, do I feel as if I'm in trouble or as if I've hurt someone I love? Lovers of God surrender their sins; they do not have them pried from their fingers. To them, sin is evil, not only because it is forbidden in Scripture, but because it is opposite the nature of God. The church father Nicolas of Cusa preached that holiness had but one fear, that of losing the friendship of God.

Do I share my resources with God, or have I drawn a clear delineation between what is mine and what is his? In this sense, a person's tithe is an index to his spiritual life. That is, we can tell the way he thinks and worships by watching the way he tithes. If he tithes grudgingly, his God is an ogre. If he tithes meticulously, down to the penny on his net income, he will be a legalist in other matters too. If he doesn't tithe at all, it is because religion is a trivial matter to him (in spite of what he says) and he has yet to cast his vote in its favor. For years, I took the tithe (or tenth) as a ballpark figure. That changed when I noticed myself taking the same liberty with other passages of Scripture. For me, as for everyone else, the matter of stewardship was a clue to my inner motivation.

Hell for Christians

But just as marriage is not all that it can be when either party remains only because it's best for all involved, neither is Christianity all it can be until we pass from guilt or duty into love. Our religion will take a new turn whenever we can say, and mean, "I love you, Lord."

Have you noticed that this very emotion (love) was the one element absent from every sinner depicted in the Gospels? Some were self-righteous and others unrighteous, but all of them were void of love. For instance, in the synoptic Gospels no one even uses the term, except for Jesus, the Father, and one inquirer on his way to conversion. "You are right," he told Jesus, "to love [God] with all of your heart . . . and to love your neighbor as yourself is more important than all burnt offerings and sacrifices" (Mark 12:32–33).

For this, the inquirer (a Pharisee) was told that he was "not far from the kingdom of God" (12:34). It was his answer, and not the question, that impressed Jesus. The Pharisees whom Jesus condemned were those who "neglect[ed] justice and the love of God" (Luke 11:42).

The rich young ruler was told to keep the commandments and to love his neighbor as himself, and he answered that he had done all of this. Yet when he was told to sell all he had and give to the poor, he went away sad. Read the commandments again, and notice that the only one he could not keep was the commandment of love: he could not love the poor the way he loved himself, since he kept his money for himself.

The elder brother of the prodigal son is another example. He possessed all the virtues of holiness—honesty, ambition, integrity, loyalty, and a profound sense of justice—but he could not bring himself to love his younger brother. He could not imagine how someone could stoop to do all that his brother had done. He could not move beyond the hurt his brother inflicted on the family. The German writer Helmut Theilicke explains his problem with painful accuracy.

> Because he was so frightfully untouched and so entirely without love in the crucial moment, his heart could not beat with his father's. As he withdrew from his brother, he also, unwittingly, withdrew from his own father. And finally, he was the one who, in a very subtle way, went to a far country. From this foreign land, however, there was no returning.

The loveless cannot find a way back.[2] If there is a hell for Christians, this must be it.

"Thought, purpose, logic, industriousness, but without radiance or love . . . think of it," says William Sullivan, "isn't that an accurate description of Satan?"[3]

To love appears to be the one thing the unregenerate heart cannot do. Is this, then, the miracle of conversion? Is this the heart of flesh where once only stone existed? Is this the welling "spring of water" Jesus promised the woman at the well? Is this "life more abundant"? Is this holiness?

HOLINESS AS PERFECT LOVE

Yes, holiness is first and always about love. Anything else is a rabbit trail. We will speak often of holiness as living with power, or as living without sin, or as a baptism of the Spirit, but in its purest form holiness is a matter of love. Even before the Fall it was not that Adam dotted his i's and crossed his t's, but that he actually loved him who walked at night in the Garden. In sin, a friendship is broken, an intimacy mocked, a trust betrayed, a warm heart turned cold. It was not that Adam's perfect record was marred. It was that he was separated from God, in whose image he had shined. He was now left to himself, and every consequence of his sin—the selfishness, the cover-up, the blame, the rebellion—was because of the absence of God. From this angle, God's persistent attempt to restore the fallen person is an attempt to restore him to loving fellowship, the perfection of which is Christian holiness.

It was for love that God righted the wrongs of the Garden, or what is the difference between Adam and Lucifer? Adam was sought, disciplined, clothed, and forgiven in a way that Lucifer was not, even though their crimes were similar (compare Gen. 3:5 and Isa. 14:13–14) because Adam was the object of God's love. It was for love that God punished Cain but did not kill him. It was love that saved the lives of eight people aboard an ark when, only moments before, God had promised to wipe them all from the earth (Gen. 6:7–8). It was love that made a rebellious Israel God's son. And it was because of love that God could never walk away from Israel's descendants—though he threatened to—but tried and tried again to restore them. For if one has loved with a pure love, he can never walk away. He may decide to spank the errant ones or to leave them in their mess. But he cannot choose to stop caring. Love binds the lover to his beloved. And God is love.

Holiness is first and always about love.

This love was a dominant theme in early holiness literature. Each time John Wesley was asked to define his newfangled theory of holiness, he replied that it meant only to "love the Lord your God with all your heart, soul, mind and strength; and to love your neighbor as yourself." He was charged with teaching everything from sinless perfection (which he denied) to a second blessing. In each case, his accusers were met with the same response: holiness is perfect (or mature) love.

It is worth noting that there is nothing in this definition about the absence of sin or the infusion of power. To be sure, these may be implied, but they are conspicuously absent from the definition, crafted by a man who usually had no trouble expressing himself. As with so many theological turning points, it would take another long generation to spell out the ramifications of Wesley's definition of holiness.

One generation after Wesley's death, a different emphasis was heard from Methodist pulpits. As preachers worked out the meaning of Wesley's thought (according to some, it was because Wesley had not worked out the meaning himself), they concluded that holiness really meant two things: purity of heart and power for service. This was reflected in the language of nineteenth century holiness literature (have you crucified the old man? are you baptized in the Spirit?).[4]

Occasionally, Wesley's students paid lip service to the idea that holiness is perfect love, but this was cloaked in the language of a second blessing so it is hard to know whether, by love, the writers meant a growing marriage to Christ or only the wedding. Beyond this, I notice the penchant of some preachers to connect the idea of love immediately to its utilitarian purpose—that of cleansing the *old man* (purity) and fitting him for service (power). And right here is the problem. Given years of this otherwise good teaching, it is possible—even likely—that many whose lives are clean and whose calendars are crammed *still* have not discovered the fundamental emotion behind all of the emphasis on holiness. For while it has many faces, love is a heart. So when we define holiness in terms of sin, we have followed a rabbit trail away from our discussion of true, authentic Christianity. In fact, a Christian might occasionally sin just as a mourner might laugh at a funeral. To sin is surely out of character with the tenor of the Christian, and it is peculiar behavior indeed to anyone watching, but it does not, in itself, spell the end of his holiness or the beginning of his slide into Abaddon.

In other words, there is more to being healthy than not being sick, just as there is more to marriage than monogamy. We may set high standards and meet them. We may stay busy with church business and be genuinely committed to doing good. But until we have loved God, we have settled for a form of religion while denying the power thereof.

People of every age have sought to capture the essence of true spirituality by devoting themselves to something such as order (the monks) or faith (the martyrs) or knowledge (the Jesuits) or the church (the Reformers). And people today define their spirituality by good clean living. But this, too, is a rabbit trail. Today, as in every age, the true measure of a Christian is love.

"How simple this truth is," wrote Madam Guyon three hundred years ago. "Even the uneducated may learn to live in love [and] my own heart is burdened when I think of how easily the entire church could be transformed if only they would love. But will they? Will you?"[5]

THE EXPRESSIONS OF LOVE

Whenever one says he loves God, and means it, he has turned a corner in his religion, and that will be manifested in one (or all) of three ways. Put another way, there are three instances in the Gospels where someone is said to love Jesus, and in each instance love is expressed differently. So while true love may have many expressions, these three episodes provide of a baseline from which our love may be measured.

The first episode takes place in the house a good Pharisee named Simon. There a woman pours out her love on the feet of Christ (Luke 7:36–50). The second episode takes place only hours before Christ's death when he tells his disciples to show their love by obeying him (John 14:15). The third episode takes place on the shores of Galilee after the Resurrection, when Jesus answers Peter's affirmation ("Lord, you know that I love you") with the command to feed Christ's sheep (John 21:17).

Love As Pursuit of Christ

For now, let us enter the drama of the first episode. It is the story of a woman who washes, then kisses, then anoints the feet of Jesus in the presence of her enemies (Luke 7:36–50). Apparently, her love did not begin that night, for according to Luke it was when she "learned that Jesus was eating at the Pharisee's house [that] she brought an alabaster jar of perfume. . . ."

It was premeditated.

Love in the first degree.

One can picture the woman waiting for this moment. Her offering is extraordinary. It is well known that her tears that evening came not from her eyes but from a small clay vial of the type the ancients used to collect their tears—both real and symbolic. These clay vials were often buried with the dead as an apt summary of their lives. These were the memories of their hopes, hurts, frustrations, fears, and joys. For this woman to pour out the vial was to empty her whole life onto the feet of one she had likely never met.

From here, she breaks protocol three times. First, she wipes his feet with her hair. Jewish women were forbidden to let their hair down in public since this was the practice of prostitutes. Second, she kisses his feet. On rare occasions a disciple might kiss the feet of a rabbi, but never in public. And third, she anoints his feet with oil. Most anointing was given to the head, and always by menial slaves. Jesus drew attention to this, saying to Simon, "You did not put oil on my *head,* but she has poured perfume on my *feet"* (Luke 7:46 emphasis added). So she, who came as a guest, knelt as a slave and left in peace.

In the brief parable that follows, Jesus alludes to two debtors and asks which would be more grateful when his loan was cancelled. When Simon answers, "The one who had the bigger debt," Jesus notes that the sinful woman's many sins had been forgiven—*for she loved much.*

This is the first measure of love: that we spend ourselves in pursuit of Christ. We try to take hold of him who has taken hold of us. And it is Christ we are after, not merely his church, his mission, or his agenda.

Is this true of us? Are we wearing ourselves out on Christ? Do we worship him with our bodies? Do we ever break a sweat for his name's sake? Do we count all things loss for the sake of knowing him? Do we extend ourselves financially? Are we ever tired in the morning for having stayed up the night before to pray or to meditate rather than to worry?

Love As Surrender of Self

To love another is to surrender self. We move ourselves out of the center of our lives in order that a new obsession may take our place.

> There is always room in our brain for a little diversion.

The great missionary Frank Laubach made it a practice to ask himself every fifteen minutes of the day whether his actions, words, or disposition at the moment were pleasing to Christ. "Since I began this practice," he wrote, "I have discovered that not everyone does this."

Do we?

Most of us are busy, but there is always room in our brains for a little diversion. Even the disciplined mind of a surgeon or a stockbroker is capable of thinking about one thing while doing something else. Perfect love collects these loose ends and bridles their energy in pursuit of God.

Of course, one might argue that we need not discipline ourselves in this way in order to be holy. Yet this is one way of pouring ourselves out at the feet of Christ.

Brother Lawrence made it his practice never to get out of bed before uttering the prayer, "Jesus, Son of David, have mercy on me." It was his way of loving much. In this, he never forgot how great a debt his master forgave. The holiness scholar Melvin Dieter has said that "gratitude is what keeps our holiness alive."

In short, we cannot pretend to love Christ most if we think about other things more. We cannot speak of consecration while we give ourselves in large measure to other things. The early Christian knew this, so when nearly three hundred delegates gathered for the council at Nicea, it is said that the number of them who were not missing an eye, a limb, or a member of their family could be counted on two hands. When John Wycliffe began his translation of Scripture, he was joined by a cadre of scholars, none of whom would see his thirty-fifth birthday. These people knew what it meant to pour themselves out at the feet of Christ. When persecution did not destroy them, exhaustion did.

The earliest preachers of Methodism lived fast and furious for the same cause. According to one historian,

> Of the first 737 members of the Conference (up to 1847), nearly half died before they were thirty years old and two-thirds died before they could render twelve years of service. True, some lived to a ripe old age, but most burned themselves out for God. No insurance company would have offered them a "preferred risk" policy.[6]

John "Praying" Hyde is another of the many whom we admire more than imitate. Dead from sarcoma at age thirty-nine, Mr. Hyde more likely prayed himself into the ground. Friends watched him kneel in prayer for ten hours without moving a muscle, and his monthlong fasts, sleepless nights, and agitated, heavy spirit were well known to many who came to him for prayer. In Hyde's waning years, one doctor reported:

> Your heart is in an awful condition. I have never come across such a bad case as this. It has been shifted out of its natural position on the left side to a place over on the right side. Through stress and strain it is in such a bad condition that it will require months and months of strictly quiet life to bring it back again to anything like its normal state. What have you been doing with yourself?[7]

Mr. Hyde thanked the good doctor, then ignored his advice. He spent his remaining years in pursuit of holiness. He "never preached much about his personal experience of sanctification," wrote his lifetime friend and biographer, "but he lived the sanctified life."[8]

THE THINGS WE DO FOR LOVE

Like you, I will soon leave the office and return home to a comfortable family and a quiet evening. I have lived past the age of thirty-five and have no visible scars to show for my faith in Jesus. Like you, I may question the wisdom—even the spirituality—of people who waste their God-given health and families for pursuits like missions or building the church. If they want to miss both dinner and sleep for the sake of these things, let them. As for me, I will have my cake and eat it too.

Yet there is this ominous, almost instinctive, fear that one hundred years from now, I would rather be them than me.

What has your love of Christ cost you, really?

Is it only that you, who are already rich, could be even richer were it not for your modesty and your tithe?

What do you endure, what cross do you bear because of your devotion to Christ that the world does not?

Do you love him?

How do you know?

The great Francis of Assisi was terrified of leprosy. And one day while walking a narrow path outside of town, he looked up to see a leper, horribly white in the sunshine, dragging himself in the opposite direction.

There was no place to go. Inwardly he recoiled and plotted a way of escape. But soon after, he rallied and, ashamed of himself, ran and threw his arms around the leper's neck and kissed him. Then he walked on. A moment later, the good saint glanced over his shoulder to watch the leper and was shocked to find there was no one there at all, only the hot, empty path he himself had just traveled. It was no leper that the Francis had encountered that day. It was Christ himself, coming as the least of these, and the good saint died believing it.

Someone has pointed out that people do what they do for one of three reasons: faith, fear, or love.

What do you do for love?

LIFE RESPONSES

1. What might motivate someone to accept Christ, even though he or she didn't truly love God?

2. Describe a person who loves God. What character traits might that person display? How might he or she behave?

3. Steve DeNeff mentioned several people who sacrificed their lives in service to God. What would motivate you to make that kind of surrender?

Chapter 5

BACKING FORWARD
The Struggle and Joy of Obedience

E very holiness writer has a favorite quote.
　　Here's mine: "I don't care if you are a little old lady. If you touch me with that umbrella again, I'm gonna deck you."
Isn't that a classic?
I should explain.
Several years ago Mother Teresa visited Washington, D.C. Spectators and journalists gathered in long lines to get a glimpse of the frail saint as she moved from her car into a building. Two of these journalists—a strong young man and a little old lady toting an umbrella—were jockeying for position in line. The man had the stature to guarantee himself a good angle, but each time he raised his camera to shoot he felt the stinging tip of an umbrella in his ribs. And so, after putting up with the nonsense long enough, he whirled around and let loose a few expletives directed at the mild-mannered matron behind him.

Of course she countered that she was there first, that he should give deference to a "little old lady," that he was tall enough to look over her anyway, and that until he decided to move it she was going to keep right on poking him in the ribs. And that was when the young journalist uttered his immortal line: "If you touch me with that umbrella again, I'm gonna deck you."

More curious than statement line itself is the timing of it. For it was not uttered at a parade or a ballgame. It did not happen at the closing of the stock market. No, it was said while two journalists were attempting to outstrip one another by catching a glimpse of holiness as she walked by.

Hidden inside that one sentence is the stark, brutal truth that human beings more often admire virtue than practice it. They cheer humility from within their prisons of self, which they have no intention of leaving.

Like spectators attending a ballgame, they will come to church and watch the antics of holy, passionate men and women and then return home to be occupied by other things. While they are watching, they will wish they were as good as their heroes on the field, yet when they get home they will not so much as practice.

This is why Jesus referred to obedience as the mark of a true disciple (Matt. 28:20). It is an expression of love and friendship. Writer John Piper calls it "the irrepressible public relations project of those who have tasted and seen that the Lord is good."[1] Three hundred years earlier, Jeremy Taylor called it a complex act of virtue because "many graces are exercised in one act of obedience."[2] He listed humility, self-denial, charity, benevolence, and order. Thomas à Kempis argued that to withdraw from obedience was to withdraw from grace itself.[3]

BACKING BACKWARD

For too long I had seen it another way. I grew up believing that salvation was something of a loan, and obedience was the payback. God forgives, we obey. Now we're even. I did not see the miracle inside conversion. Whatever was forbidden before conversion is even more forbidden afterwards, only now I was supposed to like it. But I never did. So I stood on the sidelines and admired those who were truly righteous, even as I fought with others for a better view. It was not until I became a pastor that I noticed others with the same problem.

Facing Forward, Walking Backward

The Danish philosopher Søren Kierkegaard told the parable of a visitor who backed away from his friends all the while he faced them. His smile and his footprints appeared to be moving toward them, but every step was one further away. He walked backward. Kierkegaard explained: "So it is with the one who, rich in good intentions and quick to promise, retreats backwards farther and farther from the good."[4]

Now slow down and read the rest.

> With the help of intentions and promises he maintains an orientation toward the good, and with this orientation toward the good he moves backwards farther and farther away from it. . . . As a drunkard constantly requires stronger and stronger stimulation in order to become intoxicated, the one who has fallen into intentions and promises requires more and more stimulation in order to walk backward.[5]

Because obedience is the surest sign that a person no longer has his life to himself, we have—most of us—become quite adept at walking backward.

For instance, we often mistake hearing for doing. We presume that because we can hear, understand, and even articulate something, we have done it. Like the Pharisees, we come to believe that our status and familiarity with the church or our knowledge of the Bible has somehow made us immune from the commandments given to ordinary folk.

We use mental clever arguments that are more complex than the commandments themselves in order to explain why we don't have to obey. Deitrich Bonhoeffer imagined a father sending his child to bed, only to have the boy reason to himself, "Father tells me to go to bed, but he really means that I am tired and he does not want me to be tired; [now] I can overcome my tiredness just as well if I go out and play, therefore . . . he really means, 'go out and play.'"[6]

It is chilling to remember that Jesus accused the Pharisees of failing to know the Scripture when in fact they had committed most of it to memory. That is to say, I may train myself into a knowledge of the Bible and then reason myself out of it again if I do not obey what I have already learned (see John 7:17).

> We confuse a momentary promise with daily discipline.

A simpler way of doing this, however, is to downsize the monstrous sayings of the Bible until they are bite-sized proverbs, fit for a fortune cookie. Which of us has not seen the way a Sunday school class can slaughter a text on the altar of convenience? A command like "turn the other cheek" is qualified with the proviso that if your enemy slaps the second cheek, you have license to drop him then and there. The command to eat Christ's flesh and drink his blood is reduced to symbolism because the literal explanation, we presume, is too grotesque. The call to carry the Cross is whittled down to mean going to church when most of our friends do not. And the ultimatum to choose between serving God or mammon is presumed to apply only to the filthy rich.

Recently, a layperson reminded me of Jesus' call to abandon my riches (Luke 14:33), and before he could put a period on the sentence I was looking for places to hide.

What does he mean by riches? I'm not rich. Relatively speaking, for a person with my education and experience, I have below average means.

My friend then quoted Wesley's definition of wealth: "whosoever has food to eat, and raiment to put on, with something left over, is rich." [7]

But wait a minute. It takes a certain amount of wealth just to grease the wheels. And I give a lot of money away. Abraham, Job, David, and Solomon were rich. And Jesus did not summon all of us to give up our wealth—only the rich young ruler.

I should add that all of this mental ping-pong occurred within a span of only ten seconds. I was trying to process this message from my friend without leaving any unresolved tensions. I didn't want him to think less of me, but I didn't want to give any money away either. I was facing the truth, but walking backward.

Suspended Disobedience

More sinister is our propensity for suspended disobedience. Usually this occurs with the help of good and stirring worship. It follows a predictable pattern.

Under the influence of music (usually moving in tempo from fast to slow), we are transported to a place where all is well, where everything is just the way it should be.

We hear the message and we admire the virtues of Jesus.

We compliment the pastor on his "fine sermon" so that we do not have to wrestle with it. We are only doing, after all, what the speaker really wanted. He wanted to sound eloquent, and we tell him that he did. Like snake charmers manipulating a deadly serpent, we decide to charm the sermon since we cannot defang it. This is suspended disobedience. We appear in church long enough to express our good intentions. We worship a mighty God who is bigger than life. We feel strong and confident about being Christians and are ready to take on the world. But an hour later as we sit around the dinner table discussing other things, the service seems long ago and far away, so imaginary, that it is almost like a movie. And of course, we do not obey movies, we merely attend them. And so while we worship, our disobedience is temporarily suspended by our fascination with God and the good life.

Even the altar call, if it lessens the impulse for change, can become a cheap substitute for obedience. In coming to the altar we often confuse the momentary promise to follow Christ's command with the daily discipline of obeying it. Perhaps Jesus had this in mind when he uttered the parable of two sons, one who promised to obey but did not, and another who would not promise but later obeyed.

"Which of the two did what his father wanted?" asked Jesus.

And before they could answer, he warned them, "The tax collectors

and the prostitutes are entering the kingdom of God ahead of you"
(Matt. 21:31).

Discreditation by Association

Finally, we have become adept at discreditation by association.
Nathaniel wondered if anything good could come out of Nazareth. The
Pharisees refused to listen to Jesus on the grounds that he was from Galilee.
In both instances, the prejudice of certain people nearly robbed them of the
truth. It would not be the last time. I have been advised by others not to
read certain books because their authors were divorced, or Catholic, or
liberal, any of which is the modern equivalent of living in Nazareth. Of
course, we need not accept everything these writers may offer, but it is
wrong to ignore the message simply because it is they who delivered it.
Contrary to some Protestants' belief, Catholics know a great deal about salvation, liberals have something to teach us about the heart of Jesus, some
parents of troubled children still have something to say about raising them,
and even divorced people may have valuable insights into marriage.

Those who render the message incredible because of the messenger
are like the patrons at a certain theater where fire broke out backstage.
The clown rushed frantically onstage to alert the audience, but they
laughed and mimicked him as part of the act. He was only doing what
clowns do. Rather than flee the building, the foolish patrons died, still
laughing, while the clown himself escaped. Perhaps it has not occurred
to us that some whom we consider foolish are capable of being wise,
even if only for a moment.[8] For even a stopped clock is right twice a
day. So let us lay it down as an immutable law that if the Devil himself
should command us to love the Lord our God, we would do well to
obey him—Devil or not.

"If you love me," said Jesus, "you will obey my commands" (see
John 15:12). These things—love and obedience—must always go
together in the believer's life.

There are two common ways of distorting this important truth. One is
to say that love is more important than obedience, and the other is to say
that obedience is more important than love. Let's look at each of these.

Love Without Obedience

Some take these words of Christ as a license to do things that are
forbidden in Scripture. They believe that love is more important than
obedience.

"Mine is a religion of love," they say, "I can do as I please!" But as always, the problem lies less in what they do than in what they please. They come late and lazy to church. They neglect the reading of Scripture. Their prayers are tired and worn clichés. Their tithing goes down, not up. And more often than not, these are folk who grew up in religious homes. Their upbringing was long on obedience and short on love, and now that they have heard the gospel of love, they will go short on obedience. They are like model prisoners who, after being set free, revert to the raucous lifestyle that led to their imprisonment in the first place.

The problem with these Christians, of course, is that they still serve the law even though they profess to be free from it. Now, as before, they have an unhealthy obsession with rules. At first they were slaves to the standard, and now they go out of their way to avoid it. Like a bride who flirts with men before her wedding but hides in the bathroom on her honeymoon, these people are experiencing the opposite side of the same problem: an unhealthy obsession with rules. The groom who smothers his fiancée with gifts before the wedding but ignores her afterward is making the same mistake. Underneath, he harbors the same distorted view of women. His acts of kindness before the wedding were merely the rent he figured to pay in order to gain a wife. But now that he possesses her (or she him), his weakness is laid bare.

> Obedience is natural when one person is devoted to another.

This is not the genuine work of law, but of duty. It produces nothing but a cultic religion organized around the teachings of Jesus, which is so much less—so much other—than what Jesus expected (see John 17:26). Our obedience to Christ will follow our love for him.

It was *because* of my love for my fiancée that I borrowed a ladder one night and climbed up to the second story of her dormitory window to hang a banner on the eve of her twenty-first birthday. It was for love that she went fishing with me and I went to the ballet with her. In other words, there are things which lead to love and things which follow it. There are places we avoid (keep away from there), hurtful things we never mention (are you gaining weight?), grievances we automatically forgive (I know you didn't mean it), and second miles we walk (here, you can have the rest) not *in order* to love someone but because we already do.

Surely this is the root of Christ's desire that we keep his commands. Obedience is not the eleventh commandment. It is the natural response of one person who is devoted to another. Perhaps this is why Jesus put these two sentences together in his farewell sermon: "Ask me for anything in my name, and I will do it" and "If you love me, you will obey what I command" (John 14:14–15). He will do what we ask in one verse, and we must do what he asks in the next. And because the relationship is based on love, neither side worries that the other will take unfair advantage.

Yet in spite of the fact that we have not always done our part (obedience), we are usually more concerned that Jesus has not kept his (doing what we ask). That indicates a relationship based on duty and governed by a score. And since we're keeping score, who really owes whom?

Have I truly been more obedient than he is kind?

How deep is my love given the fact that I am always eyeballing his responsibility and never my own?

Am I in this thing for him, or me?

Is my relationship strong enough to absorb the disappointment of an unanswered prayer?

Keeping score is extremely common among feuding couples. He wants to know why she is so prudish. She wants to know why he is always busy. There is no hope for resolving the tension until each is willing to stop looking at the other's alleged failures and begin to see his own responsibilities.

We must do the same with our religion. So when we are handed the blank check of asking for anything in Jesus' name, we ought to ask first for the capacity to obey. That is, before we squander Christ's offer on ourselves, we should spend it on him. This is love.

Obedience Without Love

Another way we often distort (or divorce) the connection between love and obedience is to presume that obedience is more important than love. That is to presume that we are holy because we do what holy people do. But if holiness were merely obedience, the Pharisees would be our friends and not our enemies. The rich young ruler would be in heaven and the dying thief in hell. Instead, it is love that measures conversion. And this notion is radical indeed for people, like me, who grew up born again.

Like many second or third generation believers, I was born with a King James Bible in my hand, and I wore it out on sword drills by the time I was eight. I memorized verses, even whole chapters, of the Bible. I lead my first "convert" to Christ when I was twelve.

Like others from my religious background, I learned to say I was saved by grace and that I loved Jesus, but all the while I lived according to duty. I presumed I loved God because, like the rich young ruler, I had been kept his commandments from my childhood on. The proof was in my obedience.

We should know better. Any veteran of the armed services knows he can obey one he does not love, or what is a commanding officer? Any child knows the same or what is a school principal. Any taxpayer understands this, or what is the Internal Revenue Service? So the words of Jesus indicate not only a connection between love and obedience, but also a sequence. If love does not precede obedience, love will rarely follow.

Backing Forward

Now just as there are some who walk backward, there are many others who back forward. These are they that love Christ before they learn to obey him. Like the woman at Christ's feet, they pour themselves out in worship every Sunday. They make stunning sacrifices and bold professions of faith, even though they have sinned only hours ago. Like Peter, they swear, "I'll follow you to the death," yet their next denial is only moments away. They promise to quit nagging their children or losing their tempers, but within days they're back at it. Do they love Jesus or don't they? And if they love him, why don't they quit these things? The question is so distressing that they rarely ask it. They are caught in the crossfire of high standards and low performance. From here, answers seem like excuses, so they live with the tension and die wondering about their fate.

It was these very people whom Jesus taught to pray "forgive us our debts . . . [and] deliver us from the evil one" (Matt. 6:12–13). Evidently, Christ presumed our battle with evil was not over on the day we were saved. And what is more, he presumed we would not only be tempted with evil, but would actually fall for it from time to time. Otherwise, a prayer for the forgiveness of our sins would be unnecessary (see also 1 John 2:1–2). But what, exactly, are we to do with the sin in our lives? How do we explain it? And how do we break the habit?

FOUR THEORIES ON SIN IN THE BELIEVER'S LIFE

No genuine believer is ever happy about the reality of sin in his life, yet he must either know what to do about it or how to explain it away. Historically, there have been four ways of doing this.

One Strike and Out

The most radical approach has been to deny sin any place in the believer's life. A contemporary of Wesley named Count Nicholas

Zinzendorf founded a group of pious and devout people called the Moravians on this very principle. After his studies in law and theology Zinzendorf concluded: "God has given us his Spirit and so we do not sin after conversion, since his Spirit cannot do evil nor allow it. We cannot bring forth both bitter water and sweet at the same time."[9] According to Zinzendorf, those who sin deny that the truth is in them, and those who allow for such sinning have not grasped reality, but have only dumbed down the Scriptures to their level of (dis)obedience.

The modern expression of this idea is our tendency to relabel sin as something else. So people who "love" God yet use his name in vain are said to suffer "impurities." Women who are sanctified yet lose their tempers are said to have "infirmities." Spirit-filled Christians who enjoy movies filled with sex and violence are said to "wrestle with the flesh." And those who either cannot or will not get over these "failings" are said to have a "weakness." But unfortunately, our sins do not disappear on the day we stop believing in them. Scripture, history, and experience testify to the truth that some who are really converted, who really love Christ, may at times fail to keep his commands. They are not rebelling against him. They are only caught up in the moment, or they are stuck in their habits of the past. And while we cannot excuse their behavior as a weakness or infirmity, neither should we expel them from the fellowship of those truly converted.

Crimes and Misdemeanors

For centuries the Catholics have provided another way of accounting for those who back forward. According to traditional Catholicism, sins come in two varieties: mortal, which are crimes against the church; and venial, which are misdemeanors against the law. Mortal sins require sacramental penance while venial sins require ordinary confession. Mortal sins turn us around. They intercept our salvation so that we are condemned, the same as before. Venial sins only interrupt our progress in Christian virtue; they do not turn us away from God.

For Protestants, this thinking is reflected in our tendency to treat some sins as worse than others. Many good Christians presume that one sin (say, murder) is more serious than another (say, fibbing). One will cost us our souls; the other will only slow us down. One is a train wreck; the other a speed bump. But as Wesley has noted, our doctrine of sin flows naturally from our doctrine of God, so "there can be no little sins until we find a little God."[10]

Passive Righteousness

In contrast to the Catholic view, Martin Luther blurred the lines between mortal and venial sins, arguing that all sins are an abomination to God. Advancing a more objective viewpoint, Luther said we are *simul iustus et peccator semper repentans*—at once sinner and saint—therefore, always repenting. In his preface to the commentary on Galatians, he wrote:

> Although I am a sinner by the law and under condemnation of the law, yet I despair not . . . because Christ lives, who is both my righteousness and my everlasting life. . . . I am indeed a sinner as touching this present life . . . but I have another righteousness and life, above this life, which is Christ the Son of God. . . . So both of these continue while we live here: The flesh is accused . . . but the spirit reigns, rejoices, and is saved by this passive and Christian righteousness.[11]

The impact of Luther's thought upon modern (even Wesleyan-Arminian) preachers must not be underestimated. Any talk of "sinning every day in word, thought, or deed," any idea of being "sinners saved by grace," comes straight from the well of Luther. The problem is that this is too objective. It presumes upon grace, even when it should not. John Wesley called this *fictio juris* (judicial fiction), in which God deceives himself by calling us what, in fact, we are not. But in fact, the grace of God is as real as the sin it forgives. And the cure is even more radical than the disease, for "where sin increased, grace increased all the more" (Rom. 5:20). We are not to be saints in name only, imagining that our sins have been cleansed while we continue to commit them. No, there is still another way to understand the presence of sin in our lives.

The Absence of Malice

The Wesleyan point of view is that sin resides in the heart. It is the presence of malicious (or selfish) intent that renders any act truly sinful, and while unintentional sins may be equally wrong, they are not equally harmful since they do not have the force of malicious intent. According to Wesley, "all sin is a transgression of the law, but not every transgression of the law is a sin."[12] In sin, as in righteousness, the heart of the matter is the matter of the heart. What is the motive behind the act? That is what makes any version either right or wrong.

I have a friend who travels frequently to Canada for business. He remembers one day when he stopped at a fast-food restaurant just this side of the border to get something to drink. In payment for his order, he pulled some spare change from his pocket and plunked it on the counter. The clerk suddenly sighed with frustration.

"Are you going to pay me with Canadian money again?" she blurted.

"What are you talking about?" my friend mumbled with a blank stare.

"This is the third day this week that you've come in here and bought a soft drink, then paid for it with Canadian money. There's a 25 percent exchange rate, you know."

She was right. Instead of paying her the ninety cents she had coming, he had inadvertently given her only sixty cents on three consecutive occasions. In other words, he was getting three drinks while paying for two. Of course, he was very embarrassed and he settled the matter then and there.

No one can deny that the woman was cheated, nor even that my friend was the culprit. But here is Wesley's point exactly. There were two ways to cheat the woman, one with malice and the other without it. The same is true with just about every harmful act. There are two ways to run the stop sign: one is to miss it and the other is to ignore it. And while both must be either forgiven or punished, only one of them is evil.

> All sin is transgression— not every transgression is sin.

Unfortunately, many modern students of Wesley see no malice in their actions because they have not stopped long enough to look for the self under their deeds. They promote themselves and defend themselves and concern themselves with themselves; they presume themselves to be always right. They fuss over themselves, admire themselves, speak for themselves, and value themselves. They even lie to themselves about themselves, all because they will not ask themselves: Why do you do what you do?

In spite of this, my vote is for Wesley.

We will never be absolutely perfect; we must always contend with sin—sometimes in victory, sometimes in defeat. But insofar as sin is a violation of the law of love, we may be delivered from the law of sin ("what I want to do I do not do," Rom. 7:15) in order to serve the greater law of Christ ("love your neighbor as yourself . . . carry each other's burdens," Gal. 5:14; 6:2).

For he who loves has kept the law of God (see Matt. 22:40; Rom. 13:10; Gal. 5:23).

But how can we say we love God yet continue to break his law? Simply put, the law of God is the law *of God*. It cannot be detached from the heart of the One who gave it. In the sense that one may love a person yet fail to meet that lover's expectations, we may—swallow hard!—transgress the law of God but still keep it, because love trumps all other laws.

We dare not define sin apart from an understanding of the Fatherhood of God.[13] In the Old Testament, the law of God always followed his covenant with his people—it did not precede it. Abraham was called and justified before he was told to be blameless (see Gen. 15:6 and 17:1). The Israelites were called a treasured possession before they were given the Ten Commandments. The keeping of the Sabbath was for those with whom God already had an everlasting friendship (see Exodus 31:16–17). Even in the "fear of God" we are told to love him (see Deuteronomy 10:12). Thus, loyalty to God is the loyalty of a son. When the believer sins, then, he is measured not according to the law alone but according to his relationship with the Father.

The law may reflect God, but it cannot contain him.

Even the Reformers, who would likely deny much of what I have just written, have taught us that the nature of a person determines the merit of his actions. Thus, they argued, evil people cannot commit good (or even benign) actions since all actions flow naturally from the person's nature. But that works both ways. If the person's heart is made pure, then the absence of malice has defanged the sin, and while the sin may still be judged, it will surely be judged differently and always in context of the deeper, more abiding nature of the person who committed it.

I am thinking of the little boy who wanted to please his father and so hooked the garden hose to his father's new car and gave him a full tank of, well, water!

He ruined his father's possession, but he did not sin against his father. In this sense, we may break God's law without sinning against him. And this is not because we have pitted the law against God. It is because we have transcended the law (creation) by relating to God (creator). The law of God is "holy, righteous and good" (Rom. 7:12), but it is not God himself. It expresses the will of God, and so he will write it on our hearts (Ezk. 36:26–27). But the law is like a photograph. It may adequately reflect God, but it cannot contain him—his personality, nuance, and emotion. You cannot confine the Eternal to paper or stone any more than you can hold the world on a map or contain a symphony on a musical score. Those who truly know God will cherish the photograph (the law) even as they transcend it. On those occasions when they break the law, the image of God is still deeply embedded within them. God is not so intertwined with his law that these erring saints will lose their God when they sin. For what does the apostle say? "If we are faithless, he will remain faithful, for he cannot disown himself" (2 Tim. 2:13).

Two Types of Obedience

We must be careful then, that we do not judge the whole of our Christian character on those few moments when we wander back to sin. To be sure, we are never finally holy until we have done away with sin, but we may still love God even while we struggle with it, or when were the disciples converted? According to Jesus, they had obeyed God's word even while they were confused, doubtful, and argumentative (John 17:6). Only days before Jesus made that bold assessment, they had argued over which of them was greatest. Only hours before, Peter was warned that he would disown his master three times in one night. This does not sound much like obedience. Yet here, in between Jesus' predictions and Peter's dismal failure, the disciples are said to have obeyed God's word. There is no easy explanation for this, except that obedience is at once both simple and strict.

Simple Obedience

Simple obedience is loyalty or allegiance. It is a redirection of the will. It is not measured by whether or not one has obeyed perfectly. It is measured by whether or not one wanted to, and by whether or not he tried. Simple obedience judges effort, not performance. It turns the will of a person away from himself and toward the One he obeys. If our master calls us to carry a load from one place to another, simple obedience does not consider that we may put the load down somewhere in between to rest our arms or tighten our grip. It cares only for the end result. And if it should come upon us while we are resting, simple obedience does not ask us why we are sitting. It asks only whether we intend to continue. It is the obedience of the good kings in the Old Testament who did what was right in the eyes of the Lord. It is a general observation over a long haul. Simple obedience does not measure the daily responsibilities between a husband and a wife. It cares mainly that they are still together, "til death do us part," and that neither has violated the marriage.

The danger of judging ourselves by simple obedience alone is that we may minimize our sins, or at least to stop looking for them. Gradually, we may return to our vices and presume that God is either patient enough or indifferent enough to allow it. We may be so easy on ourselves that it seems as if our Christianity has had no real, practical effect on us. This is a form of lawlessness: the hardening of our dispositions against any correction, conviction, or advice (see 2 Pet. 3:16; Jude 4).

Strict Obedience

Strict obedience, on the other hand, is a stringent compliance with the rules—*all* of them. It may be driven by love, but it is exceedingly conscientious. It is measured by the line item. It is not so interested that a couple is still together (it presumes this) as it is that each partner is carrying out his or her responsibility in the marriage. Strict obedience cares less that you are shooting and more that you are hitting the target. It wants to know why you are resting when you should be carrying the load. This is the obedience of a soldier to his country. Any momentary lapse is regarded as treason. It is more objective than simple obedience because it is based on actual performance.

The danger here is opposite that of simple obedience. An overemphasis on strict obedience may cause some to measure their faith only by their obedience. They will keep rules they do not understand and will come to depend on these rules for everything. When these folk have prayed consistently, when they have witnessed, tithed, or volunteered, they will feel themselves to be spiritual—not because God's Spirit is at work but because they have been faithful themselves. This is the threat of *legalism:* the insidious erosion of faith, love, and joy from the foundation of Christian life until there is nothing but morality left (see Matt. 23:23–24).

When Christ pronounced that his disciples had been obedient (John 17:6), it appears to me that he had simple obedience in mind. While I have no desire to let hypocrites off of the hook, it seems that obedience is love's final test, but never its first. Those who back forward—who love God even though they disobey him—will end in obedience because it is impossible for them to behave for very long in a manner inconsistent with their nature.

I have occasionally made this point by asking a group of men whether or not they love their wives. When they say they do, I quickly ask: "Do you now or have you ever lusted after another woman? Tell me the truth, gentlemen, your wives are wanting to know."

Invariably, there is an awkward silence in the room. I have set them up. They are caught in this very dilemma of simple and strict obedience. Naturally, the men themselves will interpret their love from the simple, while their wives—offended at their husbands' struggle with lust—will likely interpret it from the strict. But the other shoe fits too.

Ladies, do you love your children?

Have you ever wanted to wring their necks?

I thought you loved your children.

Here again, the ladies will judge their motherhood by simple obedience and their children will judge their mothers by the strict. In fact, children do say "you don't love me anymore" when their mothers scold them.

We need only to compare the journeys of Peter and Paul to see this occur. Peter moved from simple obedience (his decision to change occupations and follow Christ) to strict obedience (his endurance of things he once despised: suffering, denial, patience, martyrdom). But Paul moved in the opposite direction, from strict obedience (circumcised on the eighth day, a Hebrew of Hebrews) to simple obedience (a reoriented, Jesus-only evangelist for whom circumcision and the Sabbath meant little, Rom. 4:5; Gal. 6:15). The same conversion, the same Cross, made Peter conscientious and Paul free. It made Peter less selfish and Paul less legalistic. It made Peter nice and Paul genuine.

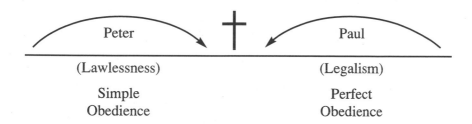

Peter	Paul
(Lawlessness)	(Legalism)
Simple Obedience	Perfect Obedience

Finding Balance

We must be careful that we find our balance between the two measures of obedience. If we begin with simple obedience and stay there, we will miss the Cross, through which we are called to be honest with our sins yet forsake them. Any repentance that does not lessen our impulse to commit the same sin again is not genuine repentance. But if we begin with strict obedience and never experience a simple and fundamental redirection of the will—that is, if we do not obey from the *inside*—we will become legalists who know the Bible thoroughly but are unfamiliar with its author. One of the truly strange ironies of the Apostle Paul's life is that prior to his conversion he professed to be "zealous for God," yet he did not recognize God when the two of them met on the road to Damascus (see Acts 22:3, 8). It would not be the last time that people would destroy the children of God in his Name. But Christ calls us to a long obedience in the same direction. So our love for him is not disqualified because of random acts of disobedience. In fact, where love rules, God's heart can absorb such failures until love finally overcomes them.

The point here is that good Christians often beat themselves up for backing forward. Most often, this is because their relationship to Christ is still based on duty rather than love. They have moved law back into the center of things and have made love only the shortcut for carrying it out. Like the doting man or the flirtatious woman, they have not gotten over their unhealthy obsession, in this case, with the rules.

BREAKING THE HABIT

But how do we learn to break the habit and back forward? How do we arrive at a view of sin in our lives that is both realistic (it still exists) and optimistic (it can be eliminated)? Rather than proposing some sort of twelve-step plan to loosen the grip of sin, I will offer a handful of observations about my own battle with the disease.

Being Hard on Self

First, I have learned that life is easier on those who are harder on themselves. For this reason, we must examine ourselves honestly and consistently. The impulse to be honest with one's self may lessen with age. Like bacteria that develop an immunity to antibiotics, sin learns to resist the prayers and confessions we used at the beginning of our Christian life. Sin goes into hiding, then later resurfaces as something else—often something noble. Lust gives rise to leadership, and leadership gives rise to stubbornness. In their youth, men may have imagined having their way with women, but now that they are old, they have put away these childish sins—so obvious to the church. Now they imagine having their own way with their peers. And when they are very old, and rottenness has settled in, they will have their own way with everything—or you will hear about it.

A hardening of the attitudes has come upon them. They are not sanctified, and never were. They do not love God more than themselves and others as much as themselves. As boys they feasted on their imagination; as adults they will feast on their image. But they have always helped themselves to others. Often these sterling personalities are leaders, elected by those with considerably less confidence, and as leaders they imagine that they have gotten over the sins of their constituents. But along with power there comes a battery of evils peculiar to leadership. If they are not continually hard on themselves, they may be taken unaware, and before they know it the Devil will be upon them with such subtlety and force that they will scarce discern his thoughts from their own. Now, in the middle or later years, the Devil will fillet them as before. Only now he will use a different knife.

"I am disappointed to learn that most of my progress in the Christian life has only been imaginary," wrote C. S. Lewis to his friend. "It is to dream that I am cleaned and shaven, only to wake up and find myself still in bed."[14]

Associating with Younger Believers

For those who find self-examination difficult, it will be well to associate with younger believers. This is likely the opposite of what we are used to hearing about spiritual growth, but there is a very good reason for it. Even as people keep a youthful outlook by chumming with youth or children, the aging saint can stay mature by associating, at least periodically, with those who are not. This is not in order to compare himself to the weaker brother. In that case the saint would be worse off than he thought. Instead, it is to catch a little of the honesty and hunger for which the young in Christ are known. As a pastor, my spiritual life is shaped, not only by preaching to my people from the platform, but also by standing with them in the trenches. There is no way to measure the impact on my spirit of a new convert telling me there is "something sneaky inside" her that makes righteousness so hard and selfishness so easy. How can I resist the charming and honest confession of a spiritual child who comes to the altar to confess his "sin of lovelessness"? Or the aging grandmother who believes she has taught her children to lie by making them apologize to one another when they're not sorry?

Truly, these young believers desire good things. If they are not far from the kingdom of God, I wonder if I have entered myself. For *I* do not desire God as I ought or love Scripture over gold and others more than self. The physician himself is sick. And I would never have known it were it not for the brave confessions of spiritual children. As a disciple for many years, I still ask questions, but most of mine are rhetorical. These novices ask them because they really want to know. How strange. How childish. They still believe that grace is a miracle and so it forgives and cleanses too. They fully expect to be delivered from sin in this life. They believe their prayers will be answered, that God will provide, that Jesus still heals, that Christ is still coming, that the church is his body. But me? I have settled into the routine. I have leveled off. I have studied questions these children do not know enough to ask. And now I must get over these questions. Do you have this problem too?

For this reason, I will always have a group of young and honest believers before me.

Confessing Often

I am learning that confession is the next best thing to innocence. If part of being smart is knowing what you don't know, then part of being holy is knowing when you're not, admitting it, then doing something about it. When the already smart learn what they do not know, they take back the turf once owned by ignorance. When the already holy see and conquer previously undiscovered sins, they take back the turf once held by carnality. In plain English, I have just said that there is room for sin, or one version of it, inside our definition of holiness.

It is possible not to sin. This is the clear teaching of Jesus (see Matt. 1:21, 5:48; John 5:14, 8:11) and his earliest followers (Rom. 6:1–2; 1 John 2:1, 3:8–9). This is also the happy experience of some in (and out of) the holiness tradition. But if we do sin "we have one who speaks to the Father in our defense" and who "[purifies] us from all unrighteousness" (1 John 2:1; 1:9) Even as intelligence is not simply the absence of ignorance but also the presence of a learning spirit, so true holiness is not merely the absence of sin but also the presence of a humble and eager soul.

This is where the desperate father of a demonic child can help us (see Mark 9:14–19). After going zero for nine with Christ's disciples, the anxious father admitted that he was somewhere between stuck and liberated. Playing off of Jesus' volley that "everything is possible for him who believes," the man confessed, "I do believe; help me overcome my unbelief."

Recently, I have begun to see the value of this stark confession. I have begun to wonder if the greater part of spirituality is really a passing from dishonesty to honesty through various shades of either in between. From this angle, what began in the Garden under a cloud of deceit (they "made coverings for themselves [and] . . . hid from the LORD God among trees of the garden," Gen. 3:7–8) steadily progresses through redemption toward a bright and clear day of self-disclosure ("then I shall know fully, even as I am fully known," 1 Cor. 13:12). This being true, any move in the direction of heaven is a move toward honesty and self-disclosure. And all dishonesty (or hiding), whether in the church or out of it, is really a move toward hell. It is a tragic irony that many who profess holiness live closer to the Garden than to the Gate.

Strangely enough, transparency often exists in opposite proportion to the amount of faith we profess. A dozen years ago, *Newsweek* magazine established an "Apology Sound-Off Line" and encouraged readers to call and anonymously speak their confessions to an answering machine. Within a few hours there were hundreds of calls from people confessing everything from tax evasion to murder. Presumably, most of these people were sinners. For when a person has nothing to lose, no image to protect, he is quite honest about his failures. But somehow the moment he believes in Christ and is accepted into a Christian community, his transparency diminishes—even if his sins do not. Perhaps this is one reason the

> **Real spirituality always moves from dishonesty to honesty.**

most grievous and entrenched forms of sin lie hidden in church leaders. Had these leaders subjected themselves to the same humiliating confessions as their rank-and-file members, they could have ended their troubles by now. All they needed was to remain teachable.

The test of our integrity, then, and the prospect of our sanctification lie in our capacity to be completely honest with ourselves before God and a few trusted others. These "trusted others" may take the form of an accountability circle, a confessional booth, a support group, or close friends. It is very important to confess sin to a few colleagues as well as to God. Those who confess only to God tend to go easy on their sins, emphasizing grace over discipline. Thus they malign the character of God, who is holy and just. Too often, these God-only confessors revert to lawlessness, so they need to surround themselves with friends from the other (strict obedience) side of the Cross (see fig. 5.1). Just as "show me" is the magic formula for learning, "forgive me" is the magic phrase for spiritual growth.

Taking Control of Life

I am learning to take control of my life by avoiding situations that are fraught with danger. Thus, I will make a "covenant with my eyes" (Job 31:1) that I will not feast on late-night television or linger over seductive advertisements in magazines. I will cautiously guard my diet of television since 85 percent of its sitcoms, 89 percent of its movies, 74 percent of its news magazine programs, and 68 percent of its general programs contain sexual content, some 90 percent of which occurs between persons who are not married.[15] Because of their failure to control their eyes, modern American Christians have reaped a thought life so impure that if their minds were to be rated like movies, most would be unfit for their children to watch.

I will "guard [my] heart [since] it is the wellspring of [my] life" (Proverbs 4:23). This means I will not indulge in the wild fantasy of repaying others for their sins against me. I will not plot ways to get even. I will neither listen to nor repeat lewd jokes. I will surround myself with things to read so my mind will not become the Devil's workshop. I will continue to memorize Scripture, songs, and proverbs from Christianity's brightest minds, thus I will gradually take back the passions and desires given to me as the image of God.

I will "beat my body and make it my slave" (1 Cor. 9:27). I will not sleep more than seven hours—or less if I can get away with it. I will eat for energy more than for pleasure or comfort. I will not enjoy alcoholic beverages—even in moderation—either in public or in private. I will physically remove myself from situations that compromise my integrity. I will watch for cycles in my life that lead to weakness, failure, or indulgence, and I will avoid the situations that activate them. I will remember that the best way to break a sinful habit is to avoid it in the first place.

For most of us, this is a slow, tedious process. Consider this "Autobiography in Five Short Chapters" from the transparent pen of someone who has felt this very pressure:

Chapter One: I walk down the street. There is a deep hole in the sidewalk. I fall in. I am lost and helpless. It isn't my fault, but it takes forever to find a way out.

Chapter Two: I walk down the same street. There is a deep hole in the sidewalk. I pretend I don't see it. I fall in again. I can't believe I'm in the same place, but it isn't my fault. It still takes a long time to get out.

Chapter Three: I walk down the same street. There is a deep hole in the sidewalk. I see it is there. I still fall in. It's a habit. My eyes are open and I know where I am. It is my fault. I get out immediately.

Chapter Four: I walk down the same street. There is a deep hole in the sidewalk. I walk around it.

Chapter Five: I walk down another street.[16]

It is often discipline that brings about the good life. And it is worth the hassle and the wait. For the pleasant surprise of holiness is that the pleasure we once enjoyed from sin is replaced by a pure and more lasting joy from within.

Asking a Different Question

Finally, I have learned to back forward by asking a different question. Rather than wondering how I will quit this or that sin, I am learning to ask how I can please the Father. Our love of Christ has been compared with marriage because the two have so much in common. Like marriage, the Christian life does not come with simple, easy instructions, and we should not reduce Scripture to such, for it does not require the Spirit of Jesus to interpret simple instructions. Speaking for himself, Jesus said, "If anyone loves me . . . my Father will love him, and we will come to him and make our home with him" (John 14:23). This is how obedience happens. It is the by-product of living together with God and his Word. During this time, God will provide for us, and we will seek to please him. New husbands understand this since many of them have endured the same dish at mealtime for several nights in a row. This is not because the new bride lacks imagination or because she is looking for the easy way out. Most often, it is because she has inadvertently landed upon a dish he enjoys—she found out what pleases him, and she is eager to repeat it.

Imagine this sign posted on your television, your mirror, your dashboard, or your desk: "Find out what pleases the Lord!" (Eph. 5:10). Sometimes, it is not that we fear the answer, but that we simply forget to ask. What an enormous difference this question would make!

Our religion would have both freedom and restraint. We would pray with a holy fear and familiarity "Father, hallowed be your name" (Luke 11:2). We would gravitate toward friends with the same passion. We would read the Bible, and, more than that, we would read it between the lines. We would spend our money differently. We would serve God by ministering to his people rather than serve his people by telling them about God (and there is a very real difference). We would forgive whom we should. We would capture every free thought and every waking moment. We would obey the rules even when there are no rules to obey. We would love God for his sake more than ours.

Aleida Huissen was seventy-eight years old when she quit smoking. For fifty years prior, she had tried to kick the habit but always slipped back. This time she succeeded. Why? Because her good friend, Leo Jansen had proposed marriage to her but refused to tie the knot until she finally quit smoking.

"Willpower never was enough to get me off the tobacco habit," said Aleida. "Love did it."

So often our problem is that our religion is fueled by will power rather than love. Willpower cannot do all that love can do, and even when it does, it can never enjoy it. It breeds pride, not affection. But what if—the next time we were tempted, or grew lazy in our devotions, or pondered a payback for some grievance, or held onto our temper by the skin of our teeth—we reminded ourselves that we love Christ, and that our obedience in this instance is a celebration of our love for him, not merely the proof? What if we truly comprehended the love that laid down its life for a friend? We might exceed what we have previously done out of obligation. We might do more with less. We might keep his commandments—even some that we have not read.

And best of all, we would no longer be stuck in line, watching holiness as it passes by.

LIFE RESPONSES

1. Steve DeNeff argues that a person's direction in relation to Christ is more important than his position. What does that mean? Do you think it's true?

2. Of the four explanations offered for sin in the life of a believer, which makes the most sense to you?

3. What are some ways that you have "backed backward," that is, pretended to be obedient while in fact disobeying God?

Chapter 6

A PLACE WE MISTAKE FOR HEAVEN
Loving God with Holy Ambitions

There was a man who died and found himself in a beautiful place, surrounded by every conceivable comfort. A white-jacketed butler with a pleasant smile stood before him waiting to take his order.

"You may have anything you choose," said the butler, "any food, any pleasure, any kind of entertainment."

For days the man sampled every delicacy and experience of which he had only dreamed while on earth. But one day he grew bored with his comfort and bid the servant to find him something to do, some deadline to meet, someone to help.

The butler sadly shook his head.

"I'm sorry, sir. That's the one thing I cannot do for you. There is no work here."

"No work? That's a fine thing," snapped the man. "I might as well be in hell."

"But sir," whispered the butler, "where do you think you are?"

One evidence of our love for Christ is that we serve one another. So it is strange indeed that we should believe heaven to be a final rest for the holy and convert it into a place where we are ministered unto but do not minister, even while we sit in Jesus' own backyard.

There is a vast difference between doing nice things for people and serving them. One is an act. The other is a disposition. One keeps score (will they give it back? did they say thank-you?). The other follows orders (what would Jesus do, whether they say thank-you or not?). So even after a person has been kind to his neighbors or put up with an ornery boss, he may still need to learn the heart of a servant if he has not done these things for the love of Christ.

THE ROOTS OF SELFISH AMBITION

Put another way, private ambition is often the last hideout for selfish desires. This is a very difficult ax to grind in a culture that already has its hands full with more obvious sins like adultery, murder, prejudice, and slander. Confess to your neighbor that you are battling the sin of selfish ambition, and he will look at you as if you are from Mars—or a monastery, which is nearly as far removed in his mind. But it was not for adultery or murder that Lucifer found himself cast out of heaven. It was for selfish ambition. He desired more for himself than God desired for him. He was created a servant, but he wanted to be served.

The same could be said of Adam and Eve, whose temptation was not the fruit itself but that they should be as gods (Gen. 3:5). This is the sin behind Saul's Gilgal and behind the Pharisees' desire for fancy titles and seats of honor. This is what made Diotrophes the overbearing bore that he was (3 John 9). It probably clouded the minds of Christ's own disciples, who believed their peculiar relationship with him rendered them more likely to receive favors. For them, apostolic rights meant a brass plate over the door. For Jesus, they were (and are) a towel and a cross: "Whoever wants to become great among you must be your servant" (Mark 10:43).

Early Beginnings

Selfish ambition is a slippery neck to pin down. Like pride, it has a thousand innocent faces. It begins as a benign game of make-believe. As children, we pretend to be movie stars, athletes, and professionals. We play lawyer, not janitor. We dress up as celebrities on Halloween. We plaster pictures of movie stars on our walls and wear the authentic jerseys of famous athletes to school. Recently, I addressed an elementary school assembly and asked the children to name their heroes. All but two children listed movie stars and athletes, neither of which represents the real and ordinary world. As we move through the middle years, we try to become these things, and if we cannot, we settle for becoming someone else—someone important. Only a few of us are conspicuous enough to be appointed drum major or labeled most likely to succeed. The rest of us will have to look elsewhere for greatness. And we would despair in our search were it not for the commencement address at our graduation, which encourages us to keep dreaming and to seize the day.

Thus encouraged, each of us will follow a graded course leading upward from the realm of the ordinary into the sphere of the gods.

The child says, "Accept me—I am loved."
The adolescent says, "Love me—I am distinct."
The youth says, "Recognize me—I am unique."
The adult says, "Honor me—I am admirable."
And the beast cries, "Glorify me—I am better than the rest."

This is a well-traveled course for people from all walks of life. The line between noble ambition and selfish ambition is so thin that most of us will not know when we have crossed it nor admit it when others tell us that we have. As young people we dream of righting the world, curing the disease, building the kingdom. But within these noble ambitions lies the proud contention that we are the ones who can pull it off. So it is not that justice has prevailed but that I have delivered it. It is not only that we cured the disease, but that we cured it in my lifetime and—let the record show this—that I myself was part of the answer.

When I was in high school, I suffered a particularly annoying lab partner who blurted "that was my idea" after nearly every discovery we made. I felt sorry that his parents did not give him the attention he thought he deserved, but why should I have to pay the rent by watching him pat himself on the back? Yet I have often found myself afflicted by this disease called "what about me?" It matters to me not only that people find Christ, but that they find him in my church. I am willing to celebrate the successes of others provided I get my share too. It really irritates me, don't you know, when big churches get even bigger—especially at my expense. Evidently, I am not alone. At least one popular pastor has confessed:

> I discovered a brutal truth about myself . . . some years ago when I suddenly realized that I rarely delighted in another person's success. In my insecurity as a young pastor, I felt that anyone else's success was a threat to my own.[1]

A young man from my hometown recently folded up after a few futile years in the ministry. The reason? "I'm tired of fighting other churches for the same people," he said. In one way, he is right. Like law and medicine, "ministry" can be a very competitive field. If one has carnal ambitions, he dare not be timid, or he will never field an audience large enough to pay the bills.

Deferred Materialism

Retirement is another place where selfish ambitions can hide. In our society, retirement has become the long weekend at the end of life, a great indulgence for those who have denied their appetites long enough. Like the man who mistook hell for heaven, some retirees invest themselves (rather than give themselves) for forty years in order to collect dividends later, which means having the power to buy without borrowing, to attend without having to participate, to complain without taking responsibility. Having spent their lives worrying about the kids and denying themselves pleasures they always thought they deserved, these people are finally ready to get something back.

As a busy pastor, I have watched some parishioners move out of ministry as soon as they retired. It is a predictable pattern. At first, they are tardy. They arrive for meetings and services only minutes before they start. Then, they resign from all committees and attend only the services. No longer producing in the ministry, they develop a consumer's disposition and critical eye. Later, they retire from all but one of the services, because they are "busier now than when they were working." They are running out of time, and what time they have is reserved for enjoying the fruit of their faithfulness over the years. Tragically, these folk have never given up their carnal ambitions. They have only deferred them until now. One example of this was the man who warned his new pastor not to call on him anymore, now that he was retired.

> Many have not surrendered their expectations, only defered them.

"Let me show you why," the fellow said. He produced a little book in which he kept the names of everyone who had worked in the church over the years and the number of hours each person had spent. Of course, his own name topped the list.

"I did it all back when the church was first built," he added. "So don't ask for any more."

It is hard to see how any one could possess the Spirit of Christ and not have his Christ's disposition. Yet I have heard the same defense ("I've done my time") from believers of all ages. In many churches, the thirty- or forty-somethings have moved beyond the nursery and onto the board, where ministry is only decided—not done. Yet the Jesus we possess warned us against the mentality of one fool who, presumably in his sunset years, boasted to himself, "You have plenty of good things laid up for many years. Take life easy; eat, drink and be merry"—not knowing that his life would end as quickly as his posh retirement had begun (Luke 12:19). What then?

The pleasure we cannot get from retirement we save for heaven. Paradise, as we call it, is interpreted as a place where all earthly dreams come true. It is a cosmic Disneyland. It is sanctified indulgence. For many, the main attractions of heaven are the streets of gold, walls of jasper, starry crowns, and mansions that tower above the shacks we've had to endure down here. One gospel song is rather brazen about our expectations for heaven.

> I heard about a mansion
>   He has built for me in glory,
> And I heard about the streets of gold
>   beyond the crystal sea.[2]

For others, the real glory of heaven is in finally getting the credit they deserve. While it was not the intent of the writer to elicit these emotions, this popular song rescued many from the despairing thought that they would be just another saint in heaven.

> One by one they came
> Far as the eye could see
> Each one somehow touched
> By your generosity
> Little things that you had done
> Sacrifices made
> Unnoticed on the earth
> In heaven now proclaimed [3]

When I was a young pastor serving a small congregation, a fellow named Carl dropped off a new stereo for our little church. He said the Lord told him to give it to us. Before he could test the spirits, I was helping him unload it. And before I could thank him, he was already looking forward to payday.

"Don't thank me," he exclaimed. "God will make it up to me in the next world. Jesus said I'd get it back pressed down, shaken together, and running over. Hallelujah!"

He was honest with me, if not with the Scriptures. Carl had not become a servant. He had merely rendered an act of kindness to a needy church. The same is true of people who let others cut in line, then holler from the back that the "last shall be first" in heaven. Like our friend who mistook hell for heaven, these poor folk have not surrendered their expectations, only deferred them to another world because, by the looks of things, they were not likely to be fulfilled in this one. If people desired on earth what they expect to receive in heaven, we would call them materialistic. Yet what difference does it make when we expect to receive them, if we desire them *for ourselves?*

The Unthinkable

What if all of the talk about star-studded crowns and streets of gold is only symbolic? That is, what if the writer of Revelation merely borrowed images familiar to his audience, as if to say, "your deepest desires will be satisfied in heaven"? What if there are no streets of gold—or anything else? What if heaven is nothing more than a wide-open space, and God says to every new resident, "Well, here it is—start over"?

Like James and John, who desired to sit on the right and left of Christ, we often desire positions or things in Christ's kingdom that are not consistent with the Kingdom itself. Peter flunked the same test on the night Jesus washed his feet.

"No, Lord," he said, "you shall never wash my feet."

It was another way of saying, "If I were the Messiah, I would never wash the feet of disciples."

But this was Jesus' point. If Peter could not stoop to wash the feet of disciples, he could not possibly be the Messiah, for that is what Messiahs do. The Anglican writer Jeremy Taylor insisted that "no man shall be fit to govern if he does not first know how to obey."[4]

So one evidence of our love for Christ is that we have the disposition of a servant.

The purest example of this came one afternoon on the shores of Galilee when Jesus asked Peter three times to love him. It was the third time in the Gospels where people were said to love Christ.

THE NATURE OF LOVE

"Do you love me?" Jesus asked, then here is the test: "Feed my sheep" (John 21:15–17).

Notice that there is a steady progression in the three evidences of love from the Gospels—the woman at Jesus' feet, the disciples in the garden of Gethsemane, and Peter on the shores of Galilee.

The first episode took place in public (Luke 7), the second setting was more private (John 14), but the third was intimate (John 21). The first evidence of our love for Christ is that we pour ourselves at his feet (Luke 7). The second evidence is that we keep his commandments (John 14). But the third is more difficult and sustained. It does not look up; it looks around. It is not a private expression between Christ and ourselves. It is expressed in public. Jesus says, If you love *me,* feed *them.*

When William Booth, founder of The Salvation Army, was unable one year to attend his denomination's conference, he was asked to send a telegram in his place. When the moment came for Booth's message to be read on the conference floor, the delegates were surprised to hear that it contained only one word: "Others." When John Wesley said that Christianity is a social religion, he meant that perfect love is not content to stay in the church and swap deep contemplations with the choir. It moves outside the church to engage the world. The end of good religion is not only that it leads us to love God with our whole heart, soul, mind, and strength, but also that it leads us to love others as we love ourselves. Any religion that does not move in this direction—from the vertical (love toward God) to the horizontal (love toward others)—is selfish and wrongheaded.

So the Ten Commandments teach us to love God first (commandments one through four), and then to love others, whether our parents (five), spouse (seven), or neighbor (ten). The Lord's Prayer follows the same progression from vertical (thy kingdom come) to the horizontal (forgive us . . . as we forgive our debtors). It is always the same sequence. Just as we cannot separate fire from its heat and light, so we will never divorce genuine, holy love from leadership, evangelism, and acts of mercy. We cannot have one without the other, though we must never mistake the expressions of love for love itself.

Love Reflected in Leadership

While the Gospels are full of ways in which Christ loved people, these narratives record only three instances in which people are said to love him. In the third such episode (John 21), Jesus plays host on the shores of Galilee.

When Jesus asked Peter whether he loved him, he was asking a question the bold apostle had already answered. Twice before, Peter had boasted a devotion that was superior to that of the other disciples.

"Even if all fall away on account of you," he promised, "I never will," (Matt. 26:33). We can imagine that he left the emphasis where he wanted it—on the "I." Later, it was the same song: "Lord, why can't I follow you now? I will lay down my life for you" (John 13:37).

To Peter, the mark of a true disciple was not measured in what Jesus had done for the him, but in what he would do for Jesus. How far would he go? How late into the night would he work? How long would he pray? How much would he endure? And so Peter misplaced the emphasis for his love, on human ingenuity. The self was served even as it served Jesus. Of course, Jesus' stunning prophecy—"you will disown me three times" (John 13:38)—signaled the end of Peter's grand delusions. The penetrating, offensive prediction that Peter would deny his Lord was painful not because it insulted Peter but because it surprised him. He would fail Christ in the very place he was most confident he could serve him: the self! He who professed a sterling devotion would be found as craven as anyone else on the day of the crucifixion— even more so. He who was brave at every other place in the Gospels became a coward down the home stretch. One moment, he chopped off the ear of Malchus, and hours later he denied even knowing the man he had just defended. The self was as capable of cowardice as courage. Yes, there was a little of Judas in the heart of Peter. After all, every Gospel records Judas's kiss and Peter's denial in the same chapter.

Later, on the shores of Galilee, Peter would have his mulligan. Three times he had denied Christ. Three times he would have the opportunity to fix it. More than this, he would learn that holy love is not something people generate in the direction of heaven, but something Christ generates in the hearts of people toward others on earth. That is, holiness is not the love of God for our sake, but the love of others for God's sake. It is a lesson that may be driven home the next time we pray for sanctification, then labor to drum up a little empathy for people on the other side of life. He who professes the greatest measure of faith is asked to love Christ's people by feeding them. The missionary E. Stanley Jones confessed that he once thought God's best virtues were put on high shelves where only the ascended masters could reach them. He later learned that God actually had put them on the lowest shelves where people had to stoop in order to find them. The curse of sin means that we were all born too tall, rather than too short, for the things of God.

People before Ministry

But if love is passion for service, we must be careful that our passion is not derailed in one of two ways. First, we must be careful we do not love the ministry more than the people. A friend of mine who cooks for a popular restaurant was lamenting the number of people she had to feed each day. From opening time to closing, people were lined up to eat. Even though this seems like a good problem for a restaurant to have, Julie was tired of it.

"But so far today," she said, "there's been nobody coming in—knock on wood—so maybe we can get some work done around here." I smiled and left. But I thought what you are probably thinking. Does she realize what she is saying? Doesn't she comprehend that she—who loves to cook—would have little cooking to do if not for those pesky patrons?

She reminds me of the Englishman hired several years ago to drive a city bus. On his first day he managed to complete his route and return to the depot at the prescribed time, but without any passengers. When asked why he didn't have any, he admitted, "I never stopped to pick them up."

"And why didn't you stop?" inquired the angry manager.

"Because," said the rookie, "I would have fallen behind in my schedule."

Every leader faces the temptation to gradually surrender his *call* in order to pursue to lesser, yet still noble, *causes*. Schools may exchange education for building self-esteem. Counselors may exchange wholeness for happiness. Armies may exchange defense for protecting civil rights. And like the bus driver, we ourselves may exchange service for management. It is more natural than carnal. A successful leader is happy with his success and does not want to squander it.

> We are born too tall, not too short to reach the things of God.

He works hard. God blesses him. People come.

He works harder, and more people come.

He works smarter, and even more people come.

But one day in the middle of the week, he begins to focus more on the work than on the people who are coming.

As my friend the cook reminded us, people complicate things. Situations arise that fall between the answers. Our horizons get broadened. Like Moses, we may still have our quiet moments with God, but they are no longer on the back of the mountain. Now they are public spectacles. We preach or testify about them. They have powerful consequences for all the people gathered at the base of the mountain. We need not obey these people, so they are not really a threat. But because we cannot ignore them, they are always a factor—always something to consider in our private as well as our public lives. The peace of anonymity is gone. Subtly, we begin to believe that God's Word is neither the last nor the only view on any subject. We take surveys. We weigh political consequences. We attend meetings and decide matters without once passing the faceless multitude with their stories and their needs before us.

As we grow older, we speak of academic degrees and salary packages. Like the misguided parishioner who recorded his hours in a little book, we track our tenure in our heads. We hang our certificates on the wall. Our call becomes our career. Our study becomes our office. Our elders become board members. Our passion ("this one thing I do") becomes a vision statement. And we speak of momentum where unction once had the day.

We must remember that, even in large and complex ministries, we are *spiritual* leaders who deal in matters that are sometimes (though not always) inconsistent with good business sense or with our standards of reporting for the conference journal. Much of what we seek after and preach about is not quantifiable. As churches, we must develop friendships that are not utilitarian. We must witness for the love of Christ, not to induce others to attend our church. We must encourage a missionary spirit that gives to those whom we have never met and who cannot repay. And as individuals, we must be willing to listen to the countless, often annoying, details of a lonely person's day—not because we need to hear but because they need to tell.

> I have seen love for ministry eclipse love for people.

I am thinking of the seminary professor who ended his exam with the peculiar question: "What is the woman's name who cleans this building every afternoon?" She was a happy but quiet middle-aged woman with glasses, hair pulled back, who wore something like a smock as she pushed her cleaning cart from classroom to office. Everyone knew her, but no one knew anything about her. Finally, one frustrated student turned in his exam with the last question still blank.

"Is this a joke?" he asked the professor, pointing to the question. "What does this have to do with the rest of the material?"

"Doris!" said the professor adamantly. "Her name is Doris! When you leave here, you are going straight into the service of a hundred people just like her. And until you can put your clever theology into a language she can understand, until you can stand it up in her backyard and move it around, you have nothing, finally, to say."

Many times I have seen my love for ministry, for speculative theology, or for writing eclipse my love for people. I have heard them say they didn't want to bother me because I was too busy. I have seen them push their children past me at the door of the church so I wouldn't have to trouble with them. And I have never felt more like a disciple and less like Jesus in my life (see Mark 10:13–16). I have enjoyed preaching fiery sermons from a pulpit almost twenty feet away from the nearest listener, but winced when one of them sought a counseling appointment. Like some of you, I am more inclined toward public than private ministry. But why? What I considered a passion for preaching was really a passion for praise. Which of my members would compliment me for a pastoral visit made at a nursing home? Who would stand in line to shake my hand after I drove two hours to Detroit to sit with a teenage mother while her baby was taken off of life support? Who would tell their friends of the way I mopped up a kitchen or vacuumed a rug?

"True service finds it almost impossible to distinguish the small from the large service," wrote Richard Foster. And where the difference is clear, he said, "the true servant seems to be often drawn to the small service . . . because he genuinely sees it as the important service."[5]

Often, our positions in the church will make this difficult, and our ambitions will make it flatly impossible. But even as Jesus did, we must find our greatness where we best express our love: at the feet of one another.

God before Others

After we have learned to love the people, we must be careful we do not love the people more than the gospel. If one temptation is to pay too little attention to our audience, the other is to pay too much. If you ask people what they want in a church or a leader, they will tell you. And while you can easily build an empire by satisfying those popular demands, you will very likely find your love distracted. For loving our neighbor, when we have not first loved our God, is mere humanitarianism. And when it is not fueled by a holy love, the church will find itself in a very competitive field. Most cities are well cared for by a long list of charities that are committed to humanitarianism, with some interest in the gospel. But the church must be committed to the gospel, with an interest in humanitarianism.

Jesus was. Matthew observed that even after healing the people's diseases (8:3, 7, 15), casting out their demons (8:16, 32), raising their dead (9:25), and touring their villages (9:35) Jesus *still* diagnosed the people as "harassed and helpless, like sheep without a shepherd" (9:36).

It is worth noting that these are primarily spiritual conditions. That is, Jesus may heal our paralysis, but he will first forgive our sin (Mark 2:5). He may give us something to drink, but he always wants to talk about our five failed marriages and our worship (John 4). He will feed us our fish and loaves, but he is never satisfied until we "work . . . for food that endures to eternal life" (John 6:27). Even when he raises our dead, it is not to cure our sorrow, but that we "would see the glory of God" (John 11:40).

Quite simply, Jesus does nothing randomly. He performs no miracle for the sake of the miracle itself, nor even for the sake of his audience. There is always another, deeper agenda: "I have not come to call the righteous, but sinners to repentance" (Luke 5:32). Small wonder, then, that he saw humanity's need as primarily spiritual. This was not the biggest problem people faced. But it was the first and this is news indeed to a culture like ours that is wrapped in therapeutic solutions.

Consistent with much of the advice often given to ministers today, one homiletician surveyed four thousand church attendees to discover their primary needs on the morning they came to church. To no one's surprise, they listed futility, loneliness, insecurity, inferiority, guilt, alcoholism, marriage, and sex as their greatest bugaboos. The good preacher then summarized his findings as follows:

> In a congregation of five hundred, it is reasonable to assume then, that one hundred people will feel a sense of loss; one third will be facing personal adjustments that weaken or destroy their home life. One half are having emotional adjustments in school, work, home, or in community that endangers their happiness. Many others are suffering from neuroses or anxiety states. At least fifteen are homosexual inclined. Twenty-five are depressed. And one hundred are suffering feelings of guilt.[6]

Of course, the preacher was appropriately shocked at the wide variety of problems filing into his pews every Sunday. But we ought to be more concerned about his diagnosis. For the problems of personal adjustments that weaken or destroy the home life, there is only a cross with God on it. For emotional adjustments or neuroses or anxiety states, there is only the hope of being reconciled to God—with all of its ramifications. But let us not preach only about the ramifications. Let us consider that one third of Matthew, one third of Mark, one fourth of Luke, and one half of John are devoted to the last twenty-four hours of Jesus' life. Then let us devote a little more time to it ourselves next Sunday. For even the psychological problems we help unravel are bound to return with seven more unless we proceed to the spiritual core of the modern person's dilemma. The former missionary Lesslie Newbigin has said this even better: "To a hungry man a good meal looks like heaven; when he has eaten it he knows that it is not."[7]

A true shepherd feeds his sheep by refusing to settle for a temporary (seen) solution and progressing deep into the eternal (unseen) ones. A true shepherd sees a person for what he is. He moves beyond what is helpful and into what is true. In chapter nine, we will see how this happens.

Focused on the Mission

Imagine a large ballroom filled with thousands of people from various backgrounds, with all kinds of incomes and all kinds of problems. Some are dancing and some are eating while the band plays. Some sit in their corners and sulk. Others are busy with private concerns. But everyone is ignorant of the one thing you know as you enter the ballroom. The house is on fire. Even now the roof is nearly gutted and ready to cave in. If you stand at the door and scream, they will trample each other on their way out—if they believe you at all. So you decide to enter the ballroom and help them, one by one, to escape the coming inferno. The first person you see recognizes you and offers a drink. You refuse and nudge him in the direction of the door. But on your way to the door, he stops you momentarily to tell about his troubled marriage and his broken heart. Of course you have something to say about that too, but you must not neglect the more urgent and fundamental matter of getting him out of the building before the roof collapses. If you fail, all of your good counsel will not help him in the grave.

One by one you move them across the floor, arousing those who will listen and escorting them toward the door. The smoke is more intense now. The fire is hotter and the hour later than when you began. But you press on, and each person you meet seizes the opportunity to tell you of his problems while you direct him or her toward the exit.

What will they do when their businesses fails?

Should they tell their spouses about their long-term affairs?

What is the matter with our government?

Do you think a person can lose his salvation?

And where do the dinosaurs fit into the Bible's view of creation?

None of this will matter the day after they are dead. But they want to talk about it now. And while you may discuss it with them, and even offer real and lasting solutions to their problems, you must never forget that your real agenda is to get them out of danger. To be sure, you want to do more than this. But you must never do less or other.

E. Stanley Jones observed:

> I once traveled during my formative evangelistic years with a very great man. I learned much from him. But when his emphasis shifted from Christ to varying emphases—antiwar programs, social justice, birth control, spiritualism—he was less than effective; he was a blur. He would exhaust these emphases in a year or two and have to shift to a new one. But you do not exhaust Christ—he is the inexhaustible. Events come and go; the Event remains unchanged amid the changeable.[8]

In our passion to serve people, we must not confuse the advice of Christ with his agenda. His advice may save our marriages and our sanity. His agenda will save our souls. His advice can be peddled by social workers and psychologists alike (and there is nothing wrong with this). But his agenda is the passion and possession of those who bring good news.

Too often it is because we love people more than the gospel that we serve them so well, even while we go without our time alone with God. It is easy to push ourselves along this path, because after all, people need the Lord. But we must not deprive ourselves of time with the Lord whom the people need. And I say this to myself. Like Martha, I lead services better than I sit in them, (see Luke 10:41–42). I am often happier that people are buying my gospel than I am concerned about which gospel I'm selling them.

But there is one more lesson to be learned about holy love and the leadership of Christ.

The First Requirement for Leadership

A few years ago I received a call from a young woman seeking a church for her children to attend.

"Do you have a good children's ministry there?" she asked.

"Yes, ma'am. We have about a hundred children, ranging from infants through sixth graders. Each age-group has its own teacher and assistant who pour themselves into teaching these kids."

"I see. Now what kind of qualifications do your teachers have?"

"What do you mean?"

"Well, I mean what qualifies them to teach children? Are they trained? Are they licensed? Do they seem to know what they're doing?"

Here was a woman who had drunk deeply from the well of modernity. She was convinced that content was not only separate from character, but superior to it as well. And while there are many things I would do differently if I could do them again, I am still satisfied with the answer I gave my grand inquisitor that evening. I said, "All of our teachers love their students."

Long ago, when people had souls and still believed in love, my simple answer would have meant more. But we have grown up. We have become taller, so tall in fact that we cannot see the simple, unchangeable virtues on the bottom shelf. We aspire to the very positions our master left in order to wash our feet. And so, contrary to the teachings of every other leadership seminar of our day, Jesus called Peter on the question of love.

"Do you love me?" is a far cry from "can you deliver?" It is not only a better question, but a more fundamental one. For if we lead without loving, we are misguided at best and tyrants at worst, who threaten the sheep rather than feed them. Other things may help us lead our people, but none are more important than love.

Like Peter, many of us believe that our love for Christ has grown beyond the usual, into the extraordinary. If it has for you, then feed his sheep.

> Whatever comes next, I must feed his sheep.

Most of us have failed Christ at least once in our lives, and we were promptly placed on probation under the watchful eye of a heavenly truant officer. We long to return and to render some valuable, if hidden, service to God. Now can we? And what must we do? In small ways or in great, we must feed his sheep.

Maybe we have worshiped Christ for years, yet stayed away from the ministries of our church. We love the Lord, but we fear his people. Now we want to move forward. We want to get beyond the routine of worship. We have learned obedience. Now it is time to feed his sheep.

Some have been busy in the church with everything from folding bulletins to serving communion. We have counseled families and chaired meetings. We have taught classes, directed choirs, visited the sick, superintended the Sunday school, and returned phone calls late into the night. Now we are tired and bored with traditional church ministry. We cannot make ourselves care about it anymore.

Are there unreached people in our church? Who are the fallen, and what is the way to restore them? Should I pray? Encourage? Write? Consult? Tithe? Lead? Follow? Whatever is next, if God is in it, I must feed his sheep.

It is the closest thing to heaven. And speaking of heaven—

According to a legend, one lucky fellow was granted a tour there and noticed a long table with seated guests, each of whom had a three-foot fork strapped his wrist. The table was laden with a delectable banquet. Not surprisingly, all of the guests ate well and looked satisfied. On his return to earth, he was granted a pass through hell, in which he observed a banquet hall arranged with the exact same setting. Only here the guests were weeping and had emaciated bodies while a full menu sat before them. Perplexed by this, the visitor asked his attendant to explain the difference. His answer?

"The long forks have made it impossible for our guests in hell to feed themselves, yet they try nonetheless. But in heaven, each guest has learned to feed his friend across the table, who in turn is feeding him."

Christian, if you love him, take care of each other. If we do not, we will find that our own longings have not been met. Or worse, we may find that they have been met—in a place we mistake for heaven.

LIFE RESPONSES

1. What do you think the author means by saying that Christians sometimes place ministry ahead of people?

2. Steve DeNeff asks us to consider whether heaven will be a place of leisure or a place of service. Which do you think it will be, and why?

3. What are you now doing that is a service to others?

Chapter 7

FOR THE LOVE OF GOD!
The Strange Company of Holiness

For me, the most unsettling thing about the Gospels is that the wrong people keep getting saved. It's never who you think it should be. It's always someone else.

The sinful woman at Jesus' feet is forgiven. The chief priests are not.

The tax collector who cheats is forgiven. The law-abiding rich young ruler is not.

Jesus forgives the paralytic, who only wants to be healed, but he dodges the extroverted man, who promises to follow him wherever he goes.

The Roman centurion gets it but Sanhedrin members do not.

One thief asks to be saved and is not. The other thief asks only to be remembered, and is saved.

The "righteous" Pharisees are excluded from the kingdom that the "poor in spirit" possess.

The simplest, most insightful explanation I have heard for this comes from my father, who suggests that people in the Gospels were converted because Jesus saw something in them that only Jesus could see.

This insight goes a long way toward explaining not only the presence of Matthew among the chosen but also the inclusion of his conversion in each of the first three Gospels.[1] To thicken the plot of Matthew's invitation into the company of disciples, consider the following ironies.

First, his story appears in all three synoptic Gospels. And why is that strange? Because all three do not relate the story of Christ's birth or ascension. Only Luke tells us of Jesus' first discourse in Nazareth. Only Matthew and Mark say he walked on water. Only Luke tells us he raised a widow's son from the dead. Few of the parables appear in all three synoptics, nor do Jesus' final words from the Cross, nor his appearance to any one person after the Resurrection. Regarding Jesus' first miracle, his encounter with

Nicodemus, and his washing of the disciples' feet, the first three gospels are completely silent. And this is peculiar indeed since all of these events seem worth remembering. Yet while each synoptic writer has forgotten to include at least one of these stories, none of them has forgotten the mundane story of Matthew. Why?

Even more peculiar is the silence of Gospel writers as to how, exactly, certain disciples were called. For instance, we are not told how Thomas, Simon the Zealot, James the son of Alphaeus, or even Judas Iscariot came to be called disciples. They just were. But this does not surprise us since we never hear from them again (except for Judas Iscariot). In fact, every disciple whose first encounter with Jesus is remembered reappears later in the Gospels. That is, every disciple except Matthew. He makes no memorable sayings. He appears in no dramatic scenes. He is the silent observer of most miracles. He says nothing while Jesus washes his feet and serves him the bread and wine. And after the resurrection, nearly half of the disciples are granted a private audience with Christ.[2] But not Matthew. Yet each synoptic writer stops to remind us of the day that Matthew was called. After that, he vanishes from the record. So why remember his conversion?

JESUS AND SINNERS

Before we unravel this, consider a third irony, which may actually help resolve the others. While each Gospel writer tends to shuffle the deck, placing the stories of Jesus' ministry in a different sequence, all three synoptic writers preface the story of Matthew's calling with the healing of the paralytic, and all three writers follow Matthew's calling with Jesus' words about wine and wineskins. They may differ as to the scope and sequence of the Sermon on the Mount. They may juggle the miracles and the pithy statements of Christ, putting them in different orders. But they all agree on the how and when of Matthew's call.

In plain English, this means that besides recording the facts of Jesus' life, our three synoptic writers had another agenda. That is, they had a reason for telling the story as they did, and in the matter of Matthew's calling, their reasons were likely the same.

Jesus Attracted to Sinners

· "You have nothing to do but save souls," was the advice of John Wesley to his ministers, "therefore spend and be spent in this work."

More recently, someone has suggested that the church exists partly for those who never go near it. And there is some biblical precedent for that statement.

To Jesus, the gospel is always for *the world* or *whosoever*. While Jesus confined his preaching to the "lost sheep of Israel" (Matt. 15:24), his gospel was no private conversation between God and the Jews. From the very beginning there were signs that it would break out into a world religion.

That Jesus spent his childhood in Egypt and in Nazareth should have been the first clue that Israel would never have him to themselves. That Jesus spent so much of his time and miraculous energy on the people of Galilee, a land with as many Gentiles as Jews, should have made it equally clear. But when the Jews missed even this indication, he was a little more direct. On the grassy slopes of Galilee, he called his disciples the "light of the world" and a "city on a hill," which was, no doubt, an alarming analogy to those whose religion was a fortress. At the Pharisee's house (what better timing!) where the sinful woman washed his feet, Jesus promised that her unselfish act would follow her, not only through the country but "throughout the *world*" (Matt. 26:13, emphasis added).[3] On two different occasions he huddled together with a handful of followers and predicted that "the gospel of the kingdom will be preached in the whole world as a testimony to all nations" (Matt. 24:14; Luke 24:47).

> Evangelism is the offensive mark of the gospel.

Even the Devil knew enough to tempt him with what he wanted most. Showing him the kingdoms of the world, Satan said, "All these things I will give you"; and it was not only that the Devil could have provided these things but that Christ truly wanted them that made the offer a legitimate temptation. For where there is no interest or desire, there is no real temptation.

Christ's own love for the world was even partly behind his explosive outburst on the day he cleansed the Temple. It was not only that the money changers were cheating innocent worshipers that made Jesus angry, but that they were doing so in the court of Gentiles, thus depriving the world of its only chance to worship. After all, said Jesus, "Is it not written, 'my house will be called a house of prayer *for all nations?*'" (Mark 11:17, emphasis added).[4] How could a Gentile pray amid that chaos? One scholar is even more direct saying that by cleansing the Temple, "Jesus seeks to make available to the Gentiles the privileges which belonged to the new age and thereby he proclaims that the time of universal worship . . . has come!"[5] Perhaps these Gentiles were the very "sheep that [were] not of this sheep pen" (John 10:16).

And so, when he stood with his disciples at the end of his journey and told them to "make disciples of all nations," Jesus was only repeating a theme that was deeply embedded in his mission.

Intentional Movement

In Matthew, he thanks the Father for having hidden the gospel from the wise and learned and for revealing it to the little children. And he said this while criticizing Capernaum in favor of Sodom. No Jew could have ignored the insult.

In Mark, he grants the request of a blind beggar, only hours after turning down his own disciples (compare 10:36–37 and 10:51). The message is clear: the blind man saw in Jesus what even his disciples could not.[6]

In Luke, he eats with one sinner while another washes his feet. The irony is rich. The "righteous" knew all about the woman touching Jesus ("she is a sinner"), but apparently did not know anything about the Jesus she was touching.

In John, he speaks to the woman at the well, who has gone 0–5 in marriage. He defends the woman caught in adultery. He rescues a thief on a cross. And after his Resurrection, he makes his first appearance to Mary Magdalene, out of whom he had driven seven demons (Mark 16:9).

In fact, Jesus' itinerary moves him outward from Jerusalem (John 2:13) to Judea (3:22) to Samaria (4:4) and, finally, to the Gentile world (4:45–46). Jesus' own charge to "open your eyes and look at the fields" was made while he stood in a Samaritan village (4:35).

Even Jesus' parables show how the gospel breaks out into the land of Gentiles, who do not deserve it. His captivating and still famous stories of the good Samaritan, the prodigal son, the great wedding feast, and the workers in the vineyard were thinly disguised warnings that the gospel was not the property of the already religious, but of "all the people [the disciples] could find, both good and bad" (Matt. 22:10).

Evangelism is the offensive mark of the Christian gospel. Other than Islam, no religion is so zealous to convert the world. Most seek only to protect themselves from being converted. And distinct even from Islam, Christianity is not tied to a culture. It belongs to the world. In fact, no other religion can separate itself from its culture and survive the way Christianity has. And so the church has missed the heart of Jesus and has squandered one of its most important distinctives if it does not capture the spirit of evangelism. Other religions are a fortress. But with our gospel, Jesus has thrown open the doors.

A Preference for Sinners

Here then, is the explanation for the peculiar place the Gospel writers have given to the calling of Matthew: Jesus is attracted to sinners! For reasons that only the holy can know, Jesus appeared at times to even prefer the company of sinners over that of the righteous, because holiness brings with it a love for people who are different. And love is the purest reason for any kind of evangelism in the first place. Simply put, we do not evangelize our neighbors in order to bring them to church or even to heaven. We do not implore them to be saved because the alternative is so much worse. In fact, we do not convert them at all—though we certainly hope and pray they will be converted. No, the bottom line for all evangelism—the holy motive behind all of the money we spend and the time we invest and the embarrassment we risk—is love. We evangelize because we love Jesus and we love others. With this motive, there is no way the evangelist can fail, though he can be more or less successful. If his neighbor converts or if he does not, the evangelist has done what every holy evangelist must do. He has loved Christ and his neighbor with an open heart—no strings attached.

Unfortunately, this thinking runs counter to common sense, so true holiness has become suspect in the very place it ought to be the most welcome—the church! Holy love frowns on the distance that we have put between ourselves and the world. Like Jesus, it embraces the leper but does not die of leprosy. It dies at the hands of those who would not touch a leper on a bet. It loves when it cannot persuade, forgives when it cannot collect, hopes when it cannot trust, and trusts when it cannot endure. And this is a very far cry from the insipid religion most of us have witnessed; therefore, "everyone who wants to live a godly life in Christ Jesus will be persecuted" (2 Tim. 3:12), and not only by the Muslims. As the holy face the world, they will be shot in the back.

Forgiveness for Sinners

It is just possible that Jesus, who had been discreet in performing miracles up to that time, was spoiling for an argument on the day he forgave the paralytic his sins. That took place in Capernaum, where Jesus first wrangled with the Pharisees. And if he was looking for an argument, he did not have to look far.

While Jesus was standing in Peter's home, the tiled roof above him was torn out, and a paralyzed man was lowered on a cot to a place where Jesus could touch him. In each Gospel, the writer observes that Jesus "saw their faith [and] said to the paralytic, . . . 'your sins are forgiven'" (Matt. 9:2). The sequence is less important than the surprise. For in this miracle, Jesus, who had previously healed the sick (4:23), touched a leper (8:3), raised a centurion's servant (8:13), and exorcised demons from two desperate men (8:32)—all without forgiving their sins—offered the paralytic what he did not appear to seek: forgiveness. And so the man had it from the best possible source that he was right with God.

Of course the Pharisees, who were experts in these matters, did not miss this bold claim and asked, "Why does this fellow talk like that?" And before anyone could answered them, they answer themselves, "He's blaspheming [for] who can forgive sins but God alone?" (Mark 2:7).

It is interesting and unsettling to follow the dreadful course of the self-righteous Pharisees from that point forward. From their *faulty presumption* ("this fellow is blaspheming," Matt. 9:3) grew a *cynical spirit,* which revealed itself only eight verses later in the acid, rhetorical question "Why does [he] eat with . . . sinners?" (9:11). Predictably, a few verses later, they betrayed their *religious bias* against Jesus by answering their own question: "It is by the prince of demons that he

> We need nothing so much as to know we're right with God.

drives out demons" (9:34). When Jesus warned them that their closed minds would cost them their souls, they stooped to *slander* by railing, "Here is a glutton and a drunkard, a friend of tax collectors and 'sinners'" (11:19). Notably, these last two conditions (bias and slander) are a malignant form of the Pharisees own faulty presumption. From there, their hatred took the form of a *conspiracy* against him. They began "looking for a reason to accuse [him] . . . and plotted how they might kill [him]" (12:10, 14).

One cannot help but wonder if the Pharisees' first question ("why does this fellow talk like that?") would have fetched a different verdict were it not tied to a narrow-minded presumption ("he's blaspheming"). The Pharisees' conclusion that only God can forgive sins (Luke 5:21) offered another possible explanation for what they witnessed. But they were unwilling to entertain the thought that Jesus might be God. Their bone of contention (that only God can forgive sins) was Jesus' very point: "the Son of man has authority on earth to forgive sins . . ." (Matt. 9:6). But it is a trademark among self-righteous people that they never soften their convictions.

We must not miss the point behind this miracle. Jesus forgives sin rather than healing disease because sin—and not sickness—is our biggest problem. Methodist missionary to India E. Stanley Jones has noted that "those who have been up against raw human need for years have learned that men need nothing, absolutely nothing, like they need to know that they are right with God." It is the same today. Our universities may train politicians to deal with society's evils. Our law schools may equip lawyers and judges to handle society's delinquents. Our brokers may conspire to preserve society's assets. Our therapists may contemplate society's behavior. But only the Christian can address society's sin. And it is ultimately our sin that gives rise to all of the other symptoms. So it is no small thing to insist that only Jesus forgives sin.

Welcome for Sinners

To the Jews of Jesus' day, the matter of taxation was a hot subject. Like all taxpayers, the Jews were suspicious of those who collected their money, and on the day their taxes to the state exceeded their tithes to the Temple, they were livid. The Pharisees' own question, "is it right to pay taxes to Caesar or not?" was probably grounded in these public debates. But the hottest criticism of their day was reserved for the tax collectors themselves, who secured their positions by outbidding the competition, then paid off their masters by cheating the people in two ways. First, tax collectors were infamous for overassessing the property in their provinces, and second, they were ever ready to loan their victims the money they needed at an astronomical rate of interest. This made tax collectors among the wealthiest people.

They were also the least favored. The term *tax collector* was synonymous with *thief*. They were not allowed in or near the Temple. They could not bear witness in court.

Yet tax collectors were in the company of Jesus one afternoon in Matthew's home. The watching, now-seething, Pharisees would not have missed the symbolism. For to eat with someone was to fellowship with him. And to host the meal was to accept and welcome that person as your friend (see Matt. 11:19). It is significant, then, that "many tax collectors and 'sinners' came and ate *with him*" (9:10, emphasis added). It was not enough that they were at the same table. To Matthew, they were the company of Jesus. Once more, Jesus threw open the doors of the gospel to the least and the lowest around him.

The same compassion that led him to feed the five thousand drove him to serve the sinners all they could eat. And he does so still, each time his people gather at the table of the Lord to eat his flesh and drink his blood.

I didn't realize that, when I received communion as a young person. Like most children of my tradition, I grew up fearing the very ominous possibility that I could be eating and drinking damnation unto myself unless I was free from sin at the moment I received the sacrament. The table of the Lord is not for sinners, we believed. Yet it was sinners that made the table necessary in the first place. To bar the sinner from the table of God seems like barring the bachelor from his own wedding ceremony. The bachelor is not there in defiance of the wedding. Rather, he is the one the wedding is for. The same is true of repentant sinners who celebrate the Eucharist. They are the ones for whom the body and the blood are shared. Who are they who come only to remember?

John Wesley noticed this when he advised the unregenerate to wait for saving grace "in the way of prayer . . . in searching the Scriptures . . . [and] in partaking of the Lord's supper."[7] The Apostle Paul saw it, too, and reminded us that it was "on the night he was betrayed," and not some other glamorous evening, that Jesus broke the bread and shared the wine. Humanity was at its worst and God at his best in the same moment.

SAINTS AND SINNERS

But the church of today expects that we appear righteous and nearly everyone knows it. Those inside the church stutter over their confessions, explaining how it is they can still do this or that and be holy. They develop clever synonyms like *weakness* and *infirmity* where sin was once the simpler, more accurate term. They speak of struggling rather than of disobedience, of addictions rather than indulgence, and of moods rather than excesses, because to 'fess up to the truth would be to deny their sanctification, as they understand it. They do not understand that Jesus is attracted to sinners, so they pretend to be something else. The irony, of course, is that in time they will become like the very people Jesus avoided.

Those outside the church also know (or have heard) of the things we expect, and they infer that they are not yet good enough to come to church, or that they cannot live the Christian life because it is too hard. They do not understand that Jesus is attracted to sinners. They fear he will ask them to clean up their lives without making them want to, so they avoid him. But there is another, more subjective side to holiness that comes out in the story of Matthew.

Saints as Sinners

True holiness, I am learning, is the capacity to celebrate the victory of forgiveness while repenting of its dreadful cost to Christ. Holiness brings the power *not* to sin. But more than this, it allows the freedom to admit it when we do. More than being well, holiness means getting better. Holiness is not reserved only for those who have finally evicted the last measure of sin from their lives. It is also for those who are still doing so. Like salvation, holiness exists in tension between the *already* and the *not yet*. It is a brokeness over the terrible toll that sin has taken on the world, yet a haunting reminder that we ourselves once contributed to this evil. It is the confidence that we are secure in Christ along with the humble realization that we cannot last without him. Martin Luther wrote:

> Dear Lord, although I am sure of my position,
>   I am unable to sustain it without Thee.
> Help Thou me, or I am lost!

It is common in some circles to confuse holiness with sinlessness. After all, if it is possible to live without sin, why wouldn't we? In this way we have made holiness either a shortcut for those desiring to get rid of their sin ("have you entered into the blessing?") or a badge worn by those who already have. But we have left precious little room in our definition of holiness for those in between, who are earnest but frail, who hate sin but commit it. The notion that holiness is sinlessness may seem more logical, but it frustrates the grace of God and those who need it. And it renders the table of the Lord a harmless memory of our past sins rather than a living application of atonement for our present needs. Luke reminds us that Matthew, who ate with Jesus once (Luke 5:29), would eat with Jesus again (22:15), and again (24:41), and again (Acts 2:42).

In holiness, we neither deny our sins ("if we claim to be without sin we deceive ourselves") nor tolerate them ("he is faithful and just and will . . . purify us from all unrighteousness"). We admit them, early and often. And we set in motion the steps necessary to conquer where we were once defeated.

Seeking the Lost

But holiness does more than make us honest about our sin, it also inspires us to seek and to save the lost. So if we are to be like Christ in true righteousness and holiness, we will prove this by our love for sinners.

Like Jesus, we will be attracted to them, and probably for the same reasons. First, because transparent sinners, like genuine saints, are the only people who are honest with themselves. In each synoptic Gospel, the calling of Matthew is surrounded by narratives involving the Pharisees. This is too important to miss, because the Pharisees are there to show contrast (see Luke 18:9–14). Why else would God insist that Gospel writers give so much space to a religious sect that, according to Josephus, numbered fewer than six thousand in Jesus' day? It could be that God wants us to notice the humility and courage of "sinners" (like Matthew) compared to the arrogant stubbornness of "saints" (like the Pharisees). Other than Christ, the sinners were the only honest people around at the time of Matthew's call. And the honest sinner will always act the sinner, just as the honest saint will always act the saint. And when he does not, he is beside himself and admits it so as to get back to his ways (whether good or evil) before too long.

Jesus desires that we be honest with ourselves.

In this sense, the first desire of Jesus was not for the world to convert, but only for people to be honest with themselves. And in this, evangelists of today would be very wise to follow Christ's example. We are not to convert people in an instant by talking them out of their evil. We are only to confront them with the gospel of Christ and urge them to be honest about its ramifications.

Remember the story in chapter two about the fellow on the flight to Atlanta? At the beginning of our conversation, he had asked the loaded question "how does a person know he's a Christian?" In response, a zealous evangelist might have produced a tract, a Bible, or a clever diagram, then culminated his efforts with a prayer—intended to be something of an open sesame into the Christian life—and ended with a promise that the "seeker" was, in fact, "saved." In a case like that, the evangelist would have gone home a winner, and the seeker would have gone home confused (or, if he'd allowed it, exploited). But whether or not conversions produced in that way are real, the matter of what, exactly, the seeker would be converted from or to is anyone's guess. Tragically, the "convert" in a case like that would become the evangelist's story to tell and someone else's problem to disciple.

But the man I met en route to Atlanta shows us it is possible to inquire of heaven without ever choosing to go. He was not unwilling to be saved. On that night, he was unable. He simply could not be saved by making only the admission that he did ("I would definitely be the selfish kind of person."). But because conversion must begin with an admission like that, he could never be saved without it. We parted in Atlanta on the heels of his promise to pray with his wife, to stay sensitive to the voice of God (whether from within or without), and to seize the day when his heart was finally changed.[8] There is something to be said for simple honesty. So I learned that night to celebrate the transparency of an honest sinner. It was like unto the honesty of Christ himself, only bent in the other direction.

A Desire to Redeem

But there is another reason why holiness is attracted to sinners. It is because the sinner calls the best out of the holy person. Just as sickness drives the physician to heal, sin motivates the holy servant to respond. He feasts on the oppression around him. He thrives on the worst of times. He is busy while the frustrated church waits for the Rapture.

It was holiness that drew William Booth to "darkest England" where "the young and the poor and the helpless go down before my eyes into the morass, trampled underfoot by beasts of prey in human shape that haunt these regions . . . fiends [who were] merciless as hell, ruthless as the grave."[9]

Prompted by holiness, Deitrich Bonhoeffer returned to Germany—though it would mean his imprisonment and death—and, ultimately, to the sick bays of Germany's prisons, where he tended to victims of war and disease. Bonhoeffer's *Letters and Papers From Prison* portray the confused mind of a servant whose theology was always in flux, but whose heart was melded to the cries of the poor and oppressed around him.

"These outcasts are to be found in all grades of society," wrote the tired theologian from prison. "In a flower-garden they grub around only for the dung on which the flowers grow."[10]

Compelled by holiness, Mother Teresa took up residency in the slums of Calcutta, India, because she believed that every person needs to die in the arms of someone who cares. In 1997, she died in the same week as another celebrity, Diana, Princess of Wales. To be sure, both the princess and the nun could hold the sick and despairing, but only one of them returned every evening to a palace. The other grabbed a cot in the corner. Both loved. One from a distance, and the other from the other end of a hug. And, let the record show, Mother Teresa died from none of the diseases she hugged. Like Paul, she was "given over to death" and died the peaceful death that comes at the end of a faithful life.

So for religious people, the test of holiness is not in whether they resist temptation. That would be too easy. Rather, holiness means loving God as only Jesus did, and loving sinners as only Jesus could.

LOVE THAT WORKS

The Presbyterian writer Donald McCullough relates the moving story of a surgeon who performed an operation on a young woman with cancer. The surgeon wrote:

> I stand by the bed where a young woman lies, her face postoperative, her mouth twisted in palsy, clownish. A tiny twig of the facial nerve, the one to the muscles of her mouth, has been severed. She will be thus from now on. The surgeon had followed with religious fervor the curve of her flesh; I promise you that. Nevertheless, to remove the tumor in her cheek, I had to cut the little nerve. Her young husband is in the room. He stands on the opposite side of the bed, and together they seem to dwell in the evening lamplight, isolated from me, private. Who are they, I ask myself, he and this wry-mouth I have made, who gaze at and touch each other so generously, greedily? The young woman speaks.
>
> "Will my mouth always be like this?" she asks.
>
> "Yes," I say, "it will. It is because the nerve was cut."
>
> She nods and is silent. But the young man smiles.
>
> "I like it," he says. "It is kind of cute."
>
> All at once I *know* who he is. I understand, and I lower my gaze. One is not bold in an encounter with a god. Unmindful, he bends to kiss her crooked mouth, and I am so close I can see how he twists his own lips to accommodate to hers, to show her that their kiss still works.[11]

In just this way, the holy church twists its preferences into a shape that seems crooked, unnatural to her, in order that she may kiss the perverted, needy mouth of the world from which she has been saved. She keeps her gospel. She even protects it. But she does not quarantine herself from those whom the gospel can save. No, Christ's love compels her.

"But for the grace of God," she says, "there go I."

And her kiss works.

LIFE RESPONSES

1. Why do you think Jesus was attracted to sinners?

2. What word do you think best describes the attitude of your church toward nonbelievers? What word best describes your own attitude?

3. What would have to change in your church (or in your life) in order to adopt the same attitude toward nonbelievers that Jesus had?

Part III
Uncommon Angles
The Seldom Seen Sides of Holiness

T he most discouraging thought I've had recently is this: If Jesus came back to earth today, he might *still* say or do something that offends me—not because I don't understand Jesus, but because I don't understand holiness. It has a darker side.

While holiness makes bad people good, it can also make good people unpredictable or angry, even a little strange.

The following chapters examine these hard-to-understand aspects of Christ's character. We'll see that he did not lay aside his holiness to embrace them. Nor should we. For there is a freedom in holiness that may put us out of step with others—but right in line with God.

Chapter 8

A MOMENTARY LAPSE OF REASON
The Contradictions of Love

The law of noncontradiction holds that something cannot be both true and false at the same time. Read in this light, the Gospels provide a fascinating ride down a very fine line for those of us committed to their infallibility. In short, there were times in Jesus' ministry when he appeared to contradict himself, saying first one thing and later something else so that the two statements can hardly be reconciled.

For centuries skeptics have used these apparent contradictions as a sort of shooting gallery, poking fun at our belief in the Bible. And if we read Scripture without thinking, it might seem that they have a point. Here's a sample:

When Jesus confronted the woman at the well (John 4), he was soft and agreeable, even though the lady's problem was her own doing. When he finally kicked open the door of her private life and exposed her five failed marriages and live-in boyfriend, she changed the subject to worship. And, to our surprise, Jesus let her. By the time the conversation ended, Jesus had said nothing about sin, repentance, restitution, integrity, or the value of a Christian family. One is tempted to believe that these things are not important to Christ, until, only a chapter later (John 5), he stumbles onto Christ's encounter with an invalid. Here was a crippled veteran of thirty-eight years' affliction, whose problem is not his own doing. After posing the rather awkward question "do you want to get well?" Jesus healed the man and then tersely commanded, "Stop sinning, or something worse may happen to you" (5:14).

Where did that come from?

Of course, Jesus may have known things about the invalid that John does not tell us, but Christ appears to be hard on the innocent (John 5) and easy on the guilty (John 4). And there is more.

One evening Jesus allowed Mary to pour an expensive perfume on his feet because, he said, "the poor you will always have with you, but you do not always have me" (John 12:8 RSV). But a chapter later, he stooped to wash his disciples feet so that he who was served was now servant. He concluded, "You will be blessed if you do [these things]." But which scene does Jesus have in mind? And how can he, who came not to be ministered unto, welcome the extravagant offering of a poor woman? And there is more.

According to Matthew, Jesus once performed a miracle in order to encourage belief (9:6). But a while later, he stopped performing miracles in Nazareth because people didn't have faith (13:58). So is it an advantage or a disadvantage to doubt? And what will the crippled of Nazareth say when they hear about this miracle in Capernaum? And there is more.

There were times when Jesus appeared to contradict himself.

According to Luke, a would-be disciple who wanted to return home long enough to bury his father was instead told to "go and proclaim the kingdom" (9:60). But when an ex-demoniac wanted to help proclaim the kingdom, he was told to return home to his family (Mark 5:19). And there is more.

In a streak of apparent schizophrenia, Jesus healed a leper and warned him *not* to tell anyone about it (Mark 1:43). Then four chapters later, Jesus cast demons out of a young man and urged him to tell his family (5:19). Had Jesus changed his mind? Three chapters later, following Peter's memorable confession of Christ, Jesus warned his disciples not to tell anyone about him (8:30). Then later, when the Pharisees complained about the disciples' noise-making during the Triumphal Entry, Jesus waved it off saying the rocks would cry out if the disciples did not
(Luke 19:40). So does he want the praise, or doesn't he? And why were people whom Christ had healed forbidden to speak of it, while others, whom Christ had only taught were allowed to speak—sometimes?

Even more confusing is the matter of whom Christ forgave, and why. Imagine a gathering in heaven of people who have crossed paths with Christ at one time or another. Each has been given eternal life. Each has had his sins forgiven. And each has a story to tell. But when the last story has been told, there is a long trail of inconsistencies.

"I was just lying there, unable to move," says the paralytic, "and suddenly I was on my feet again, carrying my cot. I did not ask or expect to be forgiven—I just was. No talk about sin or repentance. No

150

questions asked. No confrontations. No clever prayers. Guess I was in the right place at the right time. Lucky for me that Jesus was eager to make a point to the Pharisees that day, or I might not be here" (Mark 2).

The woman caught in adultery (John 8) looks confused. "I did not ask to be forgiven either," she says, "but I had to go all the way to the wall. The mob had the rocks in their hands before Jesus intervened. And Jesus told me to sin no more." She turns to the paralytic. "How did you have it so easy, while I had it so hard?"

"Hard?" says the rich young ruler, "you did not have it hard. Jesus told me to sell everything I had, give it to the poor (who did not work for it the way that I had), and then to follow him. I kept the very commandment you broke ("you shall not commit adultery"), as well as all the others, and I still had to give up my assets."

"Oh, stop it!" shouts a disciple from a corner. "Enough of all this talk about what everyone had to give up. We had to deny our very selves. We had to take up a cross. We had to 'eat his flesh and drink his blood'" (John 6:56).

"And we had to die in the jaws of beasts," say the martyrs of the first century. "Our friends were sawn in two or impaled on the horns of bulls. Our children were drowned or beheaded, sometimes in front of us. We left family and fortune in order to follow Jesus—right into the next world."

The thief on the cross is silent. He glances at the others from the corner of his eye.

"I only asked to be remembered," he mumbles, "and here I am."

The silence of the others is deafening.

LOVE VERSUS POLICY

What kind of God moves the chains for every convert? What leader insists he came to bring a sword and then tells his followers to put theirs away? What kind of savior dines with prostitutes and argues with religious people?

These contradictions illustrate God's agenda, and ours. That is, Jesus would say first one thing and then another in order to make a point that went deeper than either statement. And Jesus' agenda is deeper than ours; it is also very different, for Jesus conducted his ministry out of love. We operate from policy.

Jesus possessed tremendous powers of discernment, and his discernment was fueled by love. Everything he did sprang from his love for God and others—and always in that order.

At the seashore, he had compassion on the multitude.

At a funeral, he loved the sisters of Lazarus.

In a village, he grieved for the widow whose only son had died.

Now love is a peculiar attribute for a god to have. But it is more than an attribute for Christ: it is the epicenter of his ministry. It is the Father's grand exhibit—the vulnerability of God. And it is the common denominator that reconciles the apparent contradictions of Jesus' life.

Hundreds of years after the Father stopped talking, Jesus remembered that the greatest commandment he had given was to love. Fifty years after Jesus stopped teaching, John remembered that Christ's new commandment—and litmus test—was love. It was the very "message we have heard from the beginning," said John (1 John 3:11). It was the one thing Paul desired from new believers, the one thing early emperors noted of the church, and the most peculiar characteristic of the new believers in Acts. The contemporary apologist Francis Schaeffer has argued that the world has every right to judge the church according to its love, since that the only evidence they have that Christians are in fact the real people of God (see John 13:35).

Now where there is love, there will be few policies. But when love wanes, policies will flourish, telling people how they must act in this or in that situation. So Jesus would say that all of the law and prophets hang on a single commandment: love. And Paul would later argue that "he who loves his fellowman has fulfilled the law" (Rom. 13:8).

Just as a contract presumes that the contractor's word is suspect, laws presume that one's love has gone cold. For laws spring from the desire for fairness, but justice is grounded in love. Laws order a society; love redeems it. So where there is love, law is unnecessary; and where there is an obsession with law, love is impossible because it presumes the worst, not the best, in any situation. Speaking as an individual, the law limits my capacity to love. It zaps my joy by obsessing over failure. It destroys peace and tempts self-control (Rom. 7:7).

But if we govern ourselves by love and not policy, we probably will contradict ourselves. Our answer will be yes today and no tomorrow, and this will incur the wrath of those around us who still govern themselves by policy alone.

This is why Jesus appears to have contradicted himself so often. If we judge him according to policy, he is inconsistent and breaks precedent. If we observe him without considering his circumstances or agenda, he appears to transgresses the law of noncontradiction. Yet he is always consistent with his own desire, goal, motive, and agenda. He is motivated by love, so he will always do what is best for God and for the individual.

On certain days, love and policy may behave in the same way. But the watchword of policy is consistency; therefore it will behave the same way at all times. What is good for the goose today will always be good for the gander tomorrow. Yet the watchword of love is grace; therefore its behavior may change from day to day. In every situation it will ask, What is best for Christ and this individual at this particular time? What will move us closer to the goal—that his kingdom come, his will be done on earth as it is in heaven? These are the questions of love.

WHEN POLICY TRIUMPHS OVER LOVE

Placing love before policy is the very thing that divided Jesus from most of the do-gooders in his day. When the Pharisees forbade healing on the Sabbath, they not only ignored the first and second greatest commandments, they emphasized policy (the law) over love (caring for the sick).

When angry Jews handed Jesus over to the Romans for crucifixion, but on that same day refused to enter the Roman palace for fear of defiling themselves, they emphasized policy (their interpretation of the law) over love (a fair hearing for the still untried rabbi).

When Judas Iscariot complained about the apparent waste of good money on perfume for Jesus' feet, he wrapped his selfishness in benevolence and emphasized policy (managing the budget to the last penny) over love (the need for Mary to express her self).

In the first church I pastored there was a young man who spent his savings to buy a red sports car he had coveted for years. He would wash it, wax it, and drive it to the mall where he always parked in the most remote parking spaces. After one morning worship service in our church, he was walking his friends around the car, showing it off, when his beautiful wife twisted her high heels in the gravel parking lot, fell against the car door, and slid to the ground. The young man panicked. Quick as a jiffy he ran around the car, stood next to his fallen wife—and carefully examined the door for scratches while she lay unattended on the ground. Predictably, their troubled marriage ended a few years later.

I wonder if we are more concerned, like the inconsiderate husband, about what people do to our beloved policies than about what our policies do to the people. Which of us has not seen someone ruined by the rules? Our rules. Good rules. But rules that, like chemotherapy, weakened what they were intended to protect. There are some people and churches for whom policy is more important than people, though they will never admit it. And wherever these people work or worship, we should all find our friends somewhere else. For anytime we are interested in protocol over people, image over reputation, or form over substance, we emphasize policy over love.

More specifically, when we criticize those who wear certain clothes to church (shorts, slacks, mismatches) without first wondering whether these might be the best clothes they have, we emphasize policy over love.

When we write elaborate procedures to determine who is entitled to receive groceries from the food pantry of our church and then feed only those who meet the qualifications, we emphasize policy over love.

When we keep score of favors or offenses, when we withhold acts of kindness because the one in need did not say thank-you last time, we emphasize policy over love.

When pastors write complex policies to determine whom they will marry and whom they will not (as I have done for years, to my embarrassment), they emphasize policy over love.

When parents set rules for the household and seldom bend or break them

The watchword of love is grace.

because "you never break rules, you break yourself against them," they may intend only to be consistent, but they emphasize policy over love.

When frustrated fathers abandon their prodigal sons because the sons have "crossed the line" or stained the family name, they emphasize policy over love.

When laypeople share Christ with their friends only to fulfill the Great Commission (as if Jesus had barked these words as a drill sergeant gives an order: *You! Go make disciples!*), they emphasize policy over love. For it is not duty, but love that drives the true evangelist (see 2 Cor. 5:14, 20).

When preachers fence the communion table so that even the devout dare not receive the sacrament if they still have sin in their lives, they emphasize policy over love. What is the Eucharist if it is not the celebration of love over law? And what is so new about Christ's "new" covenant?

When perfectionist wives clarify every detail of their husband's speech until the poor man learns to keep quiet, they emphasize policy over love.

One cartoon depicted this habit perfectly by showing a man entering the kitchen one morning, adjusting his tie for work.

"Honey," he said to his wife at the counter, "I am two hundred pounds of raw nerves this morning."

"Aw Charlie," said his wife, "you weigh more than two hundred pounds!"

When we cannot read between the lines of another person's agony because we are too busy correcting his speech ("you shouldn't say that!") we emphasize policy over love.

When dominant coaches or fathers drive their frustrated sons away from the very sports they love by pounding them with the fundamentals, they emphasize policy over love.

When angry couples refuse to compromise or to learn new patterns of speech and behavior, yet remain married because "divorce is a sin," they emphasize policy over love.

When armchair politicians or disgruntled church members criticize their leader's decisions, plans, and reactions without seeking to understand the motives behind them or the forces compelling them, they emphasize policy over love.

Whenever people criticize policies more than pray for the politicians, they emphasize policy over love.

When we convert Paul's epistles of grace into unbending letters of the law (which Paul himself forbade, 2 Cor. 3:6), when we exclude certain people—by citing chapter and verse—from ministry because Paul said this or Paul wrote that, we emphasize policy over love. Of course it is possible to prove one's obstinate views through Paul's inspired works; it is also possible, as history and the Devil have proven, to quote Scripture and yet be wrong. Every heretic worth his salt has done just that over the past two thousand years. So unless one has captured the Spirit of Christ and not only his teachings, he is not of God. He is an educated or pious devil.

WHEN LOVE TRIUMPHS OVER POLICY

On June 8, 1953, at ten o'clock in the evening, the most infamous tornado in Michigan's storied history ripped a trail of terror from one end of the state to the other. Power went out. Whole city blocks were leveled. Houses, cars, and bodies were strewn from one end of the city to another. In one city the armory was converted into a morgue to house the bodies of the more than one hundred who were killed in the ten minutes it took for the cyclone to shred their neighborhoods. On a quiet dirt road just two miles from a home where I once lived, a young boy heard the approaching sound of a twister and huddled himself under the living room sofa for protection. It likely saved his life, for when the boy crawled out from under the couch there was only the sky above him. Wandering outside into the eerie silence he met his father, now coming in from the fields with a long piece of wood driven through his forearm. Moments earlier, the father had clung to the ground, watching his cattle sail overhead and out of sight.

"I better go to the hospital and get this taken care of," said the father nodding at his arm, still impaled by debris. And together they climbed into the old family truck and drove the twelve miles to the emergency room.

When they arrived, a priest met them at the door and, after seeing the anguish in the man's eyes, asked if there was anything that he needed.

"Yup," said the fellow, "a cigarette and a shot of whiskey."

"Wait here," the priest nodded, "I'll be right back." And in a few moments he returned with the goods.

I come from a people for whom it would have been very difficult to hand the man his drink. I come from a people of policy. Yet love can be demonstrated in ten different ways when it responds to ten different situations because love is not motivated by the desire to maintain a good appearance. Love is motivated by compassion for the individual, so love can offer the man a drink tonight and deny him the same drink tomorrow, and all the while hold to abstinence for itself. And this is not circumstantial ethics, as some suppose, for the circumstances do not determine the ethic. No, the ethic is the love within the believer that was there long before the circumstance arose. He loves his God and he loves his neighbor—in that order. And love knows what to do—almost instinctively—even when the individual does not. So holiness is not a perfect conformity to the rules, but a *perfect response* to the need. And while the need may shape the response, it cannot alter the heart of the one responding. No, our minds, our passions, and our judgment are captive to the heart of Jesus Christ. And he never changes, even though the situation and our response to it will change.

> Jesus is more than the sum of his teachings.

But we have to have some standards, don't we? Of course we do. But Jesus is more than the sum of his teachings. He is a living Presence inside of us. So we may do all that Jesus did and never be more Christlike than Judas unless we love with the heart of Christ. In other words, it is possible to have obedience without love (and many do), but it is not possible to have love without obedience.

If that notion is frightening, it is because we are wired more for policy than for love. We love ourselves and hold others to the line. This is why we are so forgiving of our own mistakes and so unforgiving of others'. But holiness has it the other way around. Presuming that people would always love themselves, Jesus did not tell us to love ourselves as much as our neighbor, but to love our neighbor as much as ourselves. We are born with the capacity to love ourselves. As Luther put it, "man is curved inward on himself." This self-love is at the bottom of everything we do. It drives our instinct for survival. It makes us want to be first in war, first in peace, and first in line at the checkout counter. If we are not careful, it will make us arrogant when we succeed or lower our self-esteem when we fail (low self-esteem is really pride turned inward). But either way, we will be hard to live with. Many of us grew up believing that we are the most important person in the world, which makes it very difficult to live with the six billion others who are operating under the same delusion. But all of this changes after we are consumed by Christ's love.

DISARMING POLICY

When we operate from policy, it is easy to live with *ourselves*. We can pretend that we really are captive to our faceless rules. We can convince ourselves there is not enough money in the checkbook or that people do not qualify for our compassion. We can say they have made their bed and must lie in it. But if we operate from love, it is easier to live with others because we are kind and self-giving. And so, one by one, Jesus stripped his disciples of their policies.

"Who is the greatest in the kingdom of heaven?" the disciples wondered (Matt. 18:1). It is a question of rank and protocol. It is not a question of love. The presumed answer here was that the greatest are those who have completed their assignments. They have obeyed. They have done the right things. But Jesus answered that the greatest must be the servant of all (Mark 10:35). Great people look outward, not inward.

"How many times shall I forgive my brother when he sins against me?" Peter asked. He wanted to know Jesus' policy on forgiveness. He wondered how a person could have the morals of a Christian without the heart of one. So Jesus answered that his disciples must forgive "seventy times seven" (all the time, in other words), which would seem natural to someone concerned more for his enemies than for himself. The person who has his own agenda has the hardest time forgiving, so Jesus threatened that the disciples would be punished unless they forgave their brother *from the heart* (Matt. 18:21, 35).

"We saw a man driving out demons in your name," [said John,] "and we tried to stop him because he is not one of us" (Luke 9:49). They were curved inward upon themselves. They were more concerned about the identity of their cloister-mates than about identifying with those on the outside wanting in. Some churches still have this problem. So Jesus answered that the kingdom of God is not a fraternity but an inner nature; *anyone* who offered a cup of water in Christ's name could join the rank of the disciples (Mark 9:41).

"Do you want us to call down fire from heaven" (Luke 9:54), the disciples asked Jesus with an eager look in their eyes. And Jesus rebuked them, which was a rather dramatic way of saying they were operating from the wrong premise. Policy remembered the last seven hundred years of conflict. Love let the Samaritans go.

It is significant that each of these episodes comes directly on the heels of Christ's call to deny ourselves, take up the Cross, and follow him. This was a not a tired, three-point sermon. It was a revolutionary way to live. Those who once thought only of themselves were asked, in one scenario after another, to let their policies go and to live according to self-giving love. Not surprisingly, after they were possessed by the Holy Spirit at Pentecost, the disciples gathered together (Acts 1:14; 2:1), held everything in common including their possessions (Acts 2:45; 4:34–35), and healed the suffering people who came to them (Acts 2:43; 5:15). What Jesus had described in the Gospels became reality in Acts. Those who had been curved inward were suddenly curved outward. Where policy once ruled, love flourished. As Jesus had prayed, this group of people, whose first interest had been their own places in line, suddenly gave up those places—and later their lives—for others.

LEARNING TO LOVE FIRST

It is possible to capture the spirit of love for ourselves by training our minds around three questions.

What must it be like to be the other person?

What does the other person truly need?

What do I have or what can I do that will help?

When we fail to love, it is because we are not governed by the answers to these questions, but by a blind loyalty to policy.

Pastor David Swartz remembers "Carl" who lingered at the back door one Sunday after church and apologized for not wearing a tie. Carl had lived a hard life and had even attempted suicide by hanging himself. Fortunately, he had mistakenly used an old rope that snapped after he had hung for almost two minutes.

"That's why I can't stand to wear a tie or to button my collar," Carl explained. "I can't stand anything tight around my neck." He hesitated for a moment and then, before turning to leave, he asked, "Pastor Dave, does God understand why I can't wear a tie?"[1]

Be careful how you answer that. For directly behind Carl is a long line of parishioners begging for a similar variance. And behind the parishioners are the deacons, who are watching the pastor's every move.

How should the conscientious Christian respond? How can we sort through many different circumstances with a single motive? How can we remain consistent by saying yes today and no tomorrow? Let's look at our three questions again.

Question One: What Must it Be Like to Be the Other Person?

Two psychologists, one young and the other older, boarded the same elevator at the end of a long day. As always, the young man leaned weary against the wall and stared at the floor while the older counselor stood bobbing on his feet, anxiously waiting for the elevator to land in the lobby.

"How can you do that?" asked the young and tired psychologist in a critical tone.

"Do what?"

"Stand there, so energetic and strong after listening to people's problems for eight hours."

The seasoned old man winked. "Who listens?" he said.

This amusing story paints our problem perfectly. Many of us have learned to get in and out of conversations every day without really listening. We live with our spouse and children without ever wondering what it must be like to be married to us, to have to answer to us, to fear us, or want to impress us.

We wake up every morning and get ourselves ready for the day. We make our own appointments and schedule our own routines until we become insulated by them. We are deceived into thinking that our agenda is the only one that matters.

Think of it. How much of the day is spent thinking about us?

How often do we sink ourselves into debt buying the things we want? When did someone ever borrow money to give it away?

How much of our anger is over things that have happened to us? Does it bother us that people can be cruel to others in general, or only to us in particular? Do we care that an injustice was committed, or that it was committed against us?

How much of our stress is over what others think of us?

How many of our prayers begin and end with the things we want?

How much of our conversation is about us? The telephone company knows. Many years ago one phone company tapped into conversations of several hundred people in order to learn what were the most commonly spoken words. To no one's surprise, it was the word I, by a ratio of nearly fifty to one.

But remember the first question: What must it be like to be the other person? What if we put this question before ourselves at the start of each day? What if we wondered this about every name on our prayer list? Might we then think of other things to say besides "bless them, Lord"? Would we pray longer and with greater focus?

And what if we asked that question before criticizing another person's motive or decision? What if we really were quick to listen and slow to speak? Wouldn't we then be slower to become angry or cynical?

If we started each day with this question, how much time would we then have for children or the elderly or the anonymous employee? Imagine following this question into the home of a single mom who is fretting over her weight, or into a nursing home, where time stands still and the victims of time hide behind weathered faces of distrust. Imagine asking this question in a rehabilitation center for substance abusers, or in juvenile courtrooms, or prisons, or homes for the mentally disabled.

If there is time for only one conversation, most of us will talk about ourselves. But what must it be like to be the other person? What if we had the other guy's pressure? Or parents? Or duties? Or limitations? Or tendencies?

Question Two: What Does the Other Person Truly Need?

The answer to the second question is difficult to discern because most of us accustomed to giving the other person whatever they want or whatever it takes to shut them up, regardless of what they truly need. But there are times when love will risk the entire relationship in order to purify the dross between itself and the other person. Some friends and even spouses simply coexist rather than actively love one another because neither is willing to bring up the hard subjects.

It is easier to live with a prodigal spouse than to raise the issue of trust. But love will raise it.

It is easier to maneuver around the slothful habits of a friend rather than to challenge him or her to outgrow them. But love will think first of the friend and will make the challenge.

It is easier to give money to the poor than to teach them to work. But love will do both.

It is easier to assume that there is no friction between ourselves and another person than to ask about it and know for sure. But love will leave its gift at the altar and be reconciled to a brother (Matt. 5:23–24).

It is easier to move into another church, marriage, company, or circle of friends than to begin the long journey toward wholeness where we are. But love endures.

True love does not confront merely to be heard or to make a point or to defend the truth or to teach humility. No, love confronts because it is genuinely devoted to the other person and is convinced that confrontation is the most effective way to help.

I have learned that Jesus usually does not diagnose the other person's need the way I would. He is harsh when it seems he should be gentle (see Luke 9:60), and obstinate when it seems best to comply (see Matt. 12:38–39). He is compassionate when he should be exhausted (see Matt. 9:35–36), and exhausted when he should be compassionate (see Matt. 25:24–30 and Luke 24:25). He is stern when he should be flattered (see Luke 22:31–34), and satisfied when he should be stern (see Mark 9:24–25). The point is not that Jesus is hard to figure out. (Of course he is.) The point is that Jesus is always fundamental yet specific when deciding what another person truly needs.

Jesus did not apply one diagnosis to everyone.

By fundamental, I mean that Jesus remembers the spiritual core of every problem. This is evident from way Jesus read his audience. Even after he cleansed a leper (Matt. 8:3), raised a paralytic (8:13; 9:3), cured Peter's mother-in-law (8:15), strengthened his weak-kneed disciples (8:26), drove out the demons (8:32), and argued with the oppressive Pharisees (9:13) Jesus still remembered that the people's greatest need was spiritual. He saw them as "harassed and helpless, like sheep without a shepherd" (9:36). One would think he would have come to a different conclusion, having spent the last two days as he did. Jesus' diagnoses were always fundamental: they always addressed the person's deeper, spiritual need. But they were not simple or vague. They were useful and specific.

By specific, I mean that Jesus did not apply one diagnosis to everyone. He did not tell everyone to pray or to believe or to have faith. His answers were crafted specifically for the individual in question. To assist me in doing the same, I have established the following inventory:

What is the other person's real situation (the problem behind the problem)?

What needs have arisen from it?

What powers of God are at work in this person's life to heal him?

What does the gospel call upon this person—under these circumstances—to do? What sins must they relinquish? What impossible truths must they believe?

What does faith or discipleship look like in this situation?

G. K. Chesterton noted that the most fundamental thing to be said about any person is that he has been affected by the Fall. And the most fundamental thing to be said about a disciple is that he has been redeemed from it. To develop answers from this platform, and to work out the meaning of those answers in the other person's predicament is to remain fundamentally specific in the application of truth. Thus, the gospel remains fluid enough to take the shape of any situation, and it remains substantial enough to transform it.

Question Three: What Do I Have or What Can I Do That Will Help?

While Jesus said many things that were hard to understand, his message became very clear when he showed compassion. For this is the universal language of love and thus, all "men will glorify [our] Father in heaven" the moment we put love into action. For while the death of Christ is the most talked about event in the church, it was only the last and most important act in a long history of compassion—beginning with the Incarnation: "For God so loved the world that he gave . . . " (John 3:16). In our haste to preach faith over works, we sometimes minimize (indeed, neglect) works. But works are the test of faith. While a person may occasionally act without believing, he will never truly believe without acting, for action is the manifestation of faith. So it is our random acts of kindness, our money given to the poor, the long fuse of our patience, and the resilience of our undying trust that best interpret our faith to the world.

And right here is where love hurts. For the pounding fear of those who live according to policy is that they might one day contradict themselves and fall into the hands of an angry bureau of friends. Those friends will criticize us for holding to abstinence while we offer the injured man a drink. They will wonder aloud why we tell some parishioners to dress up and let others go without a tie. But if we wish to become people who value love over policy, we must risk putting our reputations and relationships on the line.

Gordon MacDonald has told the story of a monk and his young apprentice who traveled from their abbey to a nearby village. The two parted at the village gate but agreed that they would meet in the morning for their long journey back to the abbey.

The next morning, the monk found his young apprentice to be a reluctant traveler, seldom talking but walking with his eyes toward the ground. As their journey continued, the monk noticed that his apprentice had slowed his pace considerably, putting a fair distance between himself and his mentor. Finally, just before arriving at the abbey, the young man stopped altogether.

"What is troubling you, my son?" asked the monk.

And the younger brother confessed.

"Father, last night in the village I slept with a woman and compromised my vow. I cannot continue, for I am not worthy to enter the abbey at your side."

But the wise monk put his arm around his brother and continued toward the abbey.

"Come along," he said, "together we will enter the abbey, and together we will enter the Cathedral, and together we will make confession, and no one but God will know which of the two of us has sinned."[2]

Imagine a family or church that governed itself by love and not policy. In love, the sinning saint—trapped again in the same cycle—will confess the whole truth. He will feel himself forgiven and try again. He will not be made to feel that he is running out of favors. Of course, some will take advantage of this by turning the grace of God into a license for sin. As Paul predicted and many others have observed, there will always be some who continue in sin when grace abounds. In fact, someone has noted that the way to determine whether we are preaching the gospel at all is to ask ourselves whether there are some who take advantage of it (see Rom. 5:20–6:2). In this sense, the only thing worse than a congregation where everyone sins is a congregation where no one sins.

In love, the sober spouse stands up to the prodigal partner and insists he or she find help. And by love, the prodigal sees the light, burning in the window all the while he is gone. In love, those who stay at home hold to their convictions, yet pray and reason for their beloved to return. And in love, he is welcomed home from his rebellion with no questions, no promises, no next-times; just a very glad heart with a very bad memory—ready to start over. Seventy times seven.

In love, we pray for our enemies as St. Anselm prayed for his: "Almighty and tender Lord Jesus Christ . . . if what I ask for [my enemies]

> Policy is reasonable. Love is a momentary lapse of reason.

at any time is outside the rule of charity—whether through weakness, ignorance, or malice—good Lord, do not give it to them and do not give it back to me."

Because of love, our fellow parishioners are confident and optimistic. They are not plastic or giddy. They are not just greeters at the door. They value friendships. They listen more than they talk. They enter into the drama of whoever is talking to them. They ask thoughtful questions and contemplate the answers. They get genuinely angry over the oppression of the poor. In love, they counsel and comfort the pregnant teenager—after her abortion. They weep with the woman caught in adultery and, if need be, accompany her to the pastor's office or the boardroom.

With love, our church membership is not measured by behavior, but by whether or not we have entered into the life of the congregation. Our people forget their lines when they sing or fumble their way through a testimony, yet they do not fear the ridicule of the audience. They are free; they are not enslaved to the opinions of others. And their peers love them as well in failure as in success.

In love, we settle our differences on our way to church. We keep no record of wrongs. We keep our temper. We keep our word. We give up our coat to the one who wants our shirt, and we pray for our enemies.

Policy is judgmental and defensive. Love is discerning and protective.

Policy looks at the outside. Love looks at the heart.

Policy is a fortress. Love is a county seat.

Policy is reasonable. Love is a momentary lapse of reason.

Policy is safe. Those who follow policy will always have each other. They will always be consistent, always right, always have lots of support. But they will never be free, because the moment they change their minds about anything, their comrades will eat them alive.

But love is vulnerable. It risks criticism from family and foe alike.

So policy engenders legalists, and love engenders loyalists. The former will kill for the faith, but only the latter will die for it.

Policy is thrifty; love is extravagant.

Policy worries over its reputation; love fidgets over people.

Policy punishes; love disciplines.

Policy will go to heaven because it has obeyed; love will go to heaven because it wants to see Jesus.

Most of us learned to obey before we learned to love. We learned to be home by curfew, to wash our hands, and to clean our plates. We learned to show respect to big people we cared nothing about, and never to sass the teacher we didn't like.

But God has promised that he would give us a heart of love where once only policy existed. He promised to make us givers, not takers, to shed his own love abroad in our hearts until, in love, we obey.

"Woe to the man who never contradicts himself," a friend of mine is fond of saying. He points to the fact that all who live from love will appear—at one time or another—to be inconsistent. This must be true. And if it is true of us, well, at least we will be in very good Company.

LIFE RESPONSES

1. What is the difference between the terms *policy* and *love* as used in this chapter?

2. Are you a person who usually responds more from policy or from love? How has your religious heritage shaped your thinking on this issue?

3. Have you ever been treated according to policy rather than love? Have you ever responded to someone based on policy rather than love? What might have been done differently in those situations?

Chapter 9

PERFECT HATRED
The Dark Emotion of Holiness

Ladies first.

Isn't that how it goes?

It's a lesson I wanted to teach a Greek tourist getting off a plane in New York.

We had just taxied to the terminal after a cramped, fourteen-hour flight from Israel. As usual, the moment we stopped a hundred passengers bolted for the exit. That's when I noticed a woman in the aisle, three rows ahead of me, reaching for her baggage in the overhead compartment.

"Excuse me!" said the Greek, now cutting in front of the woman.

She nodded and stepped back into her seat. "Go ahead, I'll wait." And her timid eyes gave her away. The Greek laughed as he took her place in line.

"You Americans are too nice," he said and disappeared into the traffic.

Too nice? I had it in mind to slam him against the overhead compartment.

Too nice? The woman was merely observing etiquette. He was being a jerk. In that moment, she was a better man than he.

Too nice? What did he mean by that, anyway? What's wrong with being nice? If the alternative to being nice is to live in *his* war-infested half of the world, I said to myself, I would rather be me than him. But I cannot get away from his accusation: "You Americans are too nice."

Is it even possible to be too nice? And what effect does our religion have on niceness? Have we put too much emphasis on being nice? More specifically, is there an undeclared bias against religious zeal in our country? Are moderation and tolerance now the hot dog and apple pie of Americanism? Is there still a place for passion? For anger? Is there any room for hatred in a religion of love? Do Christians have to be nice all the time?

Too often when we speak of holiness, the image that comes to mind is the mild, well-mannered gentleman with a cowboy's hands and a counselor's heart. He is the man in the big leather chair, with an unruffled veneer, who only likes to play the game but doesn't care to win. Or we think of the calm and always attractive stay-at-home mom, who never has hard feelings, whose children mind at the sound of her voice, who lives for her family, and for whom every day is a well-planned investment. She loves her God, her family, her church, and her quiet time alone. We do not think of anger or intensity or raw emotion when we think of holiness. We do not think of men with steely nerves or women with an ax to grind. In fact, we do not think much of passion at all. The man who argues and the woman who seethes are Christians who need to lighten up.

But what about it? Can holy people call for war? Can they support the death penalty? Can they ever be glad that the terrorist is dead? Can they argue with authority? Can they sue the government? Can they refuse to move to the back of the bus?

Two Sides of the Same Coin

To ask these questions is to beg either of two extremes, and already I feel the need to distance myself from both of them. One is the extreme of violence (kill 'em all; let God sort it out). The other is the extreme of passivism (let's *talk* about our differences). One is trigger happy, and the other is afraid of guns. Those guided by the first extreme will read this chapter as a license to kill and will throw themselves undiscerningly into every conflict. They will insist that they are always right, that they are only defending the truth or saying what the rest of us already think. To them, I present the Jesus of bridled anger, who stood speechless while Pilate teased, "What is truth?" If there was ever a time to answer, that was it. I present a Jesus who held all of heaven at bay while the soldiers taunted, "If you be the Son of God, come down from the cross." He who loaned these scrawny soldiers their breath surely could have made them pay for that impudence. I present the Jesus who, only hours before dying at the hands of mocking soldiers, bent down to reattach the ear of an enemy. To those who are bent toward anger, I present the brighter side of Jesus.

But there is another extreme: passivism. Those who hold this view will read these words with fear and suspicion. They will fold their arms, look down their noses, then notify the authorities that a lion has gotten out of its cage. They will fear the militia or the henchmen. They will point to the tragedies of war or to senseless killings saying, "There! Is *that* what you want?" Then they will go about the business of making other people mad. They are passive aggressive. They do not fight. They kill with kindness. They stonewall, boycott, and roll their eyes. They deny a place for anger even as they inhale it. To unsettle their calm, uncomplicated ways, I present the Jesus who carefully braids the whip because he fully intends to use it. I present One who used words that godly mothers forbid their children to use (see Matthew 23:15, 33). I present the Jesus who argued with the authorities—at least the ones on earth. I present a Jesus who will come in power and glory to judge the earth with a winnowing fork. I present the same Jesus we want our children to imitate. Only I present his darker side.

The irony, of course, is that both images present the same Jesus— and not at different times. That is, Jesus was not happy one moment and angry the next. He did not suffer mood swings, and he was not schizophrenic. Instead, his anger and his love resided in the same chest at the same time. He hated and he loved, all at once, and he never apologized for either emotion, for his anger and his love were like heads and tails on the coin of holy passion.

We must picture anger as part of a constellation of Christian virtues that make up the whole person. Rather than relegating anger to the thin border between self-control and mania, we must learn to view it as a healthy emotion that dwells between two rabid extremes, both of which represent a peculiar obsession with anger that will ruin a good person's temper in Jesus' name. The one extreme is violence, and the other is passivism. Both vie to control our anger but are in fact unhealthy reactions to it, even as gluttony and anorexia are two unhealthy (and opposite) reactions to food. The problem is not with anger anymore than it is with the food. So in troubled homes where child discipline is a problem, one parent may beat the child (violence) and the other may let him get away with murder (passivism). Both parents may have come from homes where anger was used to justify abuse, and in this sense they are very much alike, even though they are running in opposite directions.

In just this way, we have abandoned the middle way of this important subject. Afraid that people will become sinful in their anger, we have preached them out of admitting any anger at all. And so we may speak of "setting aside our sanctification" when we feel our temperature rising. We subtly lower our estimation of godly people whenever we catch them spouting off rashly. Never mind that Christian history is replete with examples of saints who did exactly that, people who were measured by their passion and purpose in life, not by the sporadic behavior that punctuated it.

A friend of mine recently said he has given up playing basketball because it was not worth "losing his sanctification" over. I have the same nervous twitch. Many times I have started over in my pursuit of holiness because I had argued with the referee the night before or used a slang word. Predictably, my friend and I are both type A personalities. We both hate losing. And we both grew up believing that holiness would make people nice even if it did not make them new. We believed our sanctification was on hold until we were serious enough to soften our edges. So if we would be like Jesus, we thought, we had better get used to losing, and liking it.

But our biases betray us. We are afraid of anger, so we have voided our lives of passion to avoid dealing with it. And when passion is gone, commitment has no source and no expression.

A THEOLOGY OF NICENESS

Much of the trouble with our concept of holiness today is that it is nearsighted. We cannot see the big picture, the ideals, the agenda for which some godly people strive, because we are so easily put off by their apparent fits of rage. The end doesn't justify the means, we say, and so the end no longer matters. We have created a society that is devoted to the means. We don't care much about where we are headed so long as no one is rocking the boat. We have a big heart and no chest. And why have we become this way? How have we grown confused? From my narrow window to the world, I detect four misbeliefs, common to our culture, that have been engrafted to form a theology of niceness.

Myth One: Anger Always Begets Violence

First, we associate anger with violence. And here is where two very powerful assumptions collide. The first is that people are the product of their environment, and the second is that every effect has a cause. Now since the cause of violence is anger, and since people become like their environment, we conclude that we'd better rid the world of anger, or we will all become violent. This means we must quarantine ourselves against anything that shortens life or impedes happiness, whether handguns, nicotine, or rhetoric. For instance, in the last two years there have been five school shootings in my country, with more than twenty people killed. According to the "experts," this is because guns are too easy to find, video games are too violent, rock music is too suggestive, children are too angry, and parents are too lax. All of these have been moved to the left of the equation that produces violence as the end result. Even though Cain killed Abel for none of those reasons, we strive to outlaw all of them because we believe that children will become like their environment. We have concluded, therefore, that the environment is the cause of violence. Some school districts have made it illegal for students to "harass" each other since, presumably, harassment will lead to violence. Subject a child to teasing long enough, we reason, and he will turn violent, because he must. So everyone must do his part. The makers of video games must soften their violent graphics. Heavy-metal rockers must cancel a few performances. Congress must make it harder to purchase guns. And lawyers must sue parents who cannot control their children. If we do these things, we will have deprived violence of its cause, and we will have rescued our children from the influence of evil. Then we will say to ourselves, "What a beautiful world!"

Hatred is evil except when opposed to evil.

But is it? Or might we wake up to find ourselves still in bed with evil? For anger need not lead to violence any more than knowledge must lead to arrogance, or passion must lead to folly. To be sure, it can, but it does not have to. In fact, in Jesus we see anger without violence. He curses the Pharisees and the fig tree, but he does not consume them. He is angry at his disciples but he does not bloody their noses. And after three years of wrangling with His enemies, he has killed no one—which is more than one can say for Moses, Joshua, and David.

The secret, I think, is to feel anger intensely and even express it, but always with restraint. Pastor Stephen Brown tells the story of a hotheaded preacher who paced back and forth in his office, railing to his staff about the antics of a family in his church. The young assistant pastor sat in quiet disbelief while the pastor pranced like a lion, with neck-swelling fury. Finally, the young assistant chided him: "Pastor, I know you are very upset, but try to restrain yourself."

"Young man," said the pastor, biting his lip, "don't tell me to restrain my anger. You are now seeing more restrained anger than you will ever see in your lifetime." [1]

The pastor is right. As a driven man under pressure, he is best to feel his anger—and even to rant and rave—but to do so in private. Because he never opens the door and clobbers the family giving him trouble, he has allowed his religion to influence his anger (rather than the other way around) and for this, he is no hypocrite. It was for him that Paul said, "Do not let your anger lead you into sin" (Eph. 4:26 TEV). It is one thing to have anger, and another to be led by it. As long as we are unable to tell the difference, as long as we see anger as a shortcut to violence, we will abort the one in fear of the other.

Myth Two: All Hatred Is Evil

Second, we associate hatred with evil. Three times I have preached on the hatred of God, and three times I have been greeted by unhappy parishioners at the door, Bibles in hand, who were certain I had just skewed the character of God. One elderly woman waited until I had finished preaching one of these harsh messages, then stood in her pew and started singing,

> Makes me love everybody,
>   makes me love everybody . . .
> 'Tis the old time religion,
>   And it's good enough for me.

Of course she stared at me while she sang until I started singing along. She was determined to have the last word. And most of us would agree with her that love is good and hatred is bad. Of course, most hatred is evil. Any hatred that broods over a grudge, contemplates a payback, sours our disposition, or separates us from the company of other happy folk is bad. The hatred that God forbids seeks revenge when it should rebuke instead (Lev. 19:17–18). It does its evil in quiet. It plots or hides or kills with kindness (Prov. 10:18; 26:24). In this sense, it is not that one hates but that he continually lies about it that ruins him. And so it is not that God is opposed to hatred but that hatred, by its haughtiness and deceit, is so often opposed to God.

But when it is not, hatred is a beneficial thing. And how can we know the difference? As a general rule, we may say that hatred is evil except on those occasions when it is opposed to evil. For hatred is an abiding disposition *against* something. It is metastasized anger. And wherever evil lives, evil deserves the hatred of righteous people.

Myth Three: All Passion Leads to Excess

What is more, we have associated passion with excess. Aldous Huxley's *Brave New World* is a short but terrifying novel about a "perfect world," where "everyone belongs to everyone else, you know." Babies are genetically manufactured and raised in an intellectual bubble in which everybody thinks alike. Those who color outside the lines are quickly identified, isolated, and sufficiently "reprogrammed." Everyone's love and passion is kept in check by the brave new world. No one is allowed to dream or to invent anything without permission from the authorities. People may think, but may not think otherwise, because the cardinal sin of the brave new world is not apathy. It is
passion and the mutiny that it breeds.

And I have just described the problem in too many churches, even whole denominations. We are afraid of wildfire, so we settle for no fire at all. If people are allowed to think for themselves they might run excess, for what is heresy but truth taken to the extreme? To avoid heresy, we temper the truth until it is soft, with smooth edges. We redefine commitment until it fits nicely within our brave new church. We make religion a servant instead of a master because the moment one of us devotes himself to a cause, he has become dangerous.

This is a form of spiritual neuropathy in which one may still use his religion even though he can no longer feel it. In the brave new church, faith in God is as helpful as any other conviction, only it is—well, painless.

Harvard law professor Stephen Carter has summarized our condition accurately.

> In contemporary American culture, the religions are more and more treated as just passing beliefs. . . . If you can't remarry because you have the wrong religious belief, well, hey, believe something else! If you can't take an exam because of a holy day, get a new holy day! If the government decides to destroy your sacred lands, just make some other lands sacred! . . . If you can't have blood transfusions because you think God forbids it, no problem! Get a new God! And through all of this trivializing rhetoric runs the subtle but unmistakable message: pray if you like, worship if you must, but whatever you do, do not on any account take your religion seriously.[2]

Of course, all great achievements have been made by people who cared more than the rest of us. And with their caring came certain and embarrassing tantrums. Beethoven screamed profanities, and Luther blurted out adjectives about the ancestry of his enemies; and because we are opposed to swearing, we will smite the genius even before he gets started. Charles Spurgeon and William Booth fought with depression while John Wesley fought with his wife. Charles Finney abandoned his new bride three days after their wedding in order to conduct revivals in New York. He did not return for six months. And because we value family, we chop these giants at the knees with Paul's warning to "manage [your] own family well" (1 Tim. 3:4). But which of us middle-class North Americans is fit to counsel those from whose springs we have drunk so freely? We oppose their excesses, yet the excesses seemed to ride tandem with their passion. For when a person is obsessed with one thing, he is usually oblivious to others. So let us never become critical of people with passion. They are the only reason the rest of us have something to do.

Myth Four: Tolerance Is Always a Virtue

There is fourth point of confusion in our theology of niceness: we associate tolerance with virtue. Therefore, we associate passivism with maturity. In his insightful analysis of modern culture, the eminent historian Arthur Schlesinger Jr. has traced our love of tolerance to the demise of Hitler's regime following the Second World War. When the war was over, according to Schlesinger, we took a hard look across the Atlantic and grew frightened of what could happen when one man sought to squeeze the whole world into his own mold.

> Hitler's racism forced Americans to look hard at their own racial assumptions. How, in fighting against Hitler's doctrine of the Master Race abroad, could Americans maintain a doctrine of white supremacy at home? . . . The re-thinking of racial issues challenged the conscience of the majority and raised the consciousness of minorities.[3]

Because of that observation we were able to embrace one another's culture. Within thirty years, this would also give new power to the cries for equality between the genders (women's rights) and the generations (youth culture). One person with his opinion was just as important as any other. And later, he was just as correct. Since then, we have learned to live and let live and to swallow hard without chewing, because if we don't we have annihilated another person's freedom.

And so, religion has been made to fit within the boundaries of tolerance. Just recently I watched a television drama about a Jewish father who learned his son was homosexual. Unable to bear the news, the father had slapped his son and walked out of the room. In the next scene, the father was alone with his physician, trying to sort out his confusion.

174

"Rabbi," said the doctor, "what is the purpose of religion—any religion—when it divides two people who love each other very much?"

The moral is clear: religion exists, not in order that people may fulfill their obligations to God, but in order that people may get along. For any religion that divides a person from his father or from his lover is not a useful religion.

It is bad enough to define religion as only the means to some greater end. It is surely worse to determine the end ourselves. We have done this and called it open-mindedness. We have surrendered the faith to behavioral scientists. Where virtue once followed conviction, we now seek virtue even when conviction is gone.

Sociologist Nancy Ammerman has called this "golden rule Christianity." According to Ammerman, golden rule Christianity is an ethic in which one's "use of Scripture is defined more by choices and practice than by doctrine."[4] Golden rule Christians do not seek a deep and coherent understanding of their faith. Instead, they want reference desk answers to the moral dilemmas they face. To them, religion is measured by its capacity to make people nice, clean, happy, or rich. It does not bother them that every false prophet of the past four thousand years has been all of these things. It is still wrong to fight, to argue, to criticize, or to hate, because these things leave room for nothing else. In golden rule Christianity, convictions do not matter. Right and wrong are reduced to actions alone. Therefore, Deitrich Bonhoeffer cannot call for the death of Hitler; Martin Luther cannot slander the pope; black slaves cannot resist their oppressors because, after all, it wouldn't be nice. And so we have morals without convictions, piety without passion, friends without enemies, bark without bite. And all of this makes me—well, upset.

> We have friends without enemies, bark without bite.

People in every generation have killed and died for religion, and the question has always been the same: were they on the right side? But today, when people have mere opinions where holy convictions once dwelled, there is no right side if there is any killing at all.

I am thinking of a Little Leage baseball game I attended with my wife while our son, Nicholas, was a child. He came steaming around third base, full speed ahead, while the ball was relayed from the outfield. As the catcher reached for the ball, our son plowed into home plate. There was dirt and equipment flying everywhere, and in the end, the umpire ruled him safe.

The home team cheered. The audience hooted. Then suddenly, my wife jumped to her feet and screamed, "Nicholas—" And then with all of the grandstand watching, she ordered, "Help that other boy up!"

I could have crawled under the bleachers. This is not the way men watch baseball. But this is the ethic of our day. Whenever two people collide over anything, it is not so important who is safe and who is out, nor how either played the game. The most important thing in life, as in Little League baseball, is whether anyone got hurt and whether or not we helped our rival up once the dust settled. Contrary to popular opinion, this is not holiness. It is only good sportsmanship. It is political correctness. Of course, to be cruel would be wrong. But one has really missed the point if he dabbles with etiquette while bigger issues are at stake.

So tolerance is no virtue if, in the end, truth does not prevail. For the only way a person can truly tolerate anything is if he first believes something else. He must know who he is. He must want what is right. He must believe in something right down to the marrow in his bones. This is his real virtue. And with his own convictions firmly in place, he is finally in a position to tolerate another person's opinion. He can walk away from a fight that could only have happened because of his virtue.

QUESTIONS ABOUT ANGER

The Psalmist said he hated with a "perfect hatred" but added, "Search me, O God, and know my heart . . . [then] lead me in the way everlasting" (Ps. 139:22–24 RSV). In spite of anger's terrifying record, it is just possible that someone may be "lead in the way everlasting" even while he nurses anger. It is possible, I say, but dangerous, since even the Psalmist's own "perfect hatred" must be searched. Yes, anger is a thin ice beneath which many have lost their souls. One should not venture onto it unaware. But there are times when one's white-hot passion will lead him into places he would not otherwise go. And when he does go, he must not be considered less holy for having walked in places most saints avoid. For the secret of holiness does not lie in our futile attempts to rid ourselves of natural, even healthy, emotions, but in sanctifying those emotions right where they are. And I write these things not in order that people may experience anger, but because they already do. And what they need is not more fuel for the fire but good and reasonable tools for keeping the fire contained.

So what is perfect hatred, and when does it cross the line? What does anger look like under the influence of love? What do we do when we have the "love of Jesus, love of Jesus down in our heart," but the blood is rushing to our head? Here are four questions to measure anger.

Question One: Am I Angry Enough?

C. S. Lewis has said that anger is the fluid love bleeds when it gets cut. True enough. Passion—and therefore his anger—follow commitment. In fact, true religion must be followed by passion (even anger and hatred), or it is only a useless hobby.

All virtues are the product of two opposing forces.[5] Just as there can be no right without a left, there is no truth without error, mercy without justice, grace without punishment, virtue without evil, passion without apathy, patience without anger, or love without hatred. For if everyone is always laughing, then nothing is truly funny since we cannot distinguish that which is humorous from that which is not. Likewise, if we tolerate everything then we truly love nothing, since there is nothing left to love. And there is nothing to defend, and nothing to defend it against. In plain language, if a person loves his marriage, he must hate those things (like adultery or divorce) that set themselves against it. It is in this sense that God is said to have hated certain people (see Prov. 6:19). And if we speak of hatred as the Bible defines it, we will find this disposition helpful. For in Scripture hatred means only that we resist something or are dug in against it. It means that we fight against it and hope to win. But it does not mean we brood over it or create mental videos to watch it suffer. It does not mean we are obsessed with destroying it. Of course we will destroy it if need be, otherwise we will avoid it like the plague. Of course, there is more to love than hating one's enemies. Yes, there is more, but never less.

This seems like common sense, but it is well worth remembering the next time we have to draw the line. There are now serious ideological differences dividing the church. Some denominations are debating the authority of Scripture. Others are fighting over the place of homosexuals in their congregations: should they be listed among the unconverted, the members, or the clergy? Still other denominations are debating the matter of women in the ministry. And when holy people decide these things they are better off to raise their voices in public than to slit each others throats, politically speaking, in private. Unfortunately, there are many denominations that seem more interested in helping each other up and dusting each other off than in whether or not they arrive at the correct conclusion. Even in our Sunday schools, many discussions about religion amount to nothing more than chat room banter or a talk show blather; a virtual carnival of values clarification.

But what about our Christian duty to "let [our] gentleness be evident to all" (Phil. 4:5), to "do good to all people" (Gal. 6:10), and to "live at peace with everyone" (Rom. 12:18)? Aren't peacemakers still the children of God? While there is not room here to debate the full implications of these passages, we must remember that one cannot be gentle or peaceable with *all* people whenever two or more of them oppose each other. As a good Samaritan, there is no way to be peaceable with the robbers who are beating the innocent traveler along the road. We may bandage his wounds and pay for his hospitalization. But if we are serious about holiness, we must also police the hills in order to catch them, or we will have a tough time convincing the traveler of our love.

The old circuit rider Peter Cartwright was a bare-fisted kind of a man. One biographer says "he was manual, muscular on occasion, and militant always."

> Once a rowdy had beaten a young preacher almost to death. Cartwright went to the circuit the next time himself and, riding along the road, he met the bully who said, "Right here I gave a little Methodist preacher one of the worst whippings a man ever got." Cartwright jerked him from his horse, beat him severely, and made him go to the church to confess and ask forgiveness.[6]

To us, this leathery old preacher may seem primitive and rude, even savage. But he cared deeply for his God and for others, which is evident from the way he protected them. We should be careful, then, before labeling such anger carnal. For when a person loves one thing passionately, and no compromise seems likely or just, he will oppose the other thing—and usually with the same fervor.

What, then, does Paul mean by telling us to be good and gentle always? Perhaps he means this in the same sense that he urged us to "pray without ceasing." He did not mean that we should never deviate from that behavior, but that this should be the place we begin and end in every situation; that this should be the general pattern of our lives, our default disposition. He meant that *gentleness* and *goodness* should be our eulogy, the tale that is told at our funeral when everything else is said and done. That is, even when gentleness cannot dictate our actions, it can still explain them. We should remember that while the anger of Christ was the anger of God, it was also the anger of a man. As the perfect God-man, he showed us that God is entitled to his anger, and that we may redeem our own.

Question Two: Is My Anger Selfish?

George Matheson used to say "there are times when I do well to be angry, but I have mistaken the times."[7]   In other words, he had the right emotion in the wrong place. And if we were honest with ourselves we would see that this is our problem too.

But the problem is more than one of timing. It is never the action that should worry us. It is always the motive underneath the action that counts. This is why good people can occasionally do bad things, and bad people can still do good things. When the good person sins, he has done so unintentionally, and this shows the moment he is confronted with his evil deed. Good people are always ready to surrender evil if they can only discover it. Bad people are always ready to cover up their sin. So while the pious look for truth, the evil look for alibis. And though they may both be doing the same thing at the same time, only one of them is a scoundrel.

Now anger works the same way. For it is never the passion behind anger that makes it sinful. It is the motivation of the anger. This is the problem with temper, slander, or bitterness. The problem with temper is not that we get mad, nor even that we break things. No, often the problem is that we ourselves feel offended because it was our rights that got revoked, our reputation that got tarnished, our plans that got changed, our voice that went unheeded.

The problem with slander is not that it is based on lies. Indeed, if all gossip were true it would still be a deadly plague because it stems from our desire to improve our reputation at the cost of another's. Slander has its hovel in pride. That is, if we were less infatuated with ourselves, we would be more tolerant of others. If we were less certain that we were always right, we would be less convinced that those who disagree with us were always wrong. For slander cannot live long where there is no rivalry.

This is the problem with bitterness—which is anger plus compounded interest. It is never that people have sinned, but that they have sinned against us. This is abundantly clear whenever I counsel people whose spouses have been unfaithful. To be sure, they are entitled to anger. They have been hurt and betrayed. They have been played the fool. The very core of their marriage—trust—has been shaken loose. But this is not the only reason they are angry. Scratch them, and you will see self just below the surface. It does not bother them that infidelity is widespread, that many spouses are breaking their vows to God, that innocent children suffer, or that the next generation will find it even easier to quit on its promises. Spouses who have been wronged are never happy to learn about these things. But what really bothers them is that it has happened to them. Many of these folk have friends who have walked away from marriage, yet they themselves have not raised an eyebrow or a voice against it. But when it happens to them, they want the punishment to be swift and certain. When it is not, they create the payback in their minds, and this is the root of bitterness.

Knowing that self is often at the bottom of anger, it is very hard to miss the fact that Jesus never got angry for himself. The money changers were whipped because they made his *Father's* house a den of thieves. The Pharisees were cursed because they "shut the kingdom of heaven in *men's* faces" (Matt. 23:13, emphasis added). The disciples were chastised because they forbade *the children* access to Jesus. It was not Jesus who needed the children, it was the children who needed Jesus. It's the same throughout the Gospels. Whenever others were oppressed, Jesus got angry. And whenever he himself was oppressed, he showed restraint (see Matt. 26:52–53); not because anger is wrong, but because one must know when to be angry.

We may hate evil more than we love God.

Question Three: Am I Motivated by Anger or by Love?

I recall hearing about the medusa snail, which is a little critter with a big bite. It's modus operandi, I've been told, is to lay on the sandy ocean floor until the jellyfish comes to eat it. Once the unsuspecting jellyfish swallows the snail, the real dinner can begin. Safely hidden inside its protective shell, the snail begins to drain the life from its host until, at last, the snail kills the jellyfish from the inside out. The hunter becomes the hunted. And in the end, the snail eats the thing that once ate it.

While there may be nothing wrong with a person having anger, it will turn sour the moment he ceases to possess the anger and is himself possessed by it. There is a blurry line between those two conditions, and I have crossed it many times. And how do I know?

Very subtly, the tone of my voice may change to become cynical or belligerent. My body language might become defensive or dogmatic. According to one study, only 7 percent of communication is based on words. The other 93 percent is grounded in expression, movement, and voice inflection. This is how we may show anger even while speaking of love. We may resent people even while we smile at them. We may become suspicious of others, celebrating their "progress" even while we doubt it. We may talk more of things that we don't agree with than those that we do. We may hate evil more than we love God. We may presume the worst in everything. Without warning, we may cease to love the world because we cannot trust it.

For years I have highlighted my sermon notes by using different colors for different ideas. In my homemade system, all main points are in blue, all illustrations are in green, all Scripture is in purple, all key observations are in yellow, and all criticism is in red. Some years ago I was explaining my little system to a group of fifth-graders. I held up a few copies of recent sermons to show them the many colors, and heard a young fellow in the back mumble, "Wow. Look at all the red."

He was right! These messages were bleeding with criticism. Without knowing it, I had built whole sermons on bashing the culture, the liberals, the Pharisees, and just about everyone else. I had become the priest to whom every cleansed leper must first show himself. I was angry. But I had disguised my anger as zeal for righteousness.

What I have learned is that even when anger is not selfish it can still control us, eating us from the inside out until it affects our entire disposition. We can become angry that the law is broken, the church is ignored, our doctrine is maligned, and our standards lowered. But this does not mean we are motivated by love. It may mean we are motivated by justice or even self. In fact, it is possible to love justice, and every other virtue, without loving people at all.

Some examples: Not long ago, I counseled the wife of a violent husband, and, in a separate circumstance, the husband of an unfaithful wife. In both cases, the conscientious stay-at-home spouses were trying to do the right thing. They were biting their tongues. They were swallowing hard. They were walking away from arguments. They were trying to stay out of the courts, but their wandering partners only added insult to injury. The offended parties would sit in my office and fidget with their fingers, reach for the Kleenex, stare in a trance out the window, and shake their heads. They were deeply wounded. They were seething. And I was nearly as mad as they were. Should I have been?

A few hours later, I moved to the side of a dying woman who had a horrible past. She told me how her first marriage ended when the manipulative grandmother who had raised her threatened to kill her and her new husband if she did not move back home. So she sat her husband down and told him it was best. She packed her bags and moved back home, trying to sustain a long-distance marriage. Predictably, he moved on to marry someone else. A few years later when she married again, grandma rose up—this time from a nursing home—and made the same idle threats. Before she could carry them out, the new husband died of cancer. As the woman sat in the corner of her dimly-lit single-wide trailer, she wove a story of heartache upon heartache. I couldn't help but imagine how different her life would have been had she been strong enough to get out from under the tyranny of an oppressive grandmother. And I felt glad that grandma was dead, so the timid granddaughter could get on with life. Was I wrong?

The following morning, I read the reports of women and children maimed in an African civil war by cold, evil killers who had ravaged a village, killing indiscriminately. The survivors are missing arms, legs, fingers, and eyes, and all they can say is, "Thank God we did not die this year." Another magazine showed pictures of Pakistani Muslim rebels dipping their swords in the chests of Christians they had killed, while they walked gleefully over their bodies. A bolt of anger ripped through me. I was livid. Someone is going to pay for this, I muttered. Was I wrong?

Of course, I would rather these evils did not exist. The classic argument is that I should separate the crime from the criminal, then hate the one while loving the other. But God himself did not always do this. It is not only the "lying tongue" that he hates, but the "man [himself] who stirs up dissension" (Prov. 6:17, 19). And besides, these crimes would never exist without their perpetrator. So can I call for the end of both of them?

In these cases, I believe my anger was improper, not because anger is wrong, but because I was motivated more by anger than love. A person's anger is wrong whenever he wants justice more than mercy, even when mercy would solve the problem. It is wrong when he wants the oppression to stop but is unwilling to help the victims—on both sides of the conflict—afterward. Passion must include pity. It must be more happy that the innocent are saved than that the wicked are punished.

Holy anger is most offended when people, and not justice, get ignored. It is not obsessed with vengeance or rebuttals. It does not have to have the last word. It need not see its enemy suffer. Holy anger comes from without and is caused by the circumstance. It seeks a solution. And it goes away whenever a solution is reached.

Carnal anger is a payback. It feasts on the memory of triumph over the enemy. It lives deep in the chest of a person, making him a crusader long after the last crusade has been fought. He becomes an argument waiting for a cause. Carnal anger rejoices in justice, but not because justice was done. Rather it rejoices because it was the one who brought justice.

Unfortunately, a person's selfish motives are not always clear to observers, so we sometimes honor those who have already honored themselves.

Question Four: Does My Anger help?

Anger itself solves nothing, and in this sense it does not produce the kind of righteous life God desires. But holy anger, like healthy fear, will motivate us to do something. It has constructive powers.

In 1834 Theodore Weld organized a debate on the subject of slavery. After only eighteen days, there was a nearly unanimous agreement that "faith without works is dead," and a group of college students voted to begin an organization for the purpose of "elevating the colored people of Cincinnati." Suddenly, these students began inviting Blacks into their homes to eat and to spend the night. They talked with black people on the street, a social taboo at that time. They founded literary classes and Sunday schools for Blacks, and formed research groups to study the social and financial struggles in black communities.

The *Cincinnati Journal* criticized the students for tarnishing the image of their college, noting that "a school to prepare pious youth for preaching the gospel has not legitimate place" for such concerns as abolitionism. And when the pressure was turned up, forty students withdrew from the college to form another assembly, later to be known as Oberlin College. Here they would guarantee the freedom of speech and the right of Blacks to attend the college. They were free at last.

But all of that changed in 1858 when a slave named John Price broke free from his southern plantation and fled to Oberlin College for safety. There he was abetted by a group of Oberlin students already familiar with his circumstances. One student had boasted of liberating forty-seven slaves. Naturally, John Price's owners wanted to protect their property, and they sent four armed men to the vicinity of Oberlin, where they paid a teenager to lure Mr. Price off the campus and into their custody. Within a few hours, the bandits had their man and were headed back to Wellington, Ohio, where they would catch the next train south. But as providence would have it, they passed a group of Oberlin students who quickly surmised what was happening and alerted others to come to the fugitive slave's defense. Within minutes, a crowd of college students gathered outside the Wellington Hotel demanding the release of John Price. When the captors refused to release him, the students stormed the building (without hurting anyone) and released the fugitive, taking him back to Oberlin.

Within hours, twenty-one Oberlinites were arrested—including a Sunday school superintendent and a professor of mental and moral philosophy. A very long, clever, and expensive trial followed, which finally fizzled after countercharges were made by the Oberlin students. Several protests, appeals, and thousands of dollars later, the charges (and countercharges) were dropped, and the students returned to their college as heroes.[8]

A hundred years before this, John Wesley said that slavery was a "trade procured by villainy" and that slaveholders were "unfeeling wretches who laugh at human nature and compassion." So when it was within their power to act, the children of Wesley put their faith into practice. But it was not without anger, since it is hardly possible to storm a hotel without at least a little resentment for the bandits inside. Yet history will judge them—and so will their God—not on their emotions, but on what kind of righteousness sprang forth. To be sure, holy anger did not liberate the fugitive that night, but it surely motivated the Christians who did.

Yes, we might become violent. We might become like our enemy in trying to destroy him, and all of this would be wrong. But is this reason enough to be passive? Is neglect a lesser evil than anger? Do people get mad anymore? Do they ever talk about it? To avoid anger because we fear violence is like avoiding love because we're afraid of lust. To become angry is a risky business, to be sure, but the other, safer course is too sterile, too stoic, too artificial.

REDEEMING HATRED

But perfect hatred has a redeeming quality about it. It is restless while the world sleeps. It integrates one's personality and passion, and brings their force to some resolution. It stands its ground. Perfect hatred marshals one's temperament, intellect, strength, and alliances against those whose malice or neglect or arrogance oppress the innocent.

Every man has his memories of life in the locker room. When I was a teen, conditions there were unusually brutal. I remember a fairly weak and timid fellow named Kent, who was in my gym class in high school. Every day, Kent changed his clothes in the corner of the locker room, by himself, without speaking to anyone. In our class, as in every school, there were a couple of thugs who enjoyed the pastime of picking on kids like Kent. They were bigger and mouthier than the rest of us, so they had the run of the place. I still remember the day when one of them walked up to Kent, still seated in the corner by himself, and tried to get something started.

"What are you looking at?" snapped the bully.

"Nothing," Kent mumbled, and steadied his gaze on the floor. But he must have known his number was up. He was about to become a victim.

"Gimme your shoe!" The bully held out his hand.

But Kent would not do it.

"Gimme your shoe or I'm gonna pound you into the floor." By now, the devil's imps were gathering around him, cheering him on. "Go on," they laughed, "pound him."

Finally, Kent relented and handed his shoe to the bully. We were sure he would never see it again.

We were wrong.

With a crowd of onlookers behind him, the bully backed up a few steps, whirled into a pitching motion and threw the shoe at the timid boy on the bench. The bully's friends erupted in joyous laughter. They had not seen anything like this since—well, yesterday.

"Now pick up your shoe and give it to me again," the bully nodded with a smile.

Kent hesitated.

"Pick it up or I'll beat you senseless."

Kent waited. Then looked at the floor. What was he going to do?

> Perfect hatred defends the poor, oppressed, and impoverished.

The bully stepped forward and slapped him with an open hand on the side of his head.

"Gimme the shoe!" And he ripped it out of Kent's hands.

He backed up, whirled into his pitching motion, and threw it again. His crowd roared.

"Now gimme your shoe."

And the scene was repeated perhaps half a dozen times until the bully had satisfied his lust for power.

The rest of us stood with an incredulous look on our faces, each knowing what he would like to do, but fearing the swift and certain reprisal from the bully and his minions.

What should we have done?

In the name of justice, I think we might have allied our strengths, jumped the bully and his friends, and cleaned their clocks. And we might not have quit beating them until we had broken the back of their arrogant will.

Every day, this same scene is played out in living rooms, battlefields, boardrooms, playgrounds, and cafés. It happens between spouses and siblings, members of gangs, and directors of large corporations. It happens in our courts of law, our jails, our chambers of commerce. It happens between fraternity brothers and between heads of state. Prompted by nature, one tries to outwit the other or to take more than he has coming. That such tyrants do not overrun their homes, communities, or the world is not due to the presence of good, but to the power of those who are righteous and who use their resolve to stem the ever-encroaching tide of evil.

Perfect hatred defends the poor, the oppressed, and the impoverished among us. It seeks justice for others first and only later for self, and then by proxy.

It confronts those who foist their convictions or tempers onto others. It uses its power to level the playing field for the powerless. It not only cries with the victim, it rises to take the victim's side in conflict. It loves, but it tells the truth. And it refuses to help those who take advantage of its aid for selfish ends.

Perfect hatred insists on change, even among the stubborn, if that change is in the cause of God and the interest of the world. And perfect hatred is willing to impose firm and serious consequences if its conditions are not met. It is patient, but never intimidated. And it endures what it cannot change.

John Stott relates the story of Henry Martyn, who turned his back on a promising career in order to sail for India to spread the gospel. Once there, he busied himself with the translation of the New Testament into Persian. Through this work he came to know many Muslims, who would gather around to engage in religious discussions. On one occasion, a Muslim boasted that "Prince Abbas Mirza had killed so many Christians that Christ from the fourth heaven took hold of Mahomet's skirt to entreat him to desist."[9] It was a stupid, incredible thing for the Muslim to say. Here was Christ begging Muhammed for mercy. The usually timid missionary became visibly upset, and when his visitor asked why he was so offended, the good saint replied, "I could not endure existence if Jesus was not glorified; it would be hell to me, if he were always thus dishonored. . . . it is because I am one with Christ that I am thus dreadfully wounded."

Stott concludes:

> I never read these words of Martyn's without being rebuked, for I do not have this passionate love for Christ's honor or feel this acute pain. Nor do I see it much (if at all) in the contemporary church.[10]

Yet if people are judged by their passion, then it will be our apathy, and not our anger, we will have to explain on judgment day. And if people are judged by their passion, then it matters less whether the good missionary wept in front of the Muslim or rose up to wring his neck. What matters more is that his love for Christ was the bedrock of every other emotion that day.

Perhaps this is where modern religion is most impotent. We have not loved as we ought, and so every other emotion is cut off from its source.

Since the introduction of Christianity in America, people have sought to separate Christian morals from their doctrinal foundations, even though this is the intellectual equivalent to having children without fathers. Predictably, this has yielded a society without convictions.

But let us resist. Moved by love, we are free to express ourselves in many different ways. We must defend the innocent who have been exploited by injustice, persecution, or heresy. But we must do it in the power of Christ, or like the crusaders of old, we will lose Christ on our way to conquer Jerusalem in his name.

LIFE RESPONSES

1. Under what circumstances do you think hatred could be constructive?

2. What do you see as the greatest danger in responding from anger? What do you see as the greatest danger in being passive?

3. What arouses your anger? How can you determine whether your passion on that issue is self*ish* or self*less?*

Chapter 10

WALKING A THIN LINE
The Outer Limits of Holiness

I t has been said that there is a very thin line between genius and insanity. That has never been truer than it is today.

It has further been said that the two conditions—genius and insanity—are closely related. Aristotle was the first to see that "there was never a genius without a tincture of madness."[1] Since then, many have undertaken to write the history of the worlds finest, deepest, most innovative minds, and sure enough, most of them were a little crazy.

For example, one of them cut his grass with a pair of scissors. Another collected unusual things, including other people's garbage. The interior of his home was a labyrinth carved through the trash. Following his death, sanitation workers removed 120 tons of junk from his house, including fourteen pianos, a dismantled Model T Ford, three thousand books, and tickets to a 1905 church gathering. Another "genius" covered his body with living pigeons while he fed others on the ground. Yet another named his teapot Charlie, his blanket, Clyde, and talked to both. In fact, several of them talked to invisible "friends." Others have suffered depression, hypochondria, obsessive-compulsive disorders, distorted views of religion, and a wide variety of phobias.

But be careful. If we cure their madness we will likely ruin the genius behind it. One seems to drive the other. And the reason is that these people often lack the usual inhibitions of common sense and courtesy. As G. K. Chesterton observed, "the madman is not the man who has lost his reason; the madman is the man who has lost everything except his reason. . . . in many ways his mind moves all the quicker for not being delayed by the things that go with good judgment."[2] That is, these folk care less than the rest of us what other people think. They are not bothered with laughter, hunger, confidence, or love. But whatever they feel, they feel strongly. Their stubborn will is shaped in the crucible of insanity. Their genius is forged in the fires most ordinary folk try to avoid. So if we level off Beethoven's incessant moodiness, we rob the world of some of its greatest symphonies.

If we cure Augustine of his navel-gazing paranoia, we lose *The Confessions,* one of the literary classics of the world.

If we rescue Vincent van Gogh from his brief stay in the psychiatric hospital, we lose nearly half of his paintings, since that is where they were painted.

JESUS ON THE EDGE

Now by all current standards, Jesus was insane. He was not merely eccentric or rebellious. He was smitten with a form of madness. Clinically speaking, he exhibited several characteristics associated with insanity. But then, this is only "clinically speaking."

His Moodiness

On the surface, there was the problem of his moodiness. He was happy while others were sad (Matt. 9:11–12), and sad while others were happy (John 16:20). He was filled with joy while he moved toward his crucifixion (Luke 9:51; John 10:21) and he bade his disciples to feel the same about their own tribulation (Matt. 5:12; John 16:33). He cursed a fig tree for not producing fruit, even though it was not the season for figs (Mark 11:13). With children on his knee, he spoke both blessing to the children ("to such belongs the kingdom of God") and cursing to the disciples ("whoever does not receive the kingdom of God like a child shall not enter it"), even though James tells us that praise and cursing should not come from the same mouth (James 3:10).

His Self-Claims

Jesus also believed he was God the same way some people believe they are Jesus (John 5:43). In my city a "crazy" man went into an adult bookstore and started torching the videotapes. He was arrested carrying his Bible, a twelve-inch knife, and several newspaper clippings. At his arraignment, he claimed to be "the son of God out to rid the world of pornography." Many who read the news report were certain the man was insane—even without investigating the case. A judge agreed and

190

ordered a year of psychological treatment. Yet Jesus marched in as the Son of God to rid the Temple of thieves, and we rightly jump to his defense, even though his claims were more preposterous than those of the lunatic from my city.

Jesus was forthright about his identity; he left no doubt about it in anyone's mind. So C. S. Lewis has noted there is no middle ground with Jesus. One cannot remain neutral after hearing his preposterous claims. One must choose a reality: either Jesus is the God he professed to be, or he is a lunatic, on par with the man who says he is a poached egg.[3]

His Language

A third characteristic of Jesus' "insanity" is that he spoke another "language" (John 8:23) and, because of this, was often unable to carry on a simple conversation (John 11:8–9). Once his disciples asked him why he was going back to Judea when the Jews had earlier tried to kill him there. He said it was because the man who walks by day will not stumble, for he sees by this world's light. What did he mean by *that?* Did he miss the question? No, in many instances Jesus gave cryptic answers that were not altogether related to the question asked. He zigged when his audience zagged. When the woman at the well wondered how Jesus could ask her (a *woman*) for a drink, he delivered a spiel about living water (John 4:9–10). And when his disciples urged him to eat, he said that his food is to do the will of God (4:33–34). Why didn't he just answer the question? When Jesus was asked to heal the centurion's servant (Matt. 8:5–9), he launched into an unprovoked tirade about the wicked, who "will be thrown outside into the darkness, where there will be weeping and gnashing of teeth" (8:12). By then the centurion, with hat in hand, must have been sorry he'd asked. Then in an instant, Jesus came back to the subject and healed the servant.

Why did he do this? Why, if he came to reveal God, did he hide him in parables (see Mark 4:10–12). If it takes the faith of a child to follow Jesus, why is he himself so complicated? Even his disciples were relieved when, at the end of his mission, he finally began "speaking clearly, and without figures of speech" (John 16:29).

His Loneliness

A fourth characteristic of his "insanity" was his loneliness. It is not uncommon for demented people to seek solitude, because they know they are peculiar. So it was not by coincidence that Jesus "often withdrew to lonely places and prayed" (Luke 5:16). It was not all for meditation. It was, at least in part, because he could not entrust himself to others (Luke 9:41; John 2:24). Most of the time Jesus was the only one of his company who had faith (e.g., Matt. 8:26). For example, he was the only one who could cast out a demon, even though he had earlier deputized his disciples to do it (see Luke 9:1, 39–40). He told the disciples about his mission again and again, and they *still* didn't get it (John 14:9). Prior to his crucifixion, Jesus asked Peter (John 13:37) and Thomas (John 11:16) to vow to go with him to the death, but before it was over, he prayed in the garden alone while the two amigos slept.

In fact, reading through the Gospels, one is struck by the number of times Jesus' audience did not understand him. The Jews did not (John 5:39–40). His boosters did not (6:14–15). His family did not (7:5). The Pharisees did not (7:47–52). Even his disciples did not (14:5–10). One remarkable irony of Jesus' ministry is that his true identity was revealed not by those who believed in him, but by those who did not. In his final days, he was revealed by each of seven sources, none of whom believed in him. These were:

The Cross imposes its will in ways we don't understand.

Pilate ("You are a king, then!" John 18:37; 19:14).

Pilate's wife ("Don't have anything to do with that innocent man" (Matt. 27:19).

The High Priest ("Are you the Christ, the Son of the Blessed One" Mark 14:61).

The elders of the people ("Are you then the Son of God?" Luke 22:70).[4]

The people themselves ("the one you call 'King of the Jews,'" Mark 15:12).

The Roman soldiers ("'Hail, king of the Jews!' they said," Matt. 27:29).

Pilate, by means of the sign posted on the cross ("Jesus of Nazareth, the King of the Jews," John 19:19).

In other words, Jesus was not revealed by those to whom he had revealed himself. As he hung suffocating on the cross, those who knew him best were nowhere in sight—save one. Jesus had eaten with the five thousand. He had preached to the hundreds, walked with the Twelve, prayed with the three; but ultimately, the Cross was his to carry alone. As it always does, the Cross imposed its will onto the holy person in ways the five thousand could not understand.

It is a lonely trail, this way called holiness. Just as the mad among us desire their solitude, the holy among us are jealous of their time alone with God. They are familiar with his voice and they find ours increasingly unfamiliar. For just this reason one is hard pressed to find anyone who truly did understand Jesus. And this is what makes him seem to be insane. He defies our definition of normality. He breaks the mold of the ordinary. He is relentlessly consistent in his assumptions, his agenda, his actions, and his words. That is, given Christ's assumptions about the world and himself, his behavior is lucid and sound. Given our assumptions, he is harmlessly insane. But that says more of us than of him.

If the strange habits of Jesus no longer surprise us, it is only because we have become too familiar with them. We have already accepted the verdict that Jesus is who he says he is. But for those trapped in the first century—without the vantage of hindsight—the matter was less clear. Even his family said he was "out of his mind" (Mark 3:21). In short, those who knew him best said he was crazy.

His Followers

So were his followers. But if we cure him or his followers of their madness, we will rob the world of true Christianity. This is more than a clever way of saying that we are odd or different from others. I mean to say that Jesus was truly abnormal; that holiness is a touch of madness and that if we ever tame the madness we will lose the genius behind it. I mean to say that the consuming fire of God will not merely burn away our rough edges so that we are nicer, or wiser, or more dignified. It will not make gentlemen out of rebels. No, it is just as likely that it will make rebels out of gentlemen. Holiness may even change the things we like most about ourselves. It may add a seriousness or a mourning to our otherwise cheerful and glib disposition, or it may give us an unnerving joy in sorrow that will render us ill company. It may help us attend to sermons we used to ignore, to sacrifice where we used to indulge, to decline an argument for sake of humility rather than win it for the sake of truth. It is not only that we will quit the sins our neighbors still enjoy: it is that we will have a growing obsession with the One who is always out of step with the world; we will always be thinking about something else, always going someplace nobody else wants to go.

In what ways does holiness remove us from the center of public opinion? How does it move us to wild extremes? There are two answers to this. One has to do with the way in which the culture views us, and the other involves the way in which we respond to the culture.

THE CHALLENGE *FROM* CULTURE

Imagine two narrow ditches with a wide grass median between them. In the median are all of the sane, ordinary folk who posses varying degrees of sanity. The ditches on either side of this median are two different forms of insanity.

One is the ditch called *futile insanity.* This is mental illness. It is stark madness; mind-bending rage. It produces suicide or disease. It is often random and always destructive. It is selfish and terminal. This is the insanity of Nero, Hitler, or Jeffrey Dahmer. It is disconnected from any genius whatsoever.

The other ditch is a *useful insanity,* which is the weird, eccentric lifestyle of an overactive mind. This madness is sporadic and often benign. It can take the form of moodiness, depression, paranoia, isolation, or fanaticism. It may be troublesome, but this insanity is integrally related to the accomplishments of the insane person. These are the ditches of insanity. One is dangerous, the other merely troublesome. One destroys; the other creates.

Futile (Bad) Insanity	MEDIAN OF SANITY (The Wideness of Normality)	Useful (Good) Insanity

While both ditches represent some degree of dysfunction, they are very different from one another. In fact, they are on opposite sides of the norm. For example, while Sigmund Freud and Ted Bundy both displayed an obsession with sex, it would be a mistake to put them into the same ditch. One of them (Freud) was productive with his obsession, while the other (Bundy) was devoured by it.

The rest of us vacillate somewhere between these two extremes—sometimes angry and conniving, other times fanatical or absentminded—but never going into the ditch on either side. We are always on the safe, wide median.

The Challenge of Modernism

But it cannot remain this way for long. Over the past three hundred years there have been two profound changes in the way sanity is defined. The first change was brought about by *modernism*. Prior to the Enlightenment, insanity was described in mystical rather than in scientific terms. For nearly 1600 years, insanity was considered a spiritual problem. Native Americans referred to it as "soul loss" or "being lost to oneself." African Americans in the eighteenth century believed it was the curse of evil spirits and, in some instances, actually invoked these spirits to bring insanity upon enemies. The Puritans of that era attributed madness to original sin, or demonic possession. The prolific writer Cotton Mather (1663–1728) blamed the madness of one preacher and the depression of another on the torment of devils. The frequent rage of his third wife, Lydia, he said was a "little short of proper satanic possession."[5]

But with the dawn of Enlightenment thinking, it became necessary to find a more rational explanation for craziness. Old-school preachers and their prayers were discarded in favor of medical doctors with a host of treatments, some as weird as the patients themselves. Some patients were confined to asylums. Others were stripped and spread-eagled, then doused with water until near dead. Still others were restrained in straitjackets, shackles, body harnesses, or coffin-like cribs until their madness wore off. In his journal, John Wesley described the conversion of a young boy whose joy was mistaken for madness. Consistent with the spirit of her age, the boy's mother called for the doctor who prescribed the cure, and "they . . . blooded him [the boy] largely, confined him to a dark room, and put a strong blister on each of his arms with another all over his head." When this did not cure the boy's "madness," the mother dismissed the good doctor and left her son alone to be "beside himself" in peace.[6]

For our purposes, it is important to observe this significant shift from religion to science, from praying to bloodletting in the treatment of insanity. And why? Because when religion is no longer the basis from which sanity is defined, religion will move closer to the ditch. That is, if having religion is not an indication of being normal, then it may be taken as an indication of abnormality. If it does not define those in the median, it may be used to define those in the ditch. One psychiatrist has already noted that "religion . . . is without question potentially harmful to the user's mental health." While he does not recommend atheism in order to save our minds, he has concluded:

> There is a common, close association between religion and psychotic disorders. . . . There is absolutely no question in my mind that many ultrafundamentalist preachers are themselves suffering from a Schizophrenic psychosis.[7]

If this is true, then the objective of those in the wide median will be to tame the wildness of religion until it is useful, nice, or domestic. In fact, this describes the tension that has existed between the church and society for the last one hundred years.

The Challenge of Postmodernism

The second profound change in the way insanity is defined was occasioned by the rise of *postmodernism*. Now we have gone beyond the shift from defining insanity in scientific rather than religious terms, and we have begun to narrow the median of sanity and widen the ditches to include behavior once considered unusual but not quite insane. For instance, in the last few years, those who show a compulsion to gamble or eat or drink or work than most other people are said to be "addicted," which means that they have slipped out of the median and into the ditch where the "sick" people are.

There are two ways of narrowing the median of sanity. One is to create a *theology of niceness* (or political correctness), which makes it unlawful to say mean things or to call people names. Those who do such things are ordered by judges to undergo "sensitivity training" in order to learn how the rest of us must feel.

The other way of narrowing the median is to create a *culture of moderation*. In a culture of moderation, one's belief is no longer the most dangerous thing about him. It is his passion we must fear. He is free to believe anything, but the moment that belief is translated into action— the moment his doctrine means the loss of revenue, freedom, or life—he is said to have gone too far, whether he is acting consistently with his beliefs or not.

Very gradually, the median of sanity has been narrowed so that the ground on either side slopes gradually into the ever-widening ditches.

Futile (Bad) Insanity	Culture of Moderation	MEDIAN OF SANITY (The Narrowing of Normality)	Theology of Niceness	Useful (Good) Insanity

Consequences of the Shifting Worldview

When Jesus' family considered him insane it was because he broke the mold; he stepped apart from the crowd. When the Pharisees called him demon possessed (John 10:20), when the crowd laughed at him (Mark 5:40), and when Peter rebuked him for his crazy predictions about dying (Mark 8:31–32) it was because they had narrowed the median to exclude anyone with the convictions that Jesus had. Rather than hear Jesus out, they quickly labeled him insane so they could get back to their normal religion and get some sleep.

Normalcy As a Virtue. Once we define spirituality according to "normal behavior," several things become clear. One is that most of us live within the narrowing confines of sanity, and what is worse, we consider it a virtue. People in the median compare themselves with each other. One person disciples another, even though both of them are about room temperature. Leaders are elected because they are a notch or two above the rest, but they had better not be too far above us or we will call them "so heavenly minded that they are no earthly good." As long as public relations plays the important part that it does among us, we will elect our leaders from within the median, because the insane are usually abrasive, dogmatic, or stubborn. They are norm busters. They will not slap our backs or kiss our babies; they will not conform to the world because they are trying to conform the world to themselves. They are both a standard and a spur. They inspire us and prod us. We admire them and hate them.

In fact, the median of sanity is quite compatible with most forms of government in which the constituents elect their leaders. Any form of church government in which leaders are elected by people of their own kind, any time the pastor is one ballot away from being forced from his church, and any time the pastor or leader needs the position he occupies, the status quo will win the day and will be hard on those few insane folk who defy the norm. The pastor may lead, but he must not get too far out in front of his people, or he will be useless to them and they will find another pastor. Any time we run the church by policy, minimize doctrine, focus on unity for unity's sake, or quarantine the Scriptures to a few scholars we will be damned to the median of sanity. We will hold the party line and, before long, the party line will hold us. We will shut ourselves off from revivalists, mystics, amateurs, lunatics or anyone else who could save us.

The Sanity Police. The median itself is usually policed by three entities: church hierarchy, educational institutions, and the mental health industry. It is not that these entities are evil, but that they exist to preserve order and to protect the masses. Michael Novak has noted that the purpose of an institution is to construct and secure a sense of reality. As the keeper of sound doctrine, the church must promulgate its beliefs (hence, the creeds and catechisms), and so it is less

Jesus was "insane" because he shattered the norm.

forgiving of those who test its boundaries. The educational institutions exist to perpetuate the culture rather than reform it (even though most reformers of the church have been tied to these institutions), and as such they cannot endorse those who challenge the current paradigms. Students may have convictions, but ultimately, must answer to the culture which is the market for their degrees. The mental health industry also protects us from the tyranny of the insane by so labeling them. "You only enter this system through the ritual of a reality test," writes one critic of the mental health establishment. "You only leave it when you have convinced the system of your submission to that reality."[8]

Once more, these entities are not themselves evil. They are the innocent victims of *group think,* which is truth by consensus. They are of the people, by the people, and for the people. As such, they cannot defy the people or be given to excess.

"Help" for the Patient. Those who venture outside the median are said to need help from those inside. We must get them back into line. We must straighten them out. And some of them surely need this. But not all of them. The person who thinks he is a poached egg is as crazy as the one who thinks he can eat Christ's flesh and drink Christ's blood, but only one of them needs a doctor. The problem with those of us in the median is that we make it our business to temper both of these people until, like the Pharisees, we have not only "shut the kingdom of heaven in

men's faces" but we have failed to enter into it ourselves (Matt. 23:13). I have a friend who scored low on a personality assessment and was told by the experts that he was depressed and needed to "take some pills and see a counselor." The "expert" who made this suggestion did so in quiet, sophisticated tones and often appealed to the assessment test, which, he admitted, was based upon the report form the 1996 U.S. census, "with certain adjustments being made for the evangelical church." If Paul was right, whenever people "compare themselves with themselves" they are crazy and not sane. But here we have it the other way around. Should we not tremble at this?

This is always the way with those in the median. They observe the masses and presume the masses are normal. Then they decide that the rest of us need to be more like the most of us—whatever that may be. Of course, it is always possible to be persecuted for our own foolish blunders, and so the godly person will be on guard for them. But today it is just as likely that those who are persecuted for righteousness sake will suffer not because they are annoying, but because they shatter the norm.

In this sense, Jesus was insane: he shattered the norm. And for the sake of holiness, he calls us out of the median of sanity and into his parade of fools.

Out of the Median

John's gospel gives the clearest description of Jesus' call to come out of the median and into the ditch. For almost five chapters, one must look hard for any signs of conflict between Jesus and his audience. It is pretty smooth sailing.

In fact, it is hard to imagine anyone being more successful or popular than Jesus had become in so short a time. Had he left Galilee and gone straight to the Cross, he might have had a few more followers at the end. But according to his nature, he was determined to separate the wheat from the tares. Very gradually, things got ugly.

Calling the Question. In John, Jesus' first public relations debacle was the healing of the invalid near the pool of Bethesda (5:2). It was the Sabbath, and because the Jews forbade healing (of people) on the Sabbath they were appropriately shocked at the miracle. When Jesus refused to bow to their traditions, they "tried all the harder to kill him" (5:18). But one chapter later, with the multitude wiping their mouths from the fish and loaves, Jesus was back in popular demand, and this time they wanted to make him king (see 6:14–15).

Still unsatisfied with the level of their faith, Jesus began to speak. It was a spin doctor's nightmare. Rather than ride the coat tails of his latest miracle (or poll), Jesus insisted that all those who feasted on the fish and loaves should "believe in the one [God] has sent" (6:29). This seems harmless enough. But Jesus was preparing to say things about himself that, up to then, only John had said of him. Of course the people grumbled (6:41). One Greek scholar has called this grumbling "the buzzing of bees."[9] It is the confused sound that runs through a crowd where people gather in angry opposition.[10] In any case, this was a relatively low (yet noticeable) level of conflict.

But Jesus continued. He declared himself the "living bread" that came down from heaven (6:51), and while the meaning of this was not completely clear to his audience, it was enough to start an argument (6:52).

Still Jesus kept talking, warning them that unless they ate his flesh and drank his blood they had no life in them (6:53). This was enough to send some packing, for "from this time many of his disciples turned back and no longer followed him" (6:66). Later they were waiting to take his life (7:1).

Jesus had called the question for those in the middle. He called them out of the wide median and into the company of fanatics. From there, they would never eat his fish and loaves again without confronting the radical insanity that made it possible. It is no wonder that the rest of John's gospel reads like a split decision.

Six times in the next four chapters (7–10) we are told that Jesus' audience was sharply divided.

Some said he was a good man, but others said he deceived the people (7:12–13).

Some tried to seize him, but others put their faith in him (7:30–31).

Some said he was a prophet. Others said he was the Christ. Still others questioned both claims, and so "the people were divided because of Jesus" (7:40–43).

He impressed the Temple guards but irritated the Pharisees (7:46, 49).

Some believed in his miracles and others did not (9:16).

Some said he was possessed by demons (10:20), and others said he was possessed by God (10:21). In the end, "the Jews were again divided" (10:19).

The Call Continued. Jesus still stands outside the median of sanity and bids us to become radical versions of what we already are: Christians. He calls us to make up our minds, to pursue the logical conclusions of our faith. He calls us to give up everything we have, to "hate" our mother and father and our money, to give those who sue us the shirt off our backs, to turn the other cheek, to eliminate the limb (or person?) that siphons our spiritual strength, to pray our best prayers in private, and to worry very little about our retirement.

Our trouble is that inside the median we have learned to tame these radical sayings until we can peacefully coexist with them. We have ways of getting around them and convincing ourselves that we are still good Christians, even though we are none of the things Jesus describes. We complain when we are persecuted. We do not love our enemies; we prosecute them. We lust and hold grudges and swear on a stack of Bibles. We meticulously record our charitable contributions for income tax purposes and even increase our giving just before the end of the year. We have more money in the bank than we'll tithe in a lifetime, yet claim we have treasures in heaven.

Yet we pretend to be living by the Sermon on the Mount. While we still admire these pithy sayings of Christ, we have reduced

Jesus beckons us from the edge.

them to wise but harmless proverbs about the good life. Jesus is our man among men, a champion of our cause, a stellar example of things we treasure most. He is modern and friendly and positive. He laughs at our jokes. He feels our pain. He does not deplore our sins; he encourages us to do better, all the while knowing that boys will be boys.

But the godly person is not deceived by this. He will pursue truth wherever it takes him. He is always prepared to change his mind or alter his lifestyle, to pull up stakes and leave with his family (or without them) in order to lay hold of that for which Christ Jesus has laid hold of him (see Phil. 3:12–13). He will suffer the scorn of a public life or the barrenness of a private one so long as he goes with God. At times he is closer to those whose doctrines are different but whose heart is one with his own. He is often a person without a church. He is otherworldly. He is a mutant. His passion has made him so. This is both painful and gratifying. It is painful because his friends no longer recognize him. It is gratifying because all of heaven finally does. And as the holy person bids farewell to his friends in the median, Jesus beckons him from the edge to join those of whom the world is not worthy (Heb. 11:38).

THE CHALLENGE *TO* CULTURE

While our shifting culture has been hard on those who are fully convinced of the truth, the convinced have also been hard on our culture.

Yet we have come by it honestly, for Jesus also confronted the culture of his day. But what, exactly, about Jesus makes him such a hard fit with the status quo? And how will these virtues be found in us as we move toward the periphery of our culture? Here are a few common denominators of his madness and ours.

Contrariness

In his book *The Price of Greatness,* psychiatrist Arnold Ludwig has done us the favor of researching the biographies of over one thousand eminent historical figures and distilling their common traits into a few categories. According to Ludwig, one such trait is their *contrariness*.

> These individuals often have an attitude that is oppositional in nature. It is almost as though this response style is part of their very natures. Given their tendencies toward iconoclasm, these individuals are often at odds with others. . . . A streak of wildness never leaves them and they are difficult to train. . . . [But] while this wild streak may have irrational roots, it is not necessarily misguided. What distinguishes these individuals from others is that they do not simply rebel. These are not just people who see that the emperor has no clothes; they offer their own brand of attire for him to wear.[11]

But we must not confuse this contrariness with lesser things. We are not talking about the moral minority. In fact, the moral minority shares a rebel's obsession with the rules. The rebel dreads the rules and breaks them. The moralist studies the rules and keeps them. But only the lunatic will argue that the rules no longer matter.[12] The rebel will vote with the liberals and the moralist with the conservatives, but the lunatic will deny them both the hope of politics. To the liberal he is conservative, and to the conservative he is liberal. This is not because he walks the fine line between them but because his holiness comes from within. He is completely free. He can do what he wants, so he is liberal. But he wants the things he does, so he is conservative. He is recklessly constrained. He will judge the rhetoric of the liberal for its content, and he will judge the rhetoric of the conservative for it apparent *lack* of content. One has gone too far for him in explaining the complexities of life, and the other has not gone far enough. One he considers vulgar and the other empty. One suffers but he does not understand; the other understands but will not suffer. The moralist will argue for circumcision and the rebel will argue against it, but the contrary person will say that neither circumcision nor uncircumcision matters at all. He will say (indeed, Paul has said) that "what counts is a new creation" (Gal. 6:15). The moralist will keep the Sabbath and the rebel will destroy it, but the lunatic will make every day his Sabbath (see Rom. 14:5).

This streak of wildness explains why Luther so vehemently opposed the church (one anecdote has someone asking Luther to take his finger out of the Pope's eyes and Luther retorting, "I would, if he would only move his face!"). It explains why Tyndale strove to make every plowman as biblically literate as the Pope; why Spurgeon fought the "downward grade" of England's religion; why Wesley found himself locked out of every church; and why A. W. Tozer could, in his words, "preach [himself] off of every Bible Conference platform in the country."[13]

Chesterton has argued that this contrariness is a badge of insanity. He imagines "an unknown man spoken of by many men . . . Some men said he was too tall and some too short; some objected to his fatness, some lamented his leanness; some thought him too dark and some too fair." Of course, the unknown man might be all of these things, and thus be very strange indeed. Or he might be none of them. He could be the one thing his accusers are supposed to be; so to those who are too tall he is short, and to those too short he is tall. To the obese he is skinny, and to the starving he is fat. The problem, of course, does not lie with the unknown man himself, but with those on either side of him. This is the matter with Jesus, and ultimately with every life he transforms. By holiness, God returns his people to their original condition, and they are despised for it by those who are not so restored.

In every generation God will raise up holy men and women who are crazy enough to defy the norms and imitate the Original. Upon their shoulders the church will finally rest. But even as drowning victims may wrestle with the lifeguard who tries to save them, the church will struggle with those sent by God to preserve it.

Changed Worldview

There is another effect of holiness: It changes our view of the world. Because of the Fall, we are born into a world that has stood heaven on its head and presumed this was normal. But it seems normal only because there are so many doing it, not because it is correct. Imagine this:

It's graduation day, and everybody's going to get a diploma but John. At the assembly, the entire senior class stands up and shouts, "Let John graduate! Let John graduate!"

The principal agrees to give John one last chance. "If I have five apples in my right hand and five apples in my left hand, John, how many apples do I have?" he asks.

John thinks long and hard, then says: "Ten."

At this, the entire senior class stands up and shouts, "Give John another chance! Give John another chance!"

Now whom do you flunk? Since the Fall we have been flunking John and promoting his classmates. It is John—or Luther or Jesus or Paul—who needs another lap around the reality track, so we think. The rest of us, whose faith and passion are pale, are free to get on with life, not knowing that our future will be tainted by the past.

But what if the answers are different in the next world? What if the graduating class moves on to college and finds that John was right after all? What if we all move into the next world and discover that Luther's passion, Jesus' insanity, and Paul's counting all things rubbish (Phil. 3:8–9) are the bare minimum requirements of holiness? What then? Indeed, I used to wonder how God was going to squeeze so many Christians into so little a space in heaven (see Revelation 21:16). But if these be the minimum requirements, if a consuming passion or an insane view of the world is really an inevitable consequence of faith, then the wonder is not that God has created so little space for his saints, but that he has created so much. C. S. Lewis explains:

> Many of us have lived in some particular pocket of human society— whether a school, college, regiment or profession where the tone was bad. And inside that pocket certain actions were regarded as normal and certain others were virtuous. But when we emerged from that society we made the horrible discovery that in the outer world, "normal" was the kind of thing no decent person would dream of doing and our virtuous was taken for granted as the standard of decency. What seemed to us to be fantastic scruples turned out to be the only moments of sanity we ever enjoyed in there.[14]

Like inmates at an asylum who mock the "insanity" of their visitors, we have come to value the abnormal since it all we have ever seen. We are color-blind, yet we mock the artist's work. We are tone deaf, yet presume it is the orchestra who is flat.

But once we discover what it is to be "hidden with Christ in God" (Col. 3:3), to be "partakers of the divine nature" (2 Pet. 1:4 RSV), "to

know [the love of God] that surpasses knowledge" (Eph. 3:19), "to have
streams of living water . . . flow from within [us]" (John 7:38), we will
not simply inch forward in this present reality. We will move into another
one. We will imitate the One who turned the world upside down.

This Jesus started in Bethlehem (population five hundred) while
Jerusalem was asleep. He arrived in a manger, not on horseback. He
spoke of a kingdom within us, of an inner versus an outer righteousness.
He preached about living through dying (John 12:24), gaining through
giving away (Luke 6:38), and achieving greatness through serving
(Mark 10:44). He said that suffering was the sacrament of joy (Matt.
5:11–12), and that he had overcome the world when the world was
about to kill him. In the Beatitudes he blessed those who seem cursed
(Matt. 5:3–10) and cursed those who seem blessed (Luke 6:24–26). He
said the poor in spirit are happy in ways that Pharisees are not. He
promised that those who mourn will find comfort, those who stay hungry will be fed, the meek will inherit the earth, and the persecuted will
rejoice. This happiness is crazy indeed—for everyone but those who
have entered into it.

And once we have entered, we will find that Jesus had it right after
all. Like the crowd who laughed at Jesus one moment ("'stop wailing,'
Jesus said, 'she is not dead but asleep' [and] they laughed at him" Luke
8:52–53) and hid its embarrassment the next, we will know that Jesus
sees what the rest of us cannot. Our first day in heaven will be something like the famous journey to Emmaus. Jesus will open our eyes to
see what he alone has seen all along (see Luke 24:31, 45).

Martin Luther provides an example of this. He was a young man
studying for the priesthood when he seized upon the idea that God is
really holy and that he is *really* present in the Eucharist. Taken together, those thoughts would lead one to tremble whenever handling the
body and blood of God. But most ministers in Luther's day (as in ours)
have put these inhibitions aside in order to dole out the elements to the
masses, now waiting to get out of church on time. According to
Luther's biographer, on that fateful day when young Martin was called
on for the first time to offer the prayer of consecration over the bread
and wine, he was so deeply affected that he was unable to finish the job.

> He froze at the altar. He seemed transfixed. His eyes were glassy, and
> beads of perspiration formed on his forehead. A nervous hush filled the
> congregation as they silently urged the young priest on. Hans Luther
> (his father) was growing uncomfortable, feeling a wave of parental
> embarrassment sweep over him. His son's lower lip began to quiver.

He was trying to speak the words of the Mass, but no words came forth from his mouth. He went limp and returned to the table where his father and the family guests were seated. He had failed. He ruined the Mass and disgraced himself and his father. Hans was furious. He had just made a generous contribution to the monastery and now felt humiliated in the very place he came to witness his son's honor.[15]

Of course, Martin had his own explanation for the debacle. He wrote:

> I was utterly stupefied and terror-stricken. I thought to myself, "With what tongue shall I address such Majesty? . . . Who am I that I should lift up mine eyes or raise my hands to the divine Majesty? The angels surround him. At his nod the earth trembles. And shall I, a miserable little pygmy, say "I want this; I ask for that?"[16]

He has a point. Yet to those in the median, Luther appears insane and his father normal. But think again. If these elements are really the body and blood of God, then the only appropriate response is to wobble our knees and get off of the platform. Meanwhile, Hans had other things in mind. Who could think of the Presence or the Cross or the unworthiness of man with something so great as protocol on his mind? Hans was angry that his generous contribution was wasted. He was ashamed on behalf of the church and embarrassed for the family. To Hans on that day, the Eucharist was all about Martin. But to Martin himself, it was all about God. To the Catholic, the death of Christ is reenacted in the Eucharist. Yet it was Martin, the madman, who mourned as he looked into the wet and dying eyes of God, while his father was concerned primarily with the funeral dinner afterwards.

And was *Martin* insane?

Perhaps. But if he was, we should pray that all of us are smitten with his disease, for only that will save us. "Our prayer," says R. C. Sproul, "is that God would send to this earth an epidemic of such insanity that we too may taste of the righteousness that is by faith alone."[17]

Beware the median. For in the median we define normality by the numbers. We do not tremble over things that are sacred. We sleep peacefully at night while the other half of the world is awake and starving. We snuggle up to a God, who is a consuming fire, we live on stolen property (the earth) and destroy it, we hold the body and blood of God in our hands and think of other things. We are content to live with our sins, even though we are headed to a place where they are not welcome. We fritter away the hours of a life that is already a vapor, seldom read the book we claim to be God's Word, and decorate the part of us that will rot in the grave while ignoring the part that will not. And is *Jesus* insane?

A Sense of Urgency

The German writer Helmut Thielicke has made the point that time is linear and not circular. That is, it moves forward and does not repeat itself. So the lost opportunity cannot be had again. Thielicke writes:

> The line of time . . . is like a long corridor with many doors. Year after year we open a new one. But on its other side there is no latch or knob. We cannot go back and begin anew, as the hand on the clock does. And one day—we know not when or where—the corridor will come to an end.[18]

This means that each new day is not just another trip around the same clock. It is another step down the corridor, and the last door is fast approaching. Even as you read this, what little sand remains in the top of your hourglass is slipping through. Knowing this, a few people capture a sense of the urgent. In order to make good on their one crack at living, they have given themselves over to one pursuit. They are not just busy; they are called, and their work is not motivated by guilt, but by passion. Their lives follow a predictable course.

Driven by Purpose. Whenever passion and urgency meet, they produce a mild form of madness that grows more intense with the lateness of the hour. It is when people care deeply and sense what Shakespeare called "the inaudible and noiseless foot of time" that they do strange things. They become obsessed. They forfeit pleasure, comfort, and sleep. They whittle years off their lives by ignoring such things. But they have a sense of eternity and so they know what time it is. They are always in haste but never in a hurry, because they do only those things they are capable of doing calmly. Life is no longer a series of compartments with a little room for work, a little more for play, and some time left for self. All time is God's and is used in pursuit of him. For those who are thus occupied, even leisure serves the purpose of sharpening the focus of work. They do not tear down their homes and build bigger ones, then say to themselves, "take life easy; eat, drink and be merry." They are not turned inward on themselves. They live for others.

Jesus was consumed by the urgent. He began by telling us he must be about his Father's business (Luke 2:49) and ended by saying "it is finished" (John 19:30). Between these bookends, he told us that "the harvest is plentiful" and already ripe (Matt. 9:37; John 4:35), so we should not stay in one place too long (Matt. 10:9). He also said that "as long as it is day, we must do the work of him who sent [us]" (John 9:4).

Before we are halfway through Luke's gospel, Jesus has "set out for Jerusalem," and from this time forward he will not go out of his way (save once, John 11:6–7) to heal or to save another person. He will travel, preach, ponder, and heal as the crow flies—in a straight line! When others around him seem distracted, he reminds them—with the subtlety of a hammer—that he has not come to win friends and influence people. He has come to win people who will then influence their friends. The woman at the well wants to give him water and the disciples want to give him food, but all he can think about is "do[ing] the will of him who sent me and to finish his work" (John 4:34). On Palm Sunday he is finally getting his fifteen minutes of fame, but he moves quickly through the parade and heads straight to the Temple to give it one more cleansing (Luke 19:38, 45).

Why doesn't Jesus take it easy and live a little?

Jesus had learned to number his days. The person in the median will argue that he probably did take it easy, but in the concise record of the Gospels we are not told of it. Yet it is just as likely that Jesus was truly different from us in many ways, including the way he managed time. It is likely that he saw the end from the beginning; that he had learned to number his days (Ps. 90:12). And even today, in a society that believes all work and no play makes Jack a dull boy, there are still a few lunatics who act as though they do not have forever to live, as though time were the dress rehearsal for eternity.

Driven Saints. Like Jesus, some of God's dearest saints have lived with a sense of urgency. Thomas à Kempis advised that our "every thought and action should be that of a man who is to die this day."[19] And some of his readers took him seriously, for a couple hundred years later, the Puritan leader Jonathan Edwards penned seventy resolutions (at the ripe age of nineteen) including "never to lose one moment of time, but to improve it in the most profitable way I can," and "never to do anything, which I should be afraid to do if it were the last hour of my life."[20]

François Fénelon, the French mystic, believed that "from the first instant of our life to the last, [God] has never designed for us a barren moment, nor one which we can consider as given up to our own discretion."[21] Such thinking greatly influenced John Wesley, who admitted: "Leisure and I have taken leave of one another: I propose to be busy as

long as I live. . . ."[22]   And Wesley lived like it. He never took more
than six hours to sleep, rising every morning at four o'clock to begin his
prayer and study. He often preached his first sermon at five o'clock in
the morning, and would sometimes return to the pulpit four more times
before the day ended.

Wesley's contemporary Hannah More, whose religious tracts sold in
the millions, argued that it was sheer madness to remain insensible to
eternal things while standing on the brink of eternity. She wrote:

> We complain that life is short, and yet throw away the best part of it, only
> giving over to religion that portion which is good for nothing else. Life
> would be long enough if we assigned its best period to the best purpose.[23]

All of these were eccentric because all of them were afraid of leaving
the world in the same condition in which they'd found it. Those in
the median of sanity are afraid only of being labeled *workaholic*—a
diagnosis invented only fifty years ago to describe some people who
throw themselves recklessly into whatever they believe.

Purposeful Pleasure. Yet, even though life is short, the eccentric
Christian plays and laughs and rests like the best (or worst) of them,
only he does so with purpose. It is not that he avoids rest, but that he
rests for the purpose of recreating his energy. He does not work in
order to pay for his next vacation. That is the curse of those in the
middle. Instead, the devoted Christian takes vacations for the purpose
of allowing his soul to catch up with his body. He frolics, but never
fritters the hours away. He is always doing something, even when he is
doing nothing, because everything in his life—from exercise to sleep—
has a purpose.

Recently, I read that Charles Darwin, in the waning years of his life,
wrote apologies to his children for living such a colorless life. Committed
to his science and the development of his theories, Darwin failed to
develop the part of him that made him useful to other people. He was a
slave to his ideas, simply because he had not learned how to play. Perhaps
very phenomenon is what Chesterton had in mind when he said that "the
madman is the man who has lost everything *except* his reason."

But the trouble with most disciples is not that they play too little or
too much. It is that they play for no apparent reason. Their pleasure is
disconnected from any spiritual pursuit, even though they claim to live
in pursuit of God.

The wonder is not that those who love and trust money neglect religion in order to earn it. What else should we expect? The wonder is that
those who love and trust Christ work so long and hard to earn money.

The wonder is not that greedy people hoard things, even each other's garbage. The wonder is that those who are "aliens and strangers on earth" should confine their charitable giving to 2.2 percent of their net income, pray less than twenty minutes a week, and remain so busy with things which they *say* don't matter. The person who says he is a lightbulb and then spends the rest of his life studying electricity is surely insane. Yet he is insane in a consistent way. But the person who says he is a Christian yet does little to pursue God is impossible to understand. There is no hope for him. In spite of what he says, his God is not a consuming fire, but a lightning bug.

OVER THE LINE

According to the *Bangor Daily News,* the band played *Nearer My God to Thee* while the ill-fated Titanic sunk out from under them. So how should one go down to his grave? What mood is the right one when fifteen hundred people are about to drown? I do not know. But if it be insane to panic and scream in a moment of terror like that, then there are two ways—and not one—to feign madness. The other is to calmly play *Nearer My God to Thee* while hell opens it black and frigid mouth to swallow you whole.

In spite of the predictions about a coming revival in North America or a growing Christian consensus, things are worse and not better for disciples of Christ at the dawn of the new millennium. Religiously speaking, this is true in nearly every country of the world. We have reached a knot in the timeline of history, as Alexander Solzhenitsyn put it, a time when issues are clarified and action is necessary.

Now is a good time for the insane among us to rise up and present themselves to a church that is clearly not ready to save the day. And will they? Or will they remain quiet, afraid of being labeled insane? Dare they say that the emperor has no clothes, or even that the clothes have no emperor? Will they continue to believe the prognosis is grim, the day urgent, and the night coming, or will they ooze back into the masses within their denominations and collect their pensions? Do they have the stamina to live out of favor with the majority? And as they emerge from their traditions, still loyal to their denominations, will they find each other in the center?

Yes, it is a very thin line between genius and insanity. One is authentic and the other foolish, but which is which? The fool is one farthest from the crowd, whose values are inverted, whose life flows from a single belief, who sees the end from the beginning. He is insane, a mutant whose answers will hold up only in the next world. And for now, well . . . he is our only hope.

> It seems I've imagined him all of my life
> as the wisest of all mankind
> But in God's holy wisdom is foolish to man
> He must have seemed out of his mind.
> For even his family said he was mad
> and the priest had the demons to blame
> But God in the form of this angry young man
> could not have seemed perfectly sane.
> And so we follow God's own Fool
> for only the fool can tell;
> Come, believe the unbelievable!
> Come, be a fool as well.
> —Michael Card, *Immanuel*

LIFE RESPONSES

1. How do you define *insanity?*

2. Have you ever refrained from taking some action that you thought was right because your family or friends might think it was strange? What was the result?

3. List some ways that you find yourself at odds with popular culture or with the church because of your faith in Christ. How might you resolve the tension in either case?

Notes

Preface

1. C. S. Lewis, *The Problem of Pain* (New York: Macmillan Publishing Company, 1977), 9.
2. A. W. Tozer, *The Pursuit of God*, (Harrisburg, Pa.: Christian Publications, 1968), 15.

Chapter One: Finding the Heart's True Home

1. William Nack, "The Ballad of Big Daddy," *Sports Illustrated* (January 11, 1999): 70–86.
2. Steele writes, "the moral intuitions, immutable and invariable, are the voice of the divine Spirit, immanent in all men, irrespective of regeneration." See Daniel Steele, *The Gospel of the Comforter* (Rochester, Pa.: H. E. Schmul Publishing Co., 1960), 146. See also John Wesley's sermon "On Conscience," in which he defines conscience as "that supernatural gift of God which we usually style, preventing grace." John Wesley, *The Works of John Wesley,* vol. 7 (Grand Rapids: Baker Book House, 1996), 189.
3. The order here is not arbitrary. Men are first lost and afterwards rebellious. Wesley insisted that sin began with unbelief (Eve "gave more credit to the word of the Devil than to the Word of God") and ended with rebellion and pain (Adam "painfully feared that God, in the love of Whom his supreme happiness before consisted"). See Wesley, "The Fall of Man," *Works,* vol. 6, 217. It is important that unbelief comes before rebellion in our understanding of sin. Men rebel because they are lost; they are not lost because they rebel. Thus, God does not make sinners want him as he would have to do if they were rebellious. He makes sinners *capable* of wanting him and presents himself to them in compelling ways so that they may find him (see 1 Chron. 28:9; Isa. 55:6). It is not possible to desire God if we are in rebellion against him. But because our souls are hurt, and not hardened, we may respond to his compelling call.
4. Viktor E. Frankl, *Man's Search for Meaning* (New York: Touchstone Books, 1984), 36.
5. See R. C. Sproul, *If There is a God Why Are There Atheists?* (Wheaton: Tyndale House Publishers, 1988), 103–106.

6. From "Letter to the Editor," *U.S. News & World Report* (May 2, 1994): 7.

7. "The Face of God," *Life* 13, no. 5 (December 1990): 64.

8. *National & International Religion Report* (November 28, 1994): 2.

9. For an apt summary and critique of Hartshorne's thought (formally known as *process theology*) see David L. Smith, *Handbook of Contemporary Theology*, (Grand Rapids: Baker Book House, 1992), 150–163.

10. *National & International Religion Report* (January 9, 1995): 6.

11. Cited by William Curry Mavis in *The Psychology of the Christian Experience*, (Grand Rapids: Zondervan Publishing House, 1963), 16.

12. Max Lucado, *No Wonder They Call Him the Savior* (Portland, Oreg.: Multnomah Publishers 1986), 43–45.

13. Garrison Keillor, "The Poetry Judge," *Atlantic Monthly* (February 1996): 95.

14. Because of its offensive nature, the title of the play has been changed.

15. Martin Luther, "Lectures on Romans," *Luther's Works*, ed. Hilton C. Oswald, vol. 25 (Saint Louis: Concordia, 1972), 291.

16. Saint John of the Cross, *Dark Night of the Soul*, trans. E. Allison Peers (New York: Image Books, 1990), 86. Specifically, see paragraph 12.

17. Martin Marty, *Context* (December 1, 1994): 6.

Chapter Two: A Miracle Named Desire

1. John Dillenberger, ed., *Martin Luther: Selections from His Writings* (New York: Anchor Books, 1962), 20.

2. John Wesley, *The Works of John Wesley*, vol. 5 (Grand Rapids: Baker Book House, 1996), 21.

3. Wesley, "On Perfection," *Works,* vol. 6, 417.

4. Wendy Murray Zoba, "Do You Believe in God? Columbine and the Stirring of America's Soul," *Christianity Today* (October 4, 1999): 37.

5. Mark Van Houten, *Profane Evangelism* (Grand Rapids: Zondervan Publishing House, 1989), 84.

6. N. T. Wright, *The Crown and the Fire: Meditations on the Cross and the Spirit* (Grand Rapids: William B. Eerdmans Publishing Co., 1992), 68.

7. Wesley referred to this as *fictio juris*, or *judicial fiction* in which "God judges . . . us contrary to the real nature of things; that He esteems us better than we really are, or believes us righteous when we are unrighteous." Instead, Wesley insisted that "the judgment of the all-wise God is always according to the truth," that is, that God actually gives us—gradually or all at once—the very righteousness he says we possess. (Wesley, "Justification by Faith," *Works,* vol. 5, 57.) In this way, Wesley is distinct from Luther, who suggested our true righteousness was "alien" and therefore unrelated to anything good within us. Compare Wesley's sermon *Justification by Faith* to Luther's sermon *Two Kinds of Righteousness* and his *Argument of the Epistle to the Galatians.*

8. Daniel Steele, *Love Enthroned* (Salem, Ohio: H. E. Schmul Publishing Co., 1961), 180.

9. I believe this was the pattern of Wesley's conversion, and it was the pattern for Wesley's friend George Whitefield as well. In fact, it is often the case that those who come to Christ from outside a religious tradition move from *the natural man* to grace, while religious people (like Luther, Wesley, and Whitefield) usually move from law to grace. Wesley has articulated this clearly in his message, *Spirit of Bondage and Adoption.* While I affirm Wesley's observation, I have seen that those of the world and those of the church typically approach saving grace from opposite paths, and that God, sin, faith, repentance, salvation, and holiness may have a different, subjective meaning to each person based on his or her perspective.

Chapter Three: The Black Hole

1. Alister McGrath, *Studies in Christian Doctrine* (Grand Rapids: Zondervan Publishing House, 1997), 24–25.

2. It may also be true that one's temperament or personality has much to do with how quickly he professes to be sanctified. I have met people whom I considered holy, but who would never admit to it themselves. This is due, at least in part, to the simple fact that they are not entirely sure about *anything*—including their own sanctification. As a rule, this self-doubt plagues those who were raised in religious homes.

3. Everett Lewis Cattell, *The Spirit of Holiness* (Grand Rapids: Zondervan Publishing House, 1963), 95.

4. For examples of this kind of literature, see E. G. Marsh, *The Old Man*; W. E. Shepard, *How to Get Sanctified*; A. M. Hill *Establishing*

Grace; Harry Jessop, *Entire Sanctification*; G. A. McLaughlin, *Inbred Sin;* and many other books from the same era.

5. It is significant that this question (or one like it) is posed to ministerial students seeking licensure or ordination, and to those seeking membership in some churches. In my experience as an interviewer of both prospective ministers and church members that most seekers will describe sanctification as an experience ("It happened on a Thursday . . ."), even though they are unsure what, exactly, sanctification is.

6. See Craig S. Keener in *The IVP Background Commentary* (Downers Grove, Ill.: InterVarsity Press, 1993). There Keener writes that the carnal people of 1 Corinthians 3 "were *acting* fleshly, not that they were flesh by nature (emphasis original). Gordon Fee agrees, saying that Paul's concern "is not to suggest classes of Christians or grades of spirituality, but to get [the Corinthians] to stop thinking like the people of the present age. See Gordon Fee, *The First Epistle to the Corinthians,* New International Commenatry to the New Testament (Grand Rapids: William B. Eerdmans Publishing Co., 1987), 122.

7. Cited by Rabbi Joseph Telushkin in *Jewish Wisdom: Ethical, Spiritual & Historical Lessons from the Great Works and Thinkers* (New York: William Morrow and Company, 1994), 176.

8. The word *disciple* (*mathetes*) occurs only four times as a verb in the New Testament; in three of those instances it is translated *teach* or *instruct.* But behind this is the New Testament belief "that *a call* is the basis of discipleship for Jesus." See Geoffrey W. Bromiley, *Theological Dictionary of the New Testament*, ed. Gerhard Kittel and Gerhard Friedrich (Grand Rapids: William B. Eerdmans Publishing Co., 1985), 562.

9. These categories of disciple in the New Testament are described more fully in *The Dictionary of Jesus and the Gospels*, ed. Joel Green, Scot McKnight, and I. Howard Marshall (Downers Grove, Ill.: InterVarsity Press, 1992), 176–177.

10. Happily, as a result of our conversation, the woman in this story began her own investigation into the life and gospel of Jesus Christ, and has since become a genuine disciple. Nevertheless, her story is a stark reminder that many of our former assumptions can no longer be taken for granted.

11. Listed in a popular catalog of Christian books and videos.

12. This is a sliding scale that allows for different levels of comprehension yet insists that some comprehension is necessary. There is an ongoing soteriological debate over how much, exactly, the seeker must

know and on what level he must know it in order to be genuinely saved. While it is important for people to truly trust Christ, that faith must be based upon some (growing) knowledge of the Christ they are trusting. On the other hand, while knowledge is vitally important to the seeker, he is not converted until that moment when the knowledge becomes personal for him. The definition offered here does not seek to end this debate, but to be a kind of portable answer and something of a middle way in the ongoing debate.

13. In Catholic thought, one belongs to the Kingdom because he belongs to the Church. This presumption underlies the Eucharist, infant baptism, and last rites (or *extreme unction*). Once the person has been baptized into the Church (an act of grace) he must busy himself with the pursuit of virtues and good works.

14. Bernard's four stages were (1) love of self for self's sake, (2) love of God for self's sake, (3) love of God for God's sake, and (4) love of self for God's sake. See Bernard of Clairveaux, *Selected Works*, trans. G. R. Evans (New York: Paulist Press, 1987), 173–205.

15. According to Bonaventure, spiritual union with God begins by passing "through his vestiges, which are material" (flesh). After this, we must "enter into our soul, which is God's image . . . within us" (spirit). Finally, we must "go beyond to what is eternal, most spiritual and above us" (mind or soul). See Bonaventure, *The Soul's Journey into God*, trans. Ewert Cousins (New York: Paulist Press, 1978), 53–116.

16. See John of the Cross, *Dark Night of the Soul*, trans. E. Allison Peers, (New York: Image Books, 1990).

17. In this spiritual classic, Teresa of Avila portrays the spiritual journey as inward progress through seven mansions, beginning with humility and ending with spiritual marriage, "where the most secret things pass between God and the soul." See Teresa of Avila, *Interior Castle*, trans. E. Allison Peers, (New York: Image Books, 1989).

18. See Alan Jones, *Soul Making: The Desert Way of Spirituality* (San Francisco: HarperSanFrancisco, 1985), 159–184.

19. Cited by J. I. Packer in *Rediscovering Holiness* (Ann Arbor: Vine Books, 1992), 12.

20. Lesslie Newbigin, *Mission in Christ's Way* (New York: Friendship Press, 1987), 9.

21. G. D. Watson, "Others May, You Cannot," *Discipleship Journal*, no. 70 (1992): 62.

Chapter Four: The Power of Love

1. C. S. Lewis, *The Screwtape Letters*, (New York: Macmillan Publishing Company, 1961), 116.

2. Helmut Thielicke, *I Believe the Christian's Creed*, trans. John Doberstein (Philadelphia: Fortress Press, 1968), 102.

3. Cited by Albert Wells, Jr. in *Inspiring Quotations* (Nashville: Thomas Nelson, 1988), 120.

4. Gospel songs such as *The Cleansing Stream* by Phoebe Palmer, *Pentecostal Power* by Charlotte Homer, *Whiter Than Snow* by James Nicholson and books such as *Holiness and Power* by A. M. Hills, *Sinning Saints* and *Must We Sin?* by Howard Sweeten, *Purity and Maturity* by J. A. Wood, *The Old Man* by E. G. Marsh, McClaughlin's *Inbred Sin*, Carroll's *The Three Baptisms*, and *The Pentecostal Experience* by C. W. Ruth are typical of much (though not all) of the literature that explained Wesley's doctrine to the generations that followed.

5. Madam Guyon, *Experiencing God Through Prayer* (New Kensington, Pa.: Whitaker House, 1984), 36.

6. Robert E. Coleman, *Nothing to Do But Save Souls* (Grand Rapids: Francis Asbury Press, 1990), 102.

7. Francis McGraw, *John Hyde: The Apostle of Prayer* (Minneapolis: Bethany House Publishers, 1970), 56.

8. Ibid., 67.

Chapter Five: Backing Forward

1. John Piper, *The Pleasures of God* (Portland: Multnomah Publishers, 1991), 242.

2. Jeremy Taylor, *Holy Living*, ed. Hal Helms (Orleans, Mass.: Paraclete Press, 1993), 92.

3. Thomas à Kempis, *The Imitation of Christ*, trans. Joseph N. Tylenda (New York: Vintage Books, 1994), 94.

4. Søren Kierkegaard, *Parables of Kierkegaard*, ed. Thomas C. Oden (Princeton: Princeton University Press, 1978), 71.

5. Ibid.

6. Dietrich Bonhoeffer, *The Cost of Discipleship* (New York: Touchstone Books, 1995), 81.

7. John Wesley, "The Danger of Riches," *The Works of John Wesley*, vol. 7 (Grand Rapids: Baker Book House, 1996), 3.

8. This parable was first offered by Søren Kierkegaard. See *Parables*, 3.

9. Zinzendorf's view is summarized by John Wesley in his sermon "On Sin in Believers." See *Works*, vol. 5, 144–156.

10. Cited in *The Wesleyan Advocate,* (July 19, 1976): 12.

11. Martin Luther, *Commentary on Galatians: Modern English Version* (Grand Rapids: Fleming H. Revell Co., 1988), 20.

12. Wesley, "On Perfection," *Works*, vol. 6, 417.

13. I am indebted to Dr. Dennis Kinlaw, who first pointed this out to me in a private conversation on sin in the believer's life.

14. C. S. Lewis, *Letter to Malcolm Muggeridge, Chiefly on Prayer.*

15. See "Vital Statistics" in *U.S. News & World Report* (February 19, 2001), 12.

16. Portia Nelson cited in "A Walk Through Life," *Pastor to Pastor* 8 (December, 1993): 2.

Chapter Six: A Place We Mistake for Heaven

1. Gordon McDonald, *Restoring Your Spiritual Passion* (Nashville: Thomas Nelson, 1986), 99.

2. Eugene M. Bartlett, "Victory in Jesus," *Sing to the Lord* (Kansas City: Lillenas Publishing Co., 1993), 352.

3. Ray Boltz, "Thank You," *Moments for the Heart* (Nashville: Word Entertainment) compact music disc, 080688612924.

4. Jeremy Taylor, *Holy Living*, ed. Hal Helms (Orleans: Paraclete Press, 1988), 92.

5. Richard Foster, *Celebration of Discipline* (Grand Rapids: Zondervan Publishing House, 1978), 112.

6. Cited by John Killenger in *Fundamentals of Preaching* (Philadelphia: Fortress Press, 1985), 27–28.

7. Lesslie Newbigin, *Missions in Christ's Way* (New York: World Council of Churches, 1987), 11.

8. Cited by Florence Bulle in *God Wants You Rich—and Other Enticing Doctrines* (Minneapolis: Bethany House Publishers, 1983), 20.

Chapter Seven: For the Love of God!

1. The first three Gospels, which provide a synopsis of Jesus' life.

2. Those disciples who were granted a private audience with the risen Christ include: Peter (1 Cor. 5:5); Thomas (John 20:19–25);

Nathaniel, James, John and two others (John 21:1–2).

3. More than the fact that a "sinful" woman washed his feet and anointed him with oil is the troubling observation that she was likely fulfilling a role of the Jewish high priest himself. According to Morna Hooker, "it was Caiaphas' responsibility to recognize the Messiah, to anoint him as king, and to proclaim him to Israel, but this he fails to do . . . [so] the anointing is carried out by a woman, while the proclamation of Jesus to Israel as king is made by Pilate and the declaration that he is the son of God by Jesus' executioner." Hooker concludes, "the irony is clear . . . the whole story is absurd—a woman and two Gentiles have usurped the high priest's powers—and yet [it is] entirely appropriate in a gospel [Mark] which is about questions expressed in service, and about the lost who came first." See Morna D. Hooker, *Not Ashamed of the Gospel* (Grand Rapids: William B. Eerdmans Publishing Co., 1994), 60.

4. It should be noted there that Jesus cited this verse from a passage in Isaiah that refers to the world—Gentiles and Jews—gathering as one for the worship of God (Isaiah 56). In Isaiah, the foreigners (or Gentiles) were not to feel excluded from the worship of God (v. 3) if they loved the Lord and held fast to the covenant (v. 6), for God would "give them joy in his house of prayer" (v. 7). Geoffrey Grogan writes that "the court of the Gentiles was a kind of symbol and earnest of this, and it is from this [court] that Christ expelled the traders" using the words of this passage. See Geoffrey Grogan, *Isaiah,* The Expositor's Bible Commentary, vol. 6 (Grand Rapids: Zondervan Publishing House, 1986), 316.

5. Cited by Walter Wessel in *Mark*, The Expositor's Bible Commentary, vol. 8 (Grand Rapids: Zondervan Publishing House, 1984), 728.

6. Interestingly, Jesus' disciples were present to hear him tell of his forthcoming crucifixion and resurrection (Mark 10:33–34), yet still referred to him as "teacher," while the blind Bartimaeus, who was not a disciple, refers to Jesus as "Son of David," a messianic title with roots in the Old Testament.

7. John Wesley, "Means of Grace," *The Works of John Wesley,* vol. 5 (Grand Rapids: Baker Book House, 1996), 185–201.

8. This, I think, was the practice of John Wesley (see "The Means of Grace," cited above) and other evangelists up until the nineteenth century. It was likely the practice of Jesus himself, who seemed to distinguish between *answering* the question (John 3:1–21) and *calling* the

question (Matt. 11:28). During the nineteenth century, revivalists compressed a year's journey toward faith into a few moments, sealed with an invitation. While this created an opportunity for genuine seekers to find Christ, it also answered for some a question they were not asking.

9. William Booth, *In Darkest England and the Way Out* (Chicago: Charles H. Sergel, 1890), 15.

10. Deitrich Bonhoeffer, *Letters and Papers from Prison* (New York: Collier Books, 1953, 1971), 345.

11. Cited by Donald McCullough in *The Trivialization of God: the Dangerous Illusion of a Manageable Deity* (Colorado Springs: NavPress Publishing Group, 1995), 147–8.

Chapter Eight: A Momentary Lapse of Reason

1. David Swartz, *The Magnificent Obsession* (Colorado Springs: NavPress Publishing Group, 1990), 167–168.

2. Cited by Max Lucado, *In the Grip of Grace* (Waco: Word Books, 1996), 91–92.

Chapter Nine: Perfect Hatred

1. Stephen Brown, *No More Mr. Nice Guy* (Nashville: Thomas Nelson, 1986), 159–160.

2. Stephen Carter, *The Culture of Disbelief* (New York: Basic Books, 1993), 14–15.

3. Arthur M. Schlesinger Jr., *The Disuniting of America: Reflections on a Multicultural Society* (New York: W. W. Norton and Co., 1992), 39–40.

4. Albert Mohler Jr., "The Faith Once For All Abandoned by the Saints," *Viewpoint* (date unknown).

5. The practice of defining virtue as to the balance between two opposites began, as best I can tell, with Aristotle and continues to the present day. This particular contrast between anger and love comes from Harry Emerson Fosdick, *The Manhood of the Master* (New York: Association Press, 1922), 38–45. While much of Fosdick's theology is debatable, his insights here are important for understanding the presence of anger in a holy person.

6. Basil Miller, *God's Great Soul Winners* (Anderson, Ind.: Warner Press, 1937), 47.

7. Fosdick, *Manhood*, 41.

8. This story is better told by the historian from whom I borrowed it. See Donald Dayton, *Discovering an Evangelical Heritage* (Peabody, Mass.: Hendrickson Publishers, 1976), 48–62.

9. John R. W. Stott, *Our Guilty Silence* (Grand Rapids: William B. Eerdmans Publishing Co., 1967), 21.

10. Ibid. 22.

Chapter Ten: Walking a Thin Line

1. Cited by Clifford A. Pickover in *Strange Brains and Genius* (New York: Plenum Trade, 1998), 255.

2. G. K. Chesterton, *Orthodoxy: The Romance of Faith* (New York: Image Books, 1959), 19.

3. Lewis writes that Jesus "was never regarded as a mere moral teacher; He did not produce that effect on any of the people who actually met him." Rather, Lewis observed that Jesus always produced one of only three responses: hatred, terror, or adoration. ". . . there is no halfway house and there is no parallel in other religions." See C. S. Lewis, *God in the Dock* (Grand Rapids: William B. Eerdmans Publishing Co., 1970), 157–158.

4. In these two instances (Mark 14:61; Luke 22:70), Jesus' inquisitors do not ask whether he *claims* to be the Son of God, but whether or not he *is* the Son of God. Jesus' response (*su legeis,* "you have said it") places the weight of this statement on Jesus' accusers. Leon Morris interprets Jesus' response as: "that is *your* word, not mine" (Leon Morris, *Luke,* Tyndale New Testament Commentary, vol. 3 (Grand Rapids: William B. Eerdmans Publishing Co., 1995), 347.

5. Cited by Lynn Gramwell and Nancy Tomes in *Madness in America: Cultural and Medical Perceptions of Mental Illness Before 1914* (Binghamton, N.Y.: Cornell University Press, 1995), 17.

6. John Wesley, *The Works of John Wesley,* 3rd ed., vol. 1 (Grand Rapids: Baker Book House, 1996), 288.

7. Cited by Thomas Szasz in *Insanity: Its Idea and Consequences* (New York: John Wiley and Sons, 1987), 68. The psychiatrist's work may be found in: Eli S. Chesen, *Religion May Be Hazardous To Your Health* (New York: Golier Books, 1972).

8. Anthony Brandt, *Reality Police: The Experience of Insanity in America* (New York, William Morrow and Co., 1975), 25.

9. A. T. Robertson, *Word Pictures in the New Testament*, vol. 4 (Grand Rapids William B. Eerdmans Publishing Co., 1954), 109.

10. Leon Morris, *New International Commentary of the New Testament: Gospel According to John*, rev. ed. (Grand Rapids: William B. Eerdmans Publishing Co., 1995), 327.

11. Arnold Ludwig, *The Price of Greatness* (New York: Guilford Publishing Co., 1995), 185–186.

12. Compare Jesus' interpretation of the rules to that of the Pharisees in the matters of picking grain (Mark 2:24–28), healing the sick (3:1–5), or washing hands before eating (7:1–5, 20–23).

13. From the preface, A. W. Tozer, *The Best of A. W. Tozer,* ed. by Warren Wiersbe (Grand Rapids: Baker Book House, 1978), 8.

14. C. S. Lewis, *The Problem of Pain* (New York: Macmillan Publishing Co., 1962), 62.

15. R. C. Sproul, *The Holiness of God* (Wheaton, Ill.: Tyndale House Publishers, 1987), 106.

16. Roland Bainton, *Here I Stand: A Life of Martin Luther* (New York: Abingdon-Cokesbury Press, 1950), 30.

17. Sproul, *Holiness*, 126.

18. Helmut Thielicke, *Christ and the Meaning of Life* (New York: Harper and Row, 1962), 31.

19. Thomas à Kempis, *The Imitation of Christ* (New York: Vintage, 1998), 34.

20. Jonathan Edwards, *The Works of Jonathan Edwards* (Carlisle, Pa.: The Banner of Truth, 1995), xx.

21. François Fénelon, *Talking with God* (Brewster, Mass.: Paraclete, 1997), 130.

22. John Telford, ed., *The Letters of the Rev. John Wesley A.M.* (London: The Epworth Press, 1931), 34.

23. Hannah More, *Religion of the Heart* (Brewster, Mass.: Paraclete Press, 1993), 192.